Pedagogies of Interconnectedness

TRANSFORMATIONS: WOMANIST, FEMINIST,
AND INDIGENOUS STUDIES

Edited by AnaLouise Keating

*For a list of books in the series, please see
our website at www.press.uillinois.edu.*

Pedagogies of Interconnectedness

Feminist-Queer Collaborative Transformation

Edited by

ISIS NUSAIR and
BARBARA L. SHAW

© 2025 by the Board of Trustees
of the University of Illinois
All rights reserved
1 2 3 4 5 C P 5 4 3 2 1
∞ This book is printed on acid-free paper.

Cataloging data available from the Library of Congress

LCCN 2024053278
ISBN 978-0-252-04647-6 (cloth : alk.)
ISBN 978-0-252-08856-8 (paper : alk.)
ISBN 978-0-252-04778-7 (ebook)

Contents

Foreword

ANALOUISE KEATING

To move from an oppositional world toward a post-oppositional one challenges us as scholars, teachers, and activists, and it also serves as the foundation for much of the work in the following pieces.
—Isis Nusair and Barbara L. Shaw

What does transformation look like? What is the relationship between language, reading, writing, and progressive social justice work? How can we use words, ideas, theories, and stories to develop inclusive, life-affirming communities? How can we enact transformation in our daily practices, our classrooms, our professional and personal partnerships, and other areas of our lives? *Transformations: Womanist, Feminist, and Indigenous Studies* has its origins in these and related questions. Grounded in the belief that radical progressive change—on individual, collective, national, transnational, and planetary levels—is urgently needed and in fact possible (although typically not easy to achieve), this book series offers new pathways for transdisciplinary scholarship informed by the theories of women of color and their post-oppositional approaches to knowledge creation and social change. *Transformations* invites authors to take risks (thematically, theoretically, methodologically, or stylistically) in their work—to draw on existing knowledge systems while simultaneously moving beyond these systems and their disciplinary- or interdisciplinary-specific academic rules—and through these risks, to invent new (transdisciplinary) perspectives, methods, and knowledge.

Books in this series foreground theorizing from women of color because these theories offer boldly innovative, though too often overlooked, perspectives on transformation. Their theories give us the intellectual grounding and visionary yet pragmatic tools to understand, challenge, and alter the existing frameworks and paradigms that structure (and all too often constrain) our lives. They are more daring, innovative, and imaginative—rich with the potential to transform. Take, for example, post-oppositionality as an alternative approach to social justice work (including progressive academic scholarship). Post-oppositionality invites us to think differently; to step beyond our conventional rules; to learn from, build on, and liberate ourselves from the oppositionally based theories and practices we generally employ. I describe these alternatives as "post-oppositional" to underscore both their relationship to oppositional thought and their visionary invitation to move at least partially through it.

Post-oppositionality enacts relational approaches to knowledge production, identity formation, and social change that borrow from but don't become trapped within oppositional thought and action. Post-oppositionality is not *anti*-oppositional; it neither completely rejects nor entirely moves beyond oppositionality but instead enacts a complex dance with it, creating new perspectives as it does so. Although post-oppositionality takes many forms, these forms typically share several interrelated traits: (1) belief in our profound interconnectedness with all that exists; (2) acceptance of paradox and contradiction; (3) the desire to be radically inclusive—to seek and create complex commonalities and broad-based alliances for social change; and (4) a relational approach to differences. As these traits suggest, post-oppositionality replaces conventional models of self-enclosed individualism that define each human being as entirely separate and distinct from all others with a relational approach that values connection, community, and collaboration.

Isis Nusair and Barbara L. Shaw's *Pedagogies of Interconnectedness: Feminist-Queer Collaborative Transformation* boldly illustrates these post-oppositional traits. This book reminds us that post-oppositionality thrives on community, relationality, and collaboration. Focusing specifically on pedagogy, the editors and contributors to this volume creatively demonstrate post-oppositionality's profound contributions to feminist classroom practices. They develop thoughtful collaborations that recognize and strive to dismantle the various systemic and personal power dynamics that impede successful collaborative work. Whether they're making new connections, forging unexpected alliances, adopting new citational practices, embracing contradictions, or creating alternative canons, contributors to this volume embolden and inspire. Drawing on post-oppositional tactics like intellectual humility, inclusivity, and mutual respect, this book is packed full of useful, experientially based teaching and learning practices. *Pedagogies of Interconnectedness* demonstrates to us that transformative collaborations (whether inside or outside conventional university classrooms) are possible when we recognize and cultivate our radical interrelatedness.

Acknowledgments

We set out to write the book that we needed for our teaching, in our communities, and to breathe life into our academic work. As we conceived its possibility, it was clear from the beginning that it would draw on deep feminist genealogies that value polyvocal perspectives and collective effort. Genuine feminist-queer collaborative work takes time and painstakingly so in a neoliberal academic landscape where so many faculty and staff are asked to do more than teaching, research, and service with fewer resources. In the last few years, the pandemic and bearing witness to political violence has made it all the more clear how much we need one another as academics and activists and interpersonally.

As such, we must begin by thanking our contributors. Their pieces are insightful and instructive; the work with students as collaborators is meaningful and has transformed how we think about our own work inside and outside the classroom. We particularly appreciate their generosity regarding the publishing process; it has buoyed us in critical moments. Over the course of many years we have been challenged by health and political issues and returned to joy in turning toward one another knowing the need for this collection. This process re-taught us that feminist-queer communities are life-giving in their collaboration.

We extend our gratitude to AnaLouise Keating for her constructive feedback and including this project in the Transformations series with the University of Illinois Press. Her *Transformation Now!* has been a text that we return to often while we think through what feminist collaboration means and how it is enacted. To move from an oppositional world toward a post-oppositional one challenges us as scholars, teachers, and activists, and it also serves as the foundation for much of the work in the following pieces.

Themes of community-building and connection; intersectional work within a transnational frame; and organic collaborations—or meeting students and audiences where they are—through classrooms, study away, undergraduate research, and performances create the coherence to the collection and, more importantly, represent well the kinds of feminist-queer work that are needed to meet this moment in higher education and in our broader political worlds.

We also would like to thank Dominique Moore and Leigh Ann Cowan at the University of Illinois Press for their generosity and assistance in shepherding this project. Our work with the press started with the support of Dawn Durante, and Dominique and Leigh Ann have walked with us through the process after its early inception.

This project emerged from intensive work with the Great Lakes College Association's (GLCA) Women's Studies Committee, and we extend our thanks to our colleagues who showed up and breathed life into an academic space that has become vital to our work and with each other. We wish to especially acknowledge our co-facilitators, Meryl Altman, Christa Craven, Elora Chowdhury, Laurie Finke, Christy Holmes, Michelle Rowley, and Marta Sierra, and the many participants who enriched our three GLCA Curriculum Transformation Institutes between 2016 and 2018. Some of the contributors to this collection began their work in these generative GLCA spaces. The funding for committee meetings, conference gatherings, and the institutes was made possible through monies and grants received from the GLCA. We thank Gregory Wegner, Simon Gray, and Derek Vaughan for their support. We wish to especially acknowledge Charla White's contributions. Without her attention to detail and her guiding presence, our meetings over the years would not have been possible.

We thank the anonymous reviewers for their constructive comments and feedback. This is a richer collection because of their time and commitment.

Isis thanks Lisa Suhair Majaj for the permission to use her poem in the chapter titled "Weaving the Maps: Tales of Survival and Resistance." She also thanks the following students at Denison University—Zoe Loitz, Aditi Agarwal, Willow McIlvaine-Newsad, Ali Imran, Reya Islam, and Seyram Sunu-Attah—for their help with research, reviewing the bibliography, and putting together a preliminary draft of key index terms, along with staff members Robin Brown and Meagan Tehua for their administrative assistance. She thanks Students for Justice in Palestine and Faculty for Justice in Palestine at Denison for their dedication and support and the Transnational Feminist Collective for its communal solidarity.

Barbara extends her thanks to Rebecca Dawson for co-creating a joyful space on the page and in the classroom. M. Soledad Caballero and Aimee

Knupsky paved the way for us to co-teach at Allegheny College; without their steadfast support, our work would not have continued after the first iteration. I am particularly grateful to have found a partner in life, Dudley Williams, who is patient, listens with care, supports each step, offers thoughts, and has weathered some of the most difficult days with love and grace, helping to make them seamlessly a part of life.

Introduction

Feminist-Queer Collaborations as Radical Interconnectedness

ISIS NUSAIR and BARBARA L. SHAW

Why this anthology? Why now?

This anthology reflects our commitments and personal/political genealogies. It started in 2018 after organizing three annual women's, gender, sexuality studies institutes on undergraduate pedagogies (2016–2018). The political chaos at the time coupled with the increasingly neoliberal logics of higher education created an urgent and lively environment for our feminist-queer collaborations to stretch across institutional boundaries. After the third and final institute, a handful of institute participants committed to translating those conversations into this publication and the two of us wrote the proposal for this collection. While working on this project, we lived through COVID-19 outbreaks; further militarization of borders; the killing of Black, Latino/a/x/e, Indigenous, nonbinary, gender-nonconforming, and trans people; the reemergence of fascist rhetoric accelerated by the US 2016, 2020, and 2024 elections; policing of communities of color; and the normalization of anti-Muslim and anti-Asian violence. Attacks on the body continue with the rollback of *Roe v. Wade* and access to abortion care, increased Black maternal mortality rates, and anti-trans access to health care. The elimination of diversity offices in a growing number of state educational systems and the too-numerous-to-count book bans that target antiracist and queer-affirming titles have circumscribed our work, creating a challenging political reality that affects our classrooms and institutions.

While not explicit, our collective work traces the impact of unthinkable violence on our communities, students, classrooms, and the things we stand for. These events follow years of post-9/11 racial profiling and the subsequent US-led invasions of Afghanistan in 2001 and Iraq in 2003. We revise this introduction as we bear witness to the Israeli genocide of Palestinian people with the Biden administration continuing to provide weapons to Israel, cutting funds to United Nations Relief and Works Agency (UNRWA), and blocking United Nations votes to call for a cease-fire. Taken collectively, systems of transnational coloniality and intersectional inequalities within the United States stand in tension with the increased institutionalization of academic women's, gender, and sexuality studies programs whereby faculty and students may be silenced in holding robust, historically informed discussions. Collaboration in this context and how we see it being developed through this anthology is about reclaiming its emphasis on political and social power and offering access to resources for learning spaces and programs. It also emphasizes the continued need for feminist-queer perspectives that challenge binaries of "us"/"them" and "here"/"there" by discussing reimagined possibilities for how this oppositional thinking might be bridged. These challenging times got us thinking about the necessary practices of feminist collaboration for resistance and survival, and it brought us back to the work of the scholar/teacher/activists who have come before us.

Our connections to one another stretch from our respective early days of having political purpose inside and outside the academy to the current moment of making meaning of solidarities and co-building a feminist-queer collective. In the process, we found ourselves clinging more to the edge of each other's battles (Abod) and returning to the coalitional approaches and collective thinking that created the Combahee River Collective, *This Bridge Called My Back*, and *This Bridge We Call Home*. We center the Combahee River Collective Statement of 1977 that articulated the notion of multiple and interlocking systems of oppression and the ways it provides integrated, collective, collaborative, systemic, and structural analysis accounting for the particularities of race, class, gender, and sexuality formations. Our sense of work is layered with insights from texts produced by women of color and transnational feminists (see Pandit). In our work with students, we have been brought back to imagining the sacred in M. Jacqui Alexander's *Pedagogies of Crossing*, the sharpened critical lens of Richa Nagar's *Muddying the Waters*, the insistences in Chandra Talpade Mohanty's *Feminism without Borders*, the reclaiming in Sara Ahmed's *Living a Feminist Life*, and the generous thinking in AnaLouise Keating's *Transformation Now!* These writings elucidate the tension between resistance and collaboration, the meaning and practice of educational justice, critique, and moving through critique toward transformation. The work in the following pages from collaborators across the United States continues this tradition and discusses how they go about designing generative spaces with colleagues, friends, and undergraduate students.

Our first step in building collaborations has been to create space to find one another. It has taken many years of gathering, sharing, and listening as we collectively name the institutional structures that keep feminist and queer pedagogies on the margins of the academy. The work has sought to lay the groundwork for transformation through collective thinking. It connects us to previous feminist coalitions by making visible the process of doing the work by sustaining friendship, an ethics of care, and our political commitments alongside salient theoretical frameworks as starting places for building solidarities. Its central pillars are intersecting the work we do inside/outside the classroom/academy, changing how we think about borders between activism, communities, and higher education, and collaboration as sustaining activism and ourselves within institutions. In "turning toward" one another, a phrase that Ann Russo and Misty DeBerry name in their piece included in this anthology, the contributors to this collection are not only addressing pedagogical approaches; they are world making in/from the academy. Realized feminist collaborations are political acts that build foundations for community within institutions and lead to the growth and survival of programs and to students' participation in transformative social change.

Grounding Feminist Collaborations

Feminist collaboration has a rich history of scholarship within women/gender/sexuality/feminist/queer/LGBTQAI+ studies. Elizabeth Peck and JoAnna Mink (1998) raise the question in the introduction to *Common Ground: Feminist Collaboration in the Academy* whether feminist collaboration is different from other forms of collaboration. With processes and dialogue as integral to the collaboration as the final product, their edited collection provides salient examples of how feminist collaborative work makes meaning outside the logics of productivity and individualism. Carey Kaplan and Ellen Rose (1993) believe that one of the major strengths of feminist scholarship is the connection between lived experience and political and critical theory. They argue that many questions remain before an adequate theory of feminist collaboration can be constructed. For example, is our collaboration extraordinary, an accidental act of grace, or could it be reproduced? Is collaboration a peculiarly female or feminist mode of production? Kaplan and Rose argue that their experience and the statements of other feminist collaborators seem to suggest that feminists find collaboration particularly congenial. However, as Diane Lichtenstein and Virginia Powell (1998) argue, there may not be value in theorizing a coherent theory of feminist collaborations because they are at their best when they remain flexible and contextual interactions based on what is needed for the process of collaboration. Mona Krook (2019) illustrates how feminist collaborations are essential for giving voice to women's experiences and mobilizing for change, and Mimi Winick (2015) shows how collaboration in the nineteenth century not only led to the writing of alternative feminist histories but also developed alternative feminist historiographical practice that saw itself as responding to and shaping the advent of a feminist new age. Collaboration is central to the political intentionality of feminist leadership (Clover et al. 2017). Yoonkyeong Nah (2015) adds that collaboration between theory and praxis or academia and field experience need to be realized not merely in name but as a concrete practice. The emphasis, according to Lori Harrison-Kahan and Karen Skinazi (2017), is on reconstructing the dialogues and generating new methods and avenues for inquiry. Collaboration in this context is a way to counteract invisibility by developing initiatives that will facilitate collaborative recovery networks.

Ziyu Long and her colleagues (2020) identify three metaphorical processes that constitute feminist collaboration: reflexive becoming, where feminist collaborators constantly make sense of what counts as feminist as the group and context evolve; proactive improvisation, describing how feminist collaborators collectively strive for everyday transformations within situated constraints; and co-learning partnerships centering feminist collaborators in relation to one another in ways that uphold commitments to reflexivity, equity, and care. They argue that enacting these processes is fraught with tensions that intertwine with one another to constrain and enable feminist collaborations. Oluwatomisin Oredein (2019) sees collaboration in terms of listening, landing, and learning. Carrie Smith and her coauthors (2020) develop insights on how to move from transformation from collaborative work and dialogue to collective thinking and action. They offer a manifesto for building feminist coalitions urging us to forge networks and build spaces for action. They call for the political potential of polyvocal and polyamorous collaborations that reach across disciplines, time zones, and borders. Eunice Kamaara and her coauthors (2012) explain how feminism of negotiation provides a way forward for intercultural feminist collaboration as it corresponds to the cultural, practical, and methodological insights of the immersion experience.

A system of collaborative activity, then, is influenced by artifacts—altered by the objects of discourse that collaborators have access to and the material realities that allow for their collaboration (Fredlund 2016). Collaborations and collaborators are influenced by the institutions and communities in which they participate and also those from which they are excluded. Katherine Fredlund adds that the goal of the collaboration is determined by the collaborators' interaction with other aspects of the activity system. Collaboration is, therefore, a fluid and dynamic process in which persons (collaborators), artifacts (objects of discourse and other material conditions), institutions (both educational and political), communities (including contributors who support and allow the collaborative practice), practices (of language and of the collaboration itself), and productions of difference (race, gender, and sexuality) interact and are woven together as a result of their interaction with the runaway object of power in order to reach a goal, be it textual, educational, or otherwise (Fredlund 2016).

We also know from our experiences and engagement with one another as well as a deep reading of intersectional and transnational feminist scholarship that collaborations can be rewarding and uneasy; discomforting and the basis for change; and joyful and sustaining. They require self-reflexivity and vulnerability and ask us to take risks and follow through on our commitments beyond research and publications. It is the work of solidarity and, in Nagar's words, "ever-evolving journeys that confront and embrace the messiness of solidarity and responsibility" (2). Our ability to practice this work of feminist collaboration and solidarity in preparation for and in the classroom, and across institutions, was made possible because of the work of grassroots collectives working to secure feminist approaches in higher education—from those who founded the first women's studies program at San Diego State College (now University) in 1970 and beyond. In a contemporary era defined by (re)entrenched heteropatriarchy, transphobia, sexism, white nationalism, settler colonialism, militarization, ableism, and neoliberalism that drives consolidations and erasures of women's/feminist/gender/sexuality/queer/LGBTQAI+ studies in higher education as well as the marketing of diversity, equity, and inclusion (albeit under fire in some states) devoid of painstakingly built solidarities, politically engaged feminist collaborations are as essential and relevant now as they were fifty years ago.

This collection draws together scholars-teachers-activists who move beyond valuing collaboration in theory to embodying, engaging, and sharing with us how they have gone about living it in their classrooms and beyond. Contributors link theory and activism or theory and practices while exploring how the personal is still political through intersectional and transnational lenses. Taken together, these pieces examine how and what it means to build feminist/women's/gender/queer/LGBTQAI+ communities within academic programs, push the boundaries of feminist practice, and engage in community-building work and praxis across siloed institutional boundaries so that we may see how we and our work are intertwined. This anthology also contributes to national efforts in thinking through relational pedagogies to building local, regional, and transnational connections that imagine their purpose beyond institutionalization and toward actively contributing to sociopolitical change during these turbulent years so that transformation is theorized, rooted, and reimagined.

Feminist pedagogical collaborations with each other and with students can create radical forms of knowledge production and activism. Jamie Barlowe and Ruth Hotte (1998) remind us, "As feminist collaborators, we must, as Adrienne Rich urged us to do . . . take ourselves seriously; in doing so, we can take our students seriously, collaborating with them and each other recursively, rereading ourselves as we reread the world" (240). Collaborations are at their best when they enliven what AnaLouise Keating theorizes as "threshold" work that embraces post-oppositional interconnectedness. In the introduction to *Transformation Now!* she writes:

> Grounded in a framework of interconnectivity . . . threshold theories are relational. Whereas border thinking generally begins from a point of breakage . . . threshold theories start elsewhere—with the presupposition that we are intimately, inextricably linked. [By] positing our radical interconnectedness, threshold theories contain but exceed . . . the principle of negative difference, and the either/or thinking found in oppositional consciousness and other Enlightenment-based worldviews. (11)

Radical interconnectedness allows for "multiple intersecting possibilities, opportunities, and challenges" and for us collectively to create collaborative spaces that exist "in-between . . . where new beginnings, and unexpected combinations can occur" (10). The beauty of Keating's work is that it accepts movement and movement building as thresholds that can hold care and community, joy and struggle, political negotiations and change, painful experiences and transformative knowledge and justice. The collective voice in this anthology constructs pedagogies that move through intellectual critique and toward radically inclusive change growing out of thinking through *what* is taught to *how* it is taught so that it sustains us as communities. As women of color, international, feminist, queer scholar-teacher-activist contributors, our pedagogical work embraces change through contradiction, building communities and solidarities with care, learning transgressive analytical thought that names and resists oppressive structures, and engaging student learning through enlivened pedagogies and community action. This book also lays out how and why we integrate intersectional, transnational, liberatory, and transdisciplinary approaches that do this perspective-changing and learning work with students.

Pedagogies of Interconnectedness insists on the polyvocal and multiply positioned perspectives that make theoretical interventions based on the contributors' cooperative and collaborative pedagogies as well as provide resources for teaching courses in a rapidly expanding field. In women's/gender/sexuality/feminist/queer/LGBTQAI+ studies programs and departments across the United States, there is desire and pressure to provide offerings that are mindful and radically inclusive of intersectional, transnational, transgender/nonbinary, anticolonial/decolonial, antiracist/critical race theory, and dis/ability studies in ways that are categorically different from even five years ago. Contributors provide insights into how we might do this work through focused approaches. For example, some discuss multiple feminist-queer theoretical frameworks they have drawn on to build courses and programs that emphasize solidarity through the digital humanities (María Claudia André), community engagement (Ariella Rotramel and Kimberly Sanchez), and study away (André; Luisa Bieri; Danielle M. DeMuth and Ayana K. Weekley; Montserrat Pérez-Toribio and M. Gabriela Torres).

Contributors to this anthology, including Andrea N. Baldwin, Isis Nusair, Barbara L. Shaw, Rebecca Dawson, Meryl Altman, and Sharon R. Wesoky, also focus on intersectional and transnational approaches to collaboration and pedagogy within higher education to provide a sense of *why* they are necessary if we seek solidarity and transformation. The pieces in this collection address the roots of inequities, state violence and repression, and transnational consolidation of power while providing students with tools to think beyond critique for its own sake and lead to more sustained cultural transformation. Doing this work in the classroom is not only more urgent; it also has become more dangerous and fraught. An easy example to point to is Florida governor Ron DeSantis's appointment of new members to the board of trustees at the New College of Florida with the goal of eliminating gender studies. It matters that this project's early life span parallels the Trump administration's rollback of human rights, intellectual inquiry, and higher education, and its advancement of white supremacy and incitements of violence aimed at women, people of color, and LGBTQAI+ communities. Certainly, these forces have since doubled down in the United States and globally. We need shared tools and a broader sense of community as we walk through it in order to sustain ourselves and the work of our programs.

The volume blends theory and practice to make clear *how* they are connected and needed as we strive for sustaining feminist-queer communities. In emphasizing collaboration across departments and institutional boundaries to create meaningful and transformative spaces for students to situate themselves and reimagine the world, the collection of authors further advances what AnaLouise Keating's post-oppositional thinking looks like in practice. Hierarchies within classrooms and the competition within and between institutions secure what she names as "binary either/ or epistemology and praxis that structures our perceptions, politics, and actions through a resistant energy—a reaction against that which we seek to transform" (2). Collaboration insists on us working within and across oppositional structures for students to understand, see, and practice that change happens if we find places of solidarity, connection, or what Eli Clare names as "interdependence" in *Brilliant Imperfections*. Collaboration also provides a lens for keeping differences and oppressive structures of power in sharp focus—it is not a facile alignment with "commonalities" that rely on universal constructions of women, gender, feminist, or queer. It is not easy work, though it is necessary work if knowledge, inquiry, creativity, and transformative justice are to move beyond the classroom. We collectively argue that *despite* the continued attacks on women's/gender/sexuality/feminist/queer/LGBTQAI+ studies, critical race theory, and transnational and postcolonial studies, there is also an opportunity to build community and connections across local, national, and transnational boundaries through our work with students and staff. Led by friendship, care, transformation, and interdependence, the foundations of which Elora Chowdhury and Liz Philipose explore in *Dissident Friendships* (2016), we can build a radically different future that sustains us. The essays in this collection begin this critical work by showing us how to do this in the classroom, through study away, undergraduate research, building community partnerships, and connecting with audiences through performance.

Genealogy of Our Collaboration: Community, Survival, Solidarity

We, the editors of this book, teach at small liberal arts colleges in Ohio and Pennsylvania. We met through and have been actively involved in the Great Lakes Colleges Association's (GLCA) Women's Studies Committee for over a decade. The Women's Studies Committee itself was created in 1976, a year before the founding of the National Women's Studies Association (NWSA), and was therefore the first consortia effort to bring together faculty interested in the then–newly emerging interdisciplinary field of women's studies. The committee's purpose was to provide administrative support to its members as faculty worked in thirteen GLCA-affiliated colleges to create new programs on their campuses. Over the next twenty-five years, the committee shared expertise; raised the consciousness on member campuses about the needs of women and queer faculty, students, staff, and administrators; familiarized faculty with the most current feminist and queer scholarship and teaching methods; and developed information and support networks. Funded by the GLCA and member colleges, the committee, which included two faculty from each institution, met three times each year. These meetings provided collegial support to faculty, who were often isolated as the only women's studies faculty on their campuses, and allowed for the planning of regular conferences and workshops. By the early 2000s, the GLCA shifted to grant work to fund this type of faculty development, and the Women's Studies Committee continued to promote consortia exchange between and among the campus programs seeking to carry forward this spirit of collaboration and networking. In 2020–2021 the committee hosted several virtual meetings to determine directions for continued growth and collaboration, especially by engaging technology to keep us connected. Those meetings led to the decision to rename the group, from the "GLCA Women's Studies Committee" to "GLCA Women's, Gender and Sexuality Studies Collective." The new name better reflects the political groundings of the group as it has evolved over the years.

This institutional genealogy does not tell our whole story. Our friendship began in 2014 when we gravitated toward one another at a weekend GLCA workshop at the College of Wooster, where we were sharing with colleagues how to sustain ourselves in our institutional homes. We worked closely over that weekend to write the seed of a GLCA Expanding Collaborations grant. In two days the committee wrote, workshopped, and read through each other's proposals, and eventually the two of us submitted the grant to build three curriculum institutes. This collection is the outgrowth of our organizing of these three GLCA women's, gender, and sexuality studies curriculum institutes (2016–2018). The first institute focused on teaching "The Introductory Course" and "Queer Studies," the second on "Transnational Feminisms," and the third on "Feminist Collaborations in Teaching and Learning." Participants in the three institutes thought through feminist-queer collaborations and pedagogies. This book expands the work started during the institutes by including contributing authors from the institutes and across the United States to develop strategies in and beyond the classroom, including in the community and fields of research.

Our ongoing collaboration has been about sustaining one another through *life* by providing emotional and material support to one another alongside creating solidarities, community, and connections in our GLCA consortia collective. This project has been a journey for us: when one of us was overwhelmed (no matter the circumstances), the other one picked up the load. Our collaboration has been a seamless understanding of the pressures under which we live and work so we prioritized supporting each other as we went through the process of thinking, writing, and editing. Together we have been carving out spaces to think about what genuinely engaged feminist collaboration could be when enacted. In "The Role of Talk in the Writing Process of Intimate Collaboration," Mary Alm names "intimate collaboration as the general term for the process of writing in the 'dialogic' collaborative mode in order to emphasize the emotional and social dimensions of such collaboration" (126). The more conscious the commitment to the process, and the more dialogic the process is, the greater the chance to translate feminist theory into feminist practice. It also means that "unlike persons who choose to collaborate because they seek an efficient way to divide the work of a large project, intimate collaborators experience the process as intense and demanding, both individuals give their whole selves to all phases of the work" (126). Our accountability to one another by cowriting rather than dividing the labor, listening across our differences based on experiences and approaches, and working closely with contributors is as meaningful to this work as sharing our collective pedagogies through this edited collection.

Our collaboration also entails continuous political work across our different institutions and throughout the years has allowed us to breathe as we support each other directly and indirectly to find spaces for healing and liberation. The collaboration for Barbara would become intellectually, politically, and personally sustaining. As a single, full-time equivalent in a small liberal arts program, the members of the GLCA collective are friends, colleagues, and mentors who saw her through tenure. The same applies to Isis, who holds a joint appointment in two very small interdisciplinary programs, Women's and Gender Studies and International Studies. Creating these kinds of solidarities that are committed to curricular and institutional change has been life-giving, especially as neoliberal regimes seek to silence cultural criticism and dissent by threatening to consolidate or eliminate programs while simultaneously marketing the diversity of institutions to attract more students. As relatively small interdisciplinary programs, women's, gender, and sexuality studies programs tend to be popular with students, underfunded and understaffed, and some of the first to be threatened with elimination despite being relatively budget neutral. This is precisely the reason why collaboration and solidarities are the necessary tools needed to meet this moment.

Elimination of programs is not just a function of changing political tides. A 2020 data brief from the NWSA provides a snapshot of the devastation that COVID-19 has brought to higher education and particularly women's, gender, and sexuality studies programs: "Although these trends are nationwide and affect nearly all sectors of the university, WGSS programs and centers, woman-identifying and Black, Indigenous, and People of Color (BIPOC) faculty and staff, and public institutions are disproportionately affected" (Nadasen et al. 3). The data shows that the public health crisis, economic climate, and political moment has intensified the shift toward a "neoliberal framework for higher education, where worth is measured in terms of productivity, certain forms of labor are devalued or unrecognized, and the financial bottom line becomes the most important factor in decision making" (4). The report goes on to argue that although "universities were never exempt from capitalist imperatives, there has been an acceleration of the damaging trends toward precarity, heightened work expectations, and treating students as customers" (4). The report questions, as we do in this anthology, whose labor is regarded as valuable and whose is expendable, and what labor counts as productive and what is made invisible. In "Feminist Collaborations in Higher Education: stretched across career stages," Maddie Breeze and Yvette Taylor (2020) stress how "collaboration across career stages is a significant empirical case for understanding how feminists work to take up space [in] higher education" (413). Their work asks how feminist collaborations "can claim and disrupt the neoliberal temporal logics of competitively achieving individuals on upward career trajectories, where academic arrival can feel permanently deferred" (412). This collection intentionally takes up that question by demonstrating how students, staff, faculty, and audiences become co-producers of knowledge and education.

Transforming Pedagogies

Teaching as a collaborative pedagogy and liberatory movement building is a theme that runs through all of the chapters in this collection, where the focus is on creating intentional spaces within the classroom and beyond. The queering of academic spaces offers pathways for teacher-scholars to navigate hierarchies, inequities, and hostilities and reimagine pedagogies to transform the world otherwise. The central question that our collective voices address is how feminist-queer praxis transforms knowledge production and students' educational experiences. Many take as their starting point that grassroots activism and connection is essential for building transgressive, transformative, and sustaining learning spaces. Some narrate how feminist-queer collaborations create local and global communities between China/US; Middle East/US; South and Central America and Mexico/US; and South Africa/US; and through the classroom, digital projects, citation practices, study away opportunities, community partnerships, and performance. There are also two chapters that are cowritten with students that reorient internships, research experiences, and group studies within women's/gender/sexuality curricula.

The sections have been organized in three parts to tell a story that moves from embodiment to transformation and done so topically as to not reify hierarchies in higher education. Part I focuses on the centrality of community building and queering bodies of knowledge with students, staff, faculty, and community partners. It begins with Misty DeBerry and Ann Russo's chapter, "Turning Toward: Teaching as Collaboration." Moving away from disembodied ways of knowing that permeate the landscape of higher education, they shift our focus to community, solidarity, accountability, and mutual responsibility. These modes of embodied processes of learning have the potential to disrupt and transform intersecting oppressions and power, and lead to communal healing and change. DeBerry and Russo address the question of how to enhance the capacity of any class to create an open learning community and how to transform the classroom from a space of unconscious acts of intellectual dominance to a site of collaboration across multiple positions gathered in the classroom. Their goal is to share new strategies for structural critique, community connectedness, and social redress. The foundation of their work is not purely intellectual but also relational. They focus on how to build learning spaces where instructors and students cultivate a sense of belonging and interconnectedness by working through the tensions and difficulties rather than avoiding them.

Andrea N. Baldwin's contribution, "Critical Transnational Black Feminist Queer Praxis: Engendering Collaborative Pedagogy through Care and Community Building," focuses on how a "critical transnational Black feminist queer praxis" centers an ethic of care and demonstrates how this praxis uses collaborative pedagogy to bring together those confined to the margins of the academy—those who are queer, Black, brown, working class, and immigrant. Baldwin argues that shared space and producing communal knowledge has the potential to create a world where we can discover and create the possibilities of connection, collaboration, and coalition leading to academic/educational justice. This piece shows us how we can challenge the capitalist logics, antisociality, and exclusion of the university structure and practices through a vision of reclaiming not only how knowledge is produced but how worlds are created on university campuses outside the institutionalization of diversity and multicultural centers. This praxis, as it unsettles, imagines, and enacts, is one of self-creation, (re)naming, and collaboration that disrupts academic space as it generates community.

In "Radical Feminist Transgressions in Teaching/Learning," Linh U. Hua and K. Melchor Quick Hall showcase the value of adjacency as an intentional politics of collaboration. Rather than work toward a static condition of "coherence," they embrace a process of "messy collaborations" and transgressive practices that challenge the boundaries of the academy.

In proposing a "liberatory, feminist andragogy," they consider both what adults bring to an educational experience and what an engagement of liberation struggles can bring to the teaching/learning environment. Hua and Hall propose five guiding principles for scholarly and activist work: radical multilingualism, transgressive borderland praxis, collective and communal knowledge traditions, oral traditions, and counter-canonical citation practices. According to these authors, this feminist approach accounts for much more of what we know and how we survive, making group knowledge and the communities from which those groups emerge important sources for knowledge creation, citation, and circulation.

In "Beyond Critique: Building a Feministqueerpublichealth Classroom," Barbara L. Shaw and Rebecca Dawson argue for the need to create new spaces from places of contradiction and connection outside of either/or thinking in order to do their work of integrating the interdisciplinary humanities and sciences. They think of their teaching collaboration as a cultural and academic borderland that has allowed them to listen carefully to each other and to the different disciplinary languages used to discuss sex, health, and, more broadly, their respective fields. In their attempt at blending feminist-queer and public health approaches, they focus on "nonhierarchical, interdependent, and collaborative thinking as practice" in their shared classroom. They argue that public health is part of the problem if not grounded in these frameworks of structural and institutional inequities, so it is necessary and meaningful to draw on the scholarly and activist work in women's, gender, and sexuality studies and Black/Africana studies. Shaw and Dawson conclude that until faculty come together intentionally and with humility across disciplinary boundaries, they have no way to anticipate the potential for these integrations and collaborations.

Ariella Rotramel and Kimberly Sanchez continue building on these themes in "Challenging Hierarchy: Feminist Praxis and Sustainable Community Collaboration" by questioning the divides between identities. Their chapter explores continuums across social categories, studies the dynamic and historically specific creation and articulation of identities, and emphasizes how multiple identities and systems of oppression interact with one another in community-engaged learning. They examine how these hierarchies can problematically permeate the development of a collaboration, as well as the expectations and dynamics within a project. Their work centers the feminist pedagogical value of reciprocal relationships utilizing an intersectional critique of identity, power, and hierarchy that emphasizes naming and understanding how structural dynamics play out in the lived experiences of communities, both inside and outside the classroom. Through building feminist experiential learning into the student curricular experience, they intentionally and iteratively address inequities that structure the roles and the dynamics within community collaborations. This praxis challenges a neoliberal consumer model that meets students where they are rather than challenges them to grow or understand themselves in relationship to others.

Part II focuses on bringing transnational approaches to feminist collaborations. Taken together, the pieces destabilize the US classroom as a centralized place for knowledge production and offer pathways for students' reflection to build connections across national borders. The transnational in this context is a site for addressing past and present relations of imperial and colonial power and emphasizes how our collective lives are entangled within them. It opens with María Claudia André's examination of the uses and applications of digital technology to foster transnational and interdisciplinary collaboration across national borders, bridge theory with practice, and mobilize knowledge-making through alternative channels of production and dissemination. In "Teaching and Learning Intersectional and Transnational Feminisms through Digital Humanities," André focuses on decolonial intersectional and transnational theory and practice to demystify the academy as the only privileged location of knowledge. The chapter emphasizes the need to teach our students new ways to establish collaborative dialogues and close relationships across geographical, social, and cultural divides and argues that faculty-student research, experiential learning, oral history narratives, and feminist digital humanities have the potential to significantly impact how students acquire knowledge and engage in cross-cultural activism. Transnational and interdisciplinary digital humanities projects offer an effective means to creatively visualize and capture the human experience from multiple perspectives to showcase the coalitions, movements, and networks women forge transnationally to resist patriarchal systems and institutions in their own communities.

Luisa Bieri builds on these themes in "Engaged Global Pedagogy: Moving from Study Abroad to Transnational Scholar-Activism" and focuses on three pedagogical principles to understand and reshape transnational solidarities: reflexivity, reciprocity, and connectivity. Each principle, according to Bieri, operates within a critical praxis that highlights experiential, engaged learning within transnational feminist pedagogy. Bieri uses Antioch College's Cooperative Education model for socially engaged global learning as a case study of pedagogical praxis and renewed understanding and commitment to scholar-activism within study abroad programs. She argues that this feminist pedagogical approach is rooted in a deep, reflexive understanding of our own positionalities, as well as the historic, social, economic, and cultural realities of others. The emphasis is on self-reflexivity, sustained dialogue, and building reciprocal relationships that connect across differences to move into collective action. Bieri concludes that the more we establish engaged global learning as an extension of efforts to teach and learn about reflexivity, antiracism, and intercultural dialogue in our classrooms, the less likely it is to be an isolated "tourist" experience—disconnected from a commitment toward shared responsibility and reciprocity with community members on and off campus.

In "Teaching Feminist China: The Dream and the Real," Meryl Altman and Sharon R. Wesoky argue that the field of women's, gender, and sexuality studies has developed a core pedagogy for undergraduate teaching with a recognizable set of transnational canonized texts and "habits of practice" for syllabus building and classroom dynamics. Informed by their collaboration that involved thinking through how to incorporate China into their own classes, the authors suggest that there is a missed opportunity when we do not focus on socialist feminisms that emerge out of China. Chinese feminisms allow students to "situate their frequent critiques of neoliberal capitalism within a complex history of socialism and post-socialism, various forms of feminist solidarity, and a deeper comprehension of the multidirectional ways that transnationalism operates in complex historical, social, and political circumstances." Since transnational feminist theory originates in many locations beyond the West, incorporating Chinese feminist theory into our syllabi can provide an example of decolonizing feminism.

Danielle M. DeMuth and Ayana K. Weekley, in "Unpack *Here*: Challenging Privilege, Increasing Empathy, and Building Solidarity through Collaborative Feminist Pedagogy," offer possibilities on how feminist-built study abroad and community engagement programs intersect with transnational approaches, arguing that many programs are often depoliticized and do not offer pathways toward solidarity. They suggest that unless students spend time examining and interrogating the context of these programs and their role in them, the structures of power and privilege remain invisible, which is a barrier to collaboration, solidarity, and social change. Based on their work with students traveling to South Africa, the authors are committed to the possibilities that may be realized when study abroad and service learning are structured according to feminist theories and methods of positionality, reflexivity, and critical transnational praxis as theorized by Richa Nagar and Amanda Lock Swarr in *Critical Transnational Feminist Praxis*. DeMuth and Weekley offer an approach that goes beyond simply humanizing others and taking an interest in their lives; it involves seeing them as equal. The authors emphasize how and why it is important to work with students to reflect on and articulate how their privilege operates in relationship to people outside the United States and why it is important to develop individual and collective accountability that is necessary to build empathy and solidarity.

In "Transcultural and Transborder Pedagogies in the Feminist Classroom," Montserrat Pérez-Toribio and M. Gabriela Torres juxtapose collaborative experiments in feminist pedagogy for teaching students to dialogue with difference. In their courses—one that was based in Miami, another in Puerto Rico—they aspired to activate a vision of publicly engaged feminist pedagogy that transgresses disciplinary boundaries to link the classroom with the outside world. These feminist pedagogies foster a "pluralistic mode" of being in the world that embraces contradiction and ambiguity by rejecting easy identity and place categories. The authors situate their courses in local-global settings where multiple positionings are possible and shape the student experiences to understand how these subject positions intersect and shape each other in struggle and in conversation. Within this context, the faculty designed classroom spaces that emphasize dialogue, negotiation, and transformation through reflexive collaboration and hands-on activism. This pedagogical practice gives students the ability to observe the co-presence of the here-and-there, the self-and-other, and the center-and-margin within geographic and discursive spaces.

In part III the focus is on organic collaborations in the classroom and with public audiences. It starts with Christine Keating's "Widening the Circle: Collaborative Learning Within, Between, and Beyond Classrooms," in which she explores the possibilities and challenges for building praxical collaborations between faculty and students. Keating argues that experiments in classroom design can help enable processes of anti-hierarchical dialogue and decision making, engagement that sharpens students' critical thinking, and community building in ways that highlight the impact of theory and activism in feminist-queer learning. Keating adds that challenging the theory-practice divide in the classroom hinges on reworking the institutionally hierarchical roles that student and teacher are expected to play toward the possibility of relations grounded in liberatory dialogue, in resistant relationality, and in deeply felt solidarity and accountability. Within this context, students are co-learners, co-resisters, co-strugglers, and co-designers of justice-centered spaces, including LGBTQAI+ and disability communities, to expand the classroom boundaries and, in turn, construct it as a democratic space. Since there is no set formula for what a feminist classroom space is, Keating urges us to talk and think together to figure out what might work best for those in the room. She adds that each time we come together in the classroom (either in-person or virtually), we have the opportunity to create the space anew, structuring possibilities for collaboration, care, and dialogue.

In ""The Most Real Experience I've Had in a Course': Disrupting Silences and Cultivating Intimacy," Emily Fairchild (faculty), Leen Alfatafta (student), Sara Youngblood Gregory (student), and Carolyn Beer (student) expand Keating's argument by showing how a course that was collaboratively designed by a faculty member and three former students actively sought transformation on their campus. Brought together after an all-male panel discussion by a collective desire to study how sexism and racism circulate through university structures (and beyond), the authors offer an example of how feminist collaborations can help us find the edges of understanding and support student growth into new ways of knowing. Their work from different subject positions navigates the terrain of student-professor inter-actions, the care labor of advising, how faculty of color on predominantly white campuses are assumed to lead the work of repair during political inflection points (such as George Floyd's murder and Black Lives Matter demonstrations), and how to be self-reflexive and cowrite this piece about what they learned. The chapter argues that intimacy, as a pedagogical goal, emphasizes emotional connection, trust, and responsibility to others. Their commitment to the course disrupted classroom hierarchies as they centered marginalized voices, crossed and questioned the boundaries of professional status, critiqued disciplinary tactics guised as "collegial" comportment, and allowed expertise to be told firsthand by the authors they read and by each other. Their narrative is a testimony to how student-faculty collaborations go beyond teaching and learning to creating relationships, networks, and skills required to build solidarity and enact change in the US higher educa-tion system and beyond.

Similarly, in "Facilitating Feminist Collaborations in Undergraduate Education: Models for Research and Internships in Gender and Women's Studies," Letizia Guglielmo (faculty), Jordyn Alderman (student), Jeremy Hall (student), Brayden Milam (student), and Andrea Putala (student) explore how students take more active roles in and responsibility for their own and their peers' learning when they are the co-designers of research and internship opportunities. The authors share and reflect on three models for undergraduate research and internship building, arguing that when these practices are created with collaborative inquiry as a primary objective and guided by a decentered feminist pedagogy, such projects have the potential to foster increased activism and engagement among undergraduate students and to support change. It was important in the authors' collaboration to have student voices and experiences validated through co-designing high-impact practices. For the faculty member, it was an act of solidarity that had feminist ethics as their foundation. Finally, and most significantly, as one of the students suggests, we cannot yet imagine the impact of inviting undergraduates to shape spaces and conversations where they previously had not seen themselves reflected. Sometimes small acts grounded in feminist pedagogy create meaningful lifelong collaborations.

Making meaning *with* audiences, not *for* audiences, guides Isis Nusair's collaboration with Laila Farah in creating the one-woman multimedia performance *Weaving the Maps: Tales of Survival and Resistance*. The performance is grounded in the narratives Nusair gathered from Iraqi, Palestinian, and Syrian women refugees over the last two decades and brings about a transnational feminist praxis that crosses boundaries in the ethical re/telling of these stories. In the process of putting together this performance, Nusair and Farah cross and blur many disciplinary and academy/community divides. Their work focuses on how to draw on a reflexive reading of power, privilege, and positionality and "learn from below" to determine how we can be inclusive and accountable to people's struggles for liberation, how to achieve an embodiment that continues to resist erasure, and how to resist erasure through creativity and collaboration. In the last segment of the performance, titled "Future Movements," they bring their own collaborations with women refugees and the audience to a new level of interconnectedness. This multilayered weaving of the maps of resilience and resistance traces the sites and routes for creating systems of accountability, movement building, coalition, and solidarity.

Conclusion

We return to questions about transformation; how we operate with one another; and the vulnerabilities, violence, and potential of the current economic, political, and social moment. It matters in how we build learning spaces when we are in the middle of struggle and how what we build can become sustainable. This collection raises questions about how we think about the state as we decolonize and queer bodies of knowledge, what is citable as fundamental to sustainable collaborations, and how to make the academy a place where pedagogical border crossings and connections are possible. It addresses the meaning of organic and transformative collaborations and the ways we engage with it as teachers and community members. The anthology examines the affective and embodied dimensions of transformative justice practices and possibilities for healing, accountability, and transformation. It opens the space for setting the modes of operation for building feminist classrooms to foster intersectional, transnational, and anti-hierarchical dialogue, decision making, and learning in ways that insist we move beyond its mere naming and recognition.

The contributors to this anthology leave us with these questions: How are we to build relationships in the classroom where people can feel vulnerable and accountable for one another across inequitable power lines and for the impact of our words and actions? What are the core values that are brought into pedagogies grounded in interconnectedness? How are we "to 'world'-travel to see our face in the heartbreak of an/other?" (Rios-Rojas 167). How are we to evoke the work of personal narratives? How could modes of listening push against power over dynamics like self-preservation, coercion, and competition, and how could they prompt groups toward empathy, accountability and sustainable collectivity? The chapters in this collection start answering these questions by bridging theory and practice drawing on intersectional, transnational, decolonial, queer, and interdisciplinary approaches to pedagogy. Our continued work will determine the kind of classroom and communities we can all help change and transform.

Works Cited

Abod, Jennifer. *The Edge of Each Other's Battles: The Vision of Audre Lorde*. Women Make Movies, 2002.

Ahmed, Sara. *Living a Feminist Life*. Duke UP, 2017.

Alexander, M. Jacqui. *Pedagogies of the Crossing: Meditations on Feminism, Sexual Politics, Memory, and the Sacred*. 1st edition. Duke UP, 2006.

Alm, Mary. "The Role of Talk in the Writing Process of Intimate Collaboration." *Common Ground: Feminist Collaboration in the Academy*, edited by Elizabeth Peck and JoAnna Mink. State U of New York P, 1998.

Altman, Meryl, and Sharon Wesoky. "Teaching Feminist China: The Dream and the Real." *Pedagogies of Interconnectedness: Feminist-Queer Collaborative Transformation*, edited by Isis Nusair and Barbara Shaw. U of Illinois P, 2025.

Anzaldúa, Gloria, and AnaLouise Keating. *This Bridge We Call Home: Radical Visions for Transformation*. 1st edition. Routledge, 2002.

Barlowe, Jamie, and Ruth Hotte. "Feminist Theory and Practice and the Pedantic I/Eye." *Common Ground: Feminist Collaboration in the Academy*, edited by Elizabeth Peck and JoAnna Mink. State U of New York P, 1998.

Breeze, Maddie, and Yvette Taylor. "Feminist Collaborations in Higher Education: Stretched across Career Stages." *Gender and Education*, vol. 32, no. 3, 2020, pp. 412–28.

Chowdhury, Elora, and Liz Philipose, eds. *Dissident Friendships: Feminism, Imperialism, and Transnational Solidarity*. U of Illinois P, 2016.

Clare, Eli. *Brilliant Imperfections: Grappling with Cure*. Duke UP, 2017.

Clover, Darlene E., Catherine Etmanski, and Rachel Reimer. "Gendering Collaboration: Adult Education in Feminist Leadership." *New Directions for Adult & Continuing Education*, vol. 156, 2017, pp. 21–31.

Combahee River Collective. "The Combahee River Collective Statement." *How We Get Free* by Keeanga-Yamahtta Taylor, Haymarket Books, 2017.

Fredlund, Katherine. "Feminist CHAT: Collaboration, Nineteenth-Century Women's Clubs, and Activity Theory." *College English*, vol. 78, no. 5, 2016, pp. 470–95.

Harrison-Kahan, Lori, and Karen E. H. Skinazi. "Feminist Collaboration in an Era of Academic Instability." *American Periodicals*, vol. 27, no. 1, 2017, pp. 16–20.

Kamaara, Eunice Karanja, Elisabeth T. Vasko, and Jeanine E. Viau. "Listening and Speaking as Two Sides of the Same Coin: Negotiating Dualisms in Intercultural Feminist Collaboration." *Journal of Feminist Studies in Religion*, vol. 28, no. 2, 2012, pp. 49–67.

Kaplan, Carey, and Ellen Cronan Rose. "Strange Bedfellows: Feminist Collaboration." *Signs*, vol. 18, no. 3, 1993, pp. 547–61.

Keating, AnaLouise. *Transformation Now!: Toward a Post-Oppositional Politics of Change*. U of Illinois P, 2013.

Krook, Mona Lena. "Global Feminist Collaborations and the Concept of Violence against Women in Politics." *Journal of International Affairs*, vol. 72, no. 2, 2019, pp. 77–94.

Liechtenstein, Diane, and Virgina Powell. "Collaborative Leadership, Feminist Possibility, Feminist Oxymoron." *Common Ground: Feminist Collaboration in the Academy*, edited by Elizabeth Peck and JoAnna Mink. State U of New York P, 1998.

Long, Ziyu, Jasmine R. Linabary, Patrice M. Buzzanell, Ashton Mouton, and Ranjani L. Rao. "Enacting Everyday Feminist Collaborations: Reflexive Becoming, Proactive Improvisation and Co-Learning Partnerships." *Gender, Work and Organization*, vol. 27, no. 4, 2020, pp. 487–506.

Mohanty, Chandra. *Feminism without Borders: Decolonizing Theory, Practicing Solidarity*. Duke UP, 2003.

Moraga, Cherríe, and Gloria Anzaldúa. *This Bridge Called My Back: Writings by Radical Women of Color*. Kitchen Table: Women of Color Press, 1983.

Nadasen, Priscilla, Jen Ash, and Briona Jones. *WGSS Programs during COVID: A Data Brief from NWSA*. National Women's Studies Association, 2020.

Nagar, Richa. *Muddying the Waters: Coauthoring Feminisms across Scholarship and Activism*. U of Illinois P, 2014.

Nah, Yoonkyeong. "Rethinking the Idiom for Feminist Pedagogy: The Collaboration of Theory and Activism." *Asian Journal of Women's Studies*, vol. 21, no. 2, 2015, pp. 147–65.

Oredein, Oluwatomisin. "Sharing Our Knowledge: Feminist Collaborations across Generations." *Journal of Feminist Studies in Religion*, vol. 35, no. 2, 2019, pp. 93–98.

Pandit, Eesha, Paula Moya, Carla Kaplan, and Suzanna Walters. "Ask a Feminist: Eesah Pandit and Paula Moya Discuss Activism and the Academy with Carla Kaplan and Suzanna Walters." *Signs*, vol. 47, no. 1, 2021, pp. 235–45.

Peck, Elizabeth G., and JoAnna Stephens Mink. *Common Ground: Feminist Collaboration in the Academy*. State U of New York P, 1998.

Rios-Rojas, Anne. "'Pedagogies of the Broken-Hearted': Notes on a Pedagogy of Breakage, Women of Color Feminist Decolonial Vovidas, and Armed Love in the Classroom/Academy." *Frontiers: A Journal of Women's Studies*, vol. 41, no. 1, 2020, pp. 161–78.

Smith, Carrie, Maria Stehle, and Beverly Weber. "Intimate Collaborations and Feminist Gatherings: A Manifesto for a Coalitional Academy." *Feminist German Studies*, vol. 36, no. 1, 2020, pp. 128–43.

Winick, Mimi. "Scholarly Collaboration for a Feminist New Age in Jane Harrison's and Jessie Weston's Alternative Histories." *Nineteenth-Century Gender Studies*, vol. 11, no. 3, 2015, pp. 45–56.

Community Building and Queering Bodies of Knowledge

1

Turning Toward

Teaching as Collaboration

MISTY DEBERRY and ANN RUSSO

Dearest reader,

We write to you in the spirit of collaboration and co-struggle and from within an unfinished project. This is to say that Annie and I have been thinking, dreaming, teaching, practicing together for—at the time of this writing—well over ten years. And we very much hope/intend to do so for many, many more years to come. That said, it may be helpful to know that when we began this essay, I had recently left Chicago for Boston on a postdoctoral opportunity. At that time, our work together was fresh on our tongues, readily available, as if we had merely stepped out of a classroom and into a breakout room to eagerly chat about what we had just observed. Four or so years have passed now. It is an unusually warm spring day in the central New England area, 2023. Annie continues the rich and nuanced work of building communities at DePaul University and the greater Chicago area. And I have moved to just outside of Hanover, New Hampshire, where I am wrapping up my last term serving as a senior lecturer in the program for WGSS at Dartmouth College. This means, our work/collaboration has come to mean incorporating/navigating ways to partner across different institutions, across different time zones, along with navigating the unfolding unpredictabilities of life, doing whatever it will—whenever it will.

At the same time, since we began this essay together, the COVID-19 pandemic era set in, setting off what we can think of now as, not so much "post-COVID times" but the afterlives of COVID-19. The implications of this last statement are as plentiful as they are troubling. Particular to our work on collaboration, for us at this moment in time, at this moment in our editing process, "the classroom"—as Annie and I recently discussed in a midweek phone call—is no longer "the classroom." At least not as it was when we began our work together, when we began this essay together—itself interrupted by logistical impossibilities, somatic evacuations, and psychic debris left in the wake of COVID-19 along with the maddening, abiding geopolitical crises particular to this second decade of the twenty-first century. So, much has changed. And what it means to collaborate with each other, in the classroom, has changed too. In our approach to final edits—the passage of many seasons in between drafts and the temporal conundrum such a task can bring—rather than picking up as if from where we left off, in the middle of a sentence some four years back, we are "staying with the trouble" of this time warp we find ourselves in (Haraway). We invite you to perhaps be in process, or bear witness in time to this unfinished work that the legacies of feminist collaborations evoke—to sit with our offerings, our thoughts below, not so much listening for a linear trajectory toward a precise conceptual or practical coordinate. Instead, we invite you to take a pause with us as we reflect—in time/over time—riffing, connecting across pedagogical collaboration, across feminist co-struggle, across dreaming together anew.

Introduction

As feminists who teach and work in the academy, we are interested in the question of what collaboration looks like inside a university classroom, one shaped by the structural realities of neoliberalism, capitalism, white supremacy, and other interlocking systems of oppression and power. Committed to the work of exploring, analyzing, unsettling, and shifting the dynamics and ongoing impacts of systemic oppression, we turn to a pedagogy of collaboration, community, and interconnectedness. We believe that a pedagogy of relationship and community disrupts how these systems thrive on individualism, competition, disconnection, so-called objectivity, and disembodied ways of knowing. Offering a pedagogy of connection creates the building blocks toward accountability, mutual responsibility, and solidarity in connection to movements for social change.

Our classes and workshops inevitably bring together people who inhabit different identities, bodies, and experiences that are interconnected and overlapping across multiple power lines. Our classroom practices are oriented toward bringing awareness of how these structures of power impact not only our bodies and feelings but our relationships to knowledge as well. These practices are grounded in the theories and approaches offered across a range of Black and women of color feminist thought, antiracist feminisms, and performance studies that have shown that embodiment, such as breath and presence (Gumbs; Jones), and feelings, such as desire or anger (Lorde; Ahmed, *Promise of Happiness*), bring the possibilities of individual and collective transformation front and center. That is, embodiment and feelings can render concepts for social transformation fleshy, alive, and corporeal, thus available for direct hands-on/heart-centered engagement (Thompson).

In this essay we explore our collaboration as friends, teachers, workshop leaders, and circle keepers while also exploring our classrooms and workshops as collaborative spaces for building community, knowledge, and change. We have been collaborating and commiserating around the embodied and affective dimensions of teaching and learning that disrupt and challenge the impact of power systems over the past thirteen years. We have organized the essay as a conversation between us in an effort to recognize that as a collaboration we ourselves bring different histories, identities, experiences, and perspectives.

We share some of the practices we draw from to create organic collaborative processes with our classroom participants as we collectively create knowledge around individual and systemic violence and trauma, the power structures that produce these occurrences, and the possibilities for healing and transformation. We reflect on our experiences with practices that center embodied feelings such as breath, presence, and softness that enable us to attend to differences, conflicts, and difficulties in ways that have the potential to disrupt and shift intersecting structures of power, dominance, and privilege within the classroom itself. We hope to show how engaging in transformative practices in community with others with attention to embodiment and feelings can relieve the oft-established rifts between theory and practice and individual and social change.

Arriving at Collaboration

Misty: So how do we know when we are in the presence of the changes we seek to realize? Where does that knowing reside in the body, somatically or experientially? What does it take for the body to develop a new habit, a shift, or a change away from harmful ways of being toward more sustainable ways of "being-with" one another? And how might the classroom act as a site to practice the worlds we long to occupy, as well as a container that may hold the somatic fallout/thaw/debris left in the wake of our longings? These questions animate my work as a scholar and artist and have taken many years across my pedagogical practices to articulate. At the time I met Ann, I was in the middle of forming these questions.

I was touring with *Milkweed*, my first original solo play, which attempted to articulate the impact of sexual violence across the intimate/mundane spaces of day-to-day survival, specifically in the lives of black queer women. I had trained extensively as a classical actor and then, later, for my MFA, as an interdisciplinary artist pursuing the relationship between art and activism. During my development as an artist and activist, the classroom was a site where groups gathered, oftentimes to discuss/analyze and redress overlapping forms of oppression and trauma. Having navigated multiple experiences with sexual harm that spanned across my early childhood to young adulthood, I had about a decade under my belt with collective healing practices, particularly those fueled by performance and other expressive arts. Although that work was fortifying, such work mostly took place in a completely different space, *away from* the classroom. So I was in want of a practice, a way of being, *specifically in the classroom* that could hold the residue from ongoing forms of trauma as well as other coercive "power-over" dynamics—spanning the economic to the religious.

For me, this meant and continues to mean devoting the first ten minutes or so of class to sincerely check in with everyone. At times the check-in prompt can be "What is one smell you enjoy," followed by two to three minutes of a guided breathing—-or "coming into presence"—exercise. The check-in prompt serves to "soften" the room, allowing for students to depart from routine modes of initiating discussion while nurturing curiosity in one another through a fun way. And such a fun prompt serves to usher students' attention toward more somatic ways of being and analysis. Facilitating a moment for students to pause and ground their breath/presence, not so much prior to class discussion but as an integral way *into and through* analysis, does the work of gesturing toward a collective container where we may attend to the psychosomatic legacies of white supremacist imperial violence and the oft-muted felt residue left in their wake.[1]

Ann: Relatedly, what are practices that might cultivate communal learning, healing, and accountability? How can we make it a collective practice to name the dynamics, tensions, and harms produced through these systems in ways that do not contribute to systemic oppression and that offer paths for social change, solidarity, and transformation? How can we build an embodied lens of interlocking systems of oppression and power into our spaces that cultivates a recognition and accountability for how we are all impacted by and implicated in, as well as contribute to, the systems of oppression and the harms they produce?

For me, my involvement in feminist, antiracist and queer movement building to end oppression and violence continues to be a place of collaborative struggle. The struggle has always been to create communal spaces that are attentive to how oppressive systems can be reproduced rather than transformed in collective praxis. As feminist teachers, activists, and organizers, I have witnessed how often we end up reproducing the very systems we are seeking to understand, disrupt, and dismantle since these systems are so embedded in every aspect of our psyches, relationships, and communities (Fellows and Razack; Russo). This is a personal as well as political struggle as we must reckon with how we have experienced oppression and violence and how we have participated in or been complicit in systemic oppression and violence. This struggle has led to the work of building learning and organizing spaces where we work collaboratively to disrupt, shift, and transform the ways these systems are operating among and between us.

When I met Misty in 2010, these questions were paramount for me in the face of the ups and downs of community accountability and transformative justice work in Chicago. I had been connected to some amazing organizing efforts through the Women and Girls Collective Action Network, Project Nia, the Young Women's Empowerment Project, and the Young Women's Action Team. Many of us had been turning to transformative justice as a praxis of collectively addressing harm that leaned toward active accountability for harm rather than punishment and more harm. While transformative justice offered many possibilities, many of us faced challenges and heartbreaks as we sought to disrupt, shift, and transform dynamics rooted in systemic oppression within some of our own relationships and organizing spaces. We struggled with how to cultivate active accountability in ways that would mend, rather than destroy, our relationships. These experiences deepened my awareness of how deeply we are differentially impacted by as well as implicated within whiteness and white supremacy and the interlocking systems of capitalism, heteronormativity, neoliberalism, and imperialism. What I realized is that we would continue to stumble into conflicts and divisions fueled by these systems of oppression if we did not build the skills to address them in ways that would allow us to mend, learn, take accountability, and continue building toward another world.

I was thrilled when Misty joined the Department of Women's and Gender Studies (WGS) as a visiting professor in 2010. I was immediately drawn to her work rooted in our mutual desire to create spaces for an embodied process of learning that had the potential to disrupt and transform intersecting lines of oppression and power. We found synchronicity across the different questions we were asking. I appreciated her attention to the interconnectedness of mind, body, and spirit, and her praxis of embodiment as a method of communal healing and change. We began turning to each other with our questions, our dilemmas, and our struggles within and outside classroom spaces with attention to our different and yet interconnected experiences, interests, and methods. We created a space in our relationship to explore our failures and breakthroughs, collectively strategize and problem-solve, and encourage each other to return to the struggle of teaching and learning renewed. We shared our mistakes and worries as spaces for struggle and growth rather than for shame or blame, and we have been growing the potential and possibilities for transforming the everyday dynamics and impacts of oppression and violence that shape our learning and educational spaces.

A Few Key Terms We Hold Dear: "Transgressive," "Building Communities," "Holding Space," "Turning Toward"

Misty: To *turn toward* feminist collaborative pedagogies is to invoke a collective process of holding space for the interrelated struggles that arise from overlapping forms of oppression, trauma, and harm across structural, material, and everyday registers. In this context, to *hold space* with Ann means to co-facilitate a conversation in the classroom while actively engaging values and methods inherent to practices in transformative justice, particularly via peace circles. Such practices are rooted in a deep, embodied listening that allows for many possibilities, like direct engagement with multiple student realities as well as tending to ongoing uncertainties. Accordingly, our collaborative approach also centers the interplay between mining structural analysis on one register while at the same time nurturing a heart-centered connectedness among all participants gathered in the room, including ourselves.

To say it another way, for me, collaborating with Ann on shaping feminist collaborative pedagogies has meant approaching the classroom much like a community action lab—a group of embodied thinkers (problem solvers, movers and shakers, artists, academics, activists) working toward making new or deeper understandings of women's lives (across femme and nonbinary flesh-based materialities) and global forms of gender-based oppression, while also dismantling oppressive forms of knowledge and ways of knowing that are endemic to the academy. I am standing on a few shoulders here, queer of color feminist thinkers, artists, and activists, a few of whom Ann and I touch on across this essay. Though, briefly, bell hooks's contributions to Black feminist pedagogy has shaped my core thoughts on approaching collaboration.

In *Teaching to Transgress: Education as the Practice of Freedom*, hooks writes about the classroom as a communal place, where everyone contributes and therein directly influences the classroom dynamic (7). This is important because hooks is arguing for teachers to engage such contributions as resources that, when used constructively, "enhance the capacity of any class to create an open learning community" (8). Such an approach is inherently transgressive because it works against the notion of the classroom as a site where "ritual acts of control" and other unconscious uses of power between students and professors are enacted (1–2). So to work with Ann toward feminist collaborative pedagogies means to—from the gate—redefine, rename, and reinvoke the site of the classroom from a space of unconscious acts of intellectual dominance between a figure backed by the institution and her students to a site of collaboration across multiple positions gathered in the classroom. The goal is to share new strategies for structural critique, community connectedness, and social redress. For me, feminist collaboration, then, acts as both a core value and primary vehicle for exploring and addressing ways in which we are imbricated and caught up in each other's struggles and therein implicated in one another's healing.[2]

Ann: Collaborating as well as commiserating with Misty has created a space to imagine and build learning spaces that use community building through and across inequitable divides as a method of enhancing collective learning and knowledge. I approach teaching from a movement-building perspective and draw from Audre Lorde's call for recognizing differences as a method of building feminist movement. In one of her signature essays, "Age, Race, Class, and Sex: Women Redefining Difference," she wrote, "It is not those differences between us that are separating us. It is rather our refusal to recognize those differences, and to examine the distortions which result from our misnaming them and their effects upon human behavior and expectation" (Lorde 115). Misty and I have both been interested in what this might look like in our classrooms. In WGS classrooms I often bump against the construction of a homogeneous "we," grounded in assumptions of sameness, be it around identity or perspective, and yet this "we" simultaneously constructs a set of borders and exclusions if one does not feel the belonging being articulated. I wanted to develop methods of nurturing a "heterogeneous we," where the differences, including the inequities, and power lines within the collective would become as important to recognize in the service of building robust connection, analysis, and action. This would mean that within any given classroom or workshop we would encourage a recognition that the "we" in the group are historically, structurally, and socially interconnected through interlocking systems of oppression and power. The differences among and between us impact how we come to the classroom, the readings, the issues at hand, as well as the stakes that we might have in what is learned and how we learn together. Naming, rather than ignoring, these differences makes disrupting, shifting, and upending the power lines that shape our relationships and understanding more possible (Razack). It means that we become better able to recognize that our relationships and how we come to know are rooted in interlocking systems of power (Carillo

Rowe; hooks, Lorde; Razack; Alexander). Teaching and learning become a collective and critical endeavor rather than an individual one. Collaborative pedagogy allows us to collectively build a complex, layered, and sometimes contradictory understanding of the world rather than a focus on honing our own individual skills and knowledge in competition with others. Hegemonic individualism, and the resulting competitive atmosphere, is embedded in academic institutions and it undermines the potential for thinking outside of our own experiences and knowledge frames.

Building such a collaborative and intentional space is challenging to say the least. Misty and I began to turn to restorative peace circle practices as one approach to cultivating such a space. We participated in a skill share offered by Ora Schub of the Chicago-based Community Justice for Youth Institute, who learned the practice from Kay Pranis, who learned it from Indigenous practitioners of the upper Yukon (Pranis). While I had been teaching in circles for many years, I found the practice of restorative peace circles more conducive to a collaborative pedagogy. I found there to be more emphasis on building relationships and community between and among all participants through an intentional process of inviting each person in the circle to share their stories, perspectives, and responses to the question at hand and to listen to those of others. This methodical process makes it more possible for us to build a deeper recognition of one another as co-contributors to the creation of knowledge and understanding. Participants are called to actively listen to one another as human beings, inseparable from our bodies, emotions, and spirits. When we disagree or when a harm of oppressive words or actions occurs, the circle is able to hold the conflict because of the relationships and community that have been fostered by the circle over time. Moreover, whatever comes up in the circle becomes a communal issue rather than an individual or interpersonal one. The classroom community can speak to the conflict at hand and everyone has an opportunity to weigh in to work toward a collective resolution.

The foundational base of feminist collaboration through circles, then, is not purely intellectual but also relational. Here I draw from Aimee Carillo Rowe's *Power Lines: On the Subject of Feminist Alliances*, where she talks about the significance of our relationships in shaping our identities and knowledge. She writes, "My argument is that whom we love is who we are becoming, that the duo power/knowledge must also account for the politics of love. . . . I mean love in the most expansive sense of whose lives matter to us. Whose well-being is essential to our own. And whose survival must 'we' overlook in order to connect to power in the ways that we do? . . . The sites of our belonging constitute how we see the world, what we value, who we are becoming" (3). She calls for a "politics of relation" within our work, our teaching, and our politics. From this, I seek to build learning spaces where we cultivate a sense of belonging, interconnectedness, and accountability among and between the students as well as the teachers.

Cultivating Reciprocity, Compassion, Accountability, and Care

Ann: All learning spaces are fraught as multiple and interconnected power lines shape what happens within them. The dynamics of power, fear, mistrust, ignorance, competition, and frustration created by these systems of power inevitably manifest in classrooms where we are exploring oppression, trauma, and violence. These can make it difficult to build the relationships that seem integral to collaborative learning for change. So the practices of cultivating relational reciprocity, compassion, accountability, and care become that much more important. In creating an intentional community space within the classroom, we can welcome participants to name the tensions rather than ignoring them, and to engage with one another through practices of reciprocity, accountability, and care rather than individualism and competition.

Giving attention to the embodiment of different ideas, experiences, and responses creates the potential to build bridges across these lines of difference without obscuring the structures of power that produce them. Sitting in a circle with no furniture in between and inviting each person to speak to the questions at hand changes the dynamics of the classroom. It can contribute to breaking down some of the walls of intellectual distance and invite a more vulnerable space for building connections. Participants can critically engage the materials and share their understandings in the presence of others who become compassionate witnesses. This practice of circle sharing can be both illuminating and incredibly uncomfortable. Misty's attention to our embodiment of trauma, conflict, discomfort, and tension is invaluable to me. Within these spaces, we can practice not running away from the discomforts, angers, and frustrations but instead practice sitting with them, breathing through them, pausing rather than quickly moving forward (Lorde). These practices of pausing, sitting, taking breaths, rather than running away, evading, or ignoring them, make it more possible for me and the rest of the class to remain present to the discomfort, even if it is not resolvable in the moment.[3]

In an antiracist feminist class, a group of student presenters shared a video of US media coverage of a scene of Iranian women being physically and verbally attacked by men on the streets of Tehran. While the student presenters intended to use the clip to illustrate the media's colonialist gaze, other students argued that the framing was insufficient and that showing the clip in class only reinforced its colonialist gaze about the trauma of "others." There was palpable tension in the classroom. To shift from a back-and-forth conflict, I had the students use a circle process whereby each student had an opportunity to speak to the impact of mass-circulated trauma images and stories of "others," including in classrooms like ours, and the problems of representation shaped by systems of power. An Iranian student in the class shared her discomfort with being in classes where stories of Iranian women, women who could easily be her aunts and community members, became the object of people's colonialist gaze. Two African American students talked about their experiences of their communities being the object of study in many classrooms, without a recognition of their humanity nor of the impact of this educational process on *their* minds, hearts, and bodies. A few white students talked about how they had never thought about the concerns raised, and had initially thought that it was important to "know" what was going on in Iran despite the colonialist gaze. As the conversation went around the circle, what emerged was a more nuanced and critical understanding of US media *and* pedagogical practices and their differential uses and impact. From this conversation, the class worked together to develop a set of guidelines grounded in this experience and in anti-imperialist and antiracist frameworks that could be used for future group presentations.

Misty: That is so beautifully said, Ann. Part of what I value about our relationship and the privilege I have had in learning from you are the ways in which you plainly name the elements that are constantly taking shape and pressing against each other beneath our practices. Elements such as pausing, sitting, taking breath, as you note, rather than running away, and the sheer difficulty to both critically and compassionately engage in such ways of being present. I think oftentimes when I mention the term "peace circle," it can evoke an easy surface way of being, a lightheartedness that prefaces a "peaceful" topical and therein, perhaps, an avoidant feeling—when in practice, the work of staying present and being willing to engage deep breathing, for example, during a moment of harm while in a peace circle can actually be quite muscular. I mean the fleshy exhaustion, uncertainty of consciously breaking learned habits of being—of relational behavior—under the strained logics of oppressive systems. I feel the need to take a moment here and offer a larger framework of who I am pulling from in these pursuits, what theories and conversations, alongside my work with you, Ann, that I stay deeply connected with.

I pull from the field of performance studies and Black feminist thought (Hartman; Fleetwood) along with other women of color feminist contributions (Al-Saji; Ahmed, *Cultural Politics*; Muñoz, *Disidentifications*). I try to hold those fields in productive tension/congress with affect and feminist phenomenology studies. I am looking to hold the ideas of these fields in tight cohabitation with their implied or directly theorized forms of embodied, felt, and shared practices. Central to my thoughts, and larger body of work, is the idea of habitual embodiment and perception. Here, José Muñoz ("Feeling Brown"), Sarah Ahmed (*Queer Phenomenology*), and others (Al-Saji; Fleetwood) write about affective accumulation—a buildup of "feeling like" registers. These scholars mean for readers to hold central across analyses of racialized dynamics the grave impact of feelings and perceptions that sediment among and on marginalized collectives, thus determining how such groups are perceived, apprehended, and therein treated (Muñoz; Ahmed, *Cultural Politics*; Al-Saji). Their theories help readers contend with the fact that historic, material, and structural experiences with "power-over" dynamics do not merely fade away with time. Rather, they remain, they "stick" (Ahmed, *Cultural Politics* 194–95), become "habituated" (Al-Saji 36). Such dynamics are as large, multivalent, and abstract as they are subtle, fine, and felt. They are embedded in the ways we imagine ourselves through to the ways we gesture (behave) across everyday spaces.

Along these lines, Ahmed, through her work in *The Cultural Politics of Emotion*, takes up the affective circulation of hate within racist group formations and discursive practices. She asserts that hatred is not an attribute that is natural to any particular individual, but rather hatred sticks to certain individuals and groups due to the impact of the circulation of racist discursive practices over time (42–46). Ahmed argues that affect builds in force, through processes of accumulation and circulation. So the daily fallout, or debris, of navigating white supremacist, anti-Black, and heteronormative institutional spaces accrete in the psyche, on the body (singular-plural), and are often circulated through habitual patterns of being with one another. To put it another way, the very dynamics we seek to dismantle are often internalized and re-performed and therefore contained in the muscularity of the everyday (collective) body/ies. As a practitioner, whether in the classroom or on the stage, I take this into account and try to interrupt some of the systems that have stuck. I evoke a conscious engagement with affective embodiment that, in my experience, helps shift, detangle, or soften some of those ingrained, habitual ways of being with one another that racial capitalism, imperialism, and white supremacy would demand. This provides a pedagogical and collaborative platform toward not only analyzing but also *feeling* our way toward alternative, less harmful (and, hopefully, more sustainable) ways of "being with" one another. The radical opportunity here is to consciously engage modes of performance/embodiment to bear emphasis on processes of world making (brown; Haines).

Opening Up and Sustaining a Transformative Classroom

Ann: In my classes, I invite class participants to a practice of recognizing that tensions and conflicts are not only inevitable but welcome. I encourage them to pay attention to the power lines that produce the tensions and to think about what it means to be in community with one another in the process of addressing them. One practice that contributes to this is that we develop collective values and practices to hold our work together and to hold whatever may come up in the process of learning together. To generate shared values and practices, I ask them to think about their past experiences in classes or groups where they felt valued and heard or where they felt invisible, diminished, or harmed. With these experiences in mind, we generate a list that can hold the complexities of our different experiences and differential relationships to power, our disagreements and conflicts.

For me, this practice is born of an understanding of the individual and collective impact of interlocking systems of power on people's identities and experiences and how that shows up in our intellectual and political work or in the ways we are represented. This process can be an important place for encouraging people's attention to and accountability for the ways in which people's dominance, hegemonic understandings, and inequitable relationships have an impact and how we might disrupt or dismantle these dynamics. When these dynamics are named through the value-setting process, class members are more able to address the power lines that structure our understanding of and relationship to one another and to the course materials (see Russo; Razack; hooks, *Teaching Community*).

Core values often include accountability, compassion, active listening, confidentiality, care, and many others that seem important to individual members. As values are brought into the circle, we invite anyone in the group, including ourselves, to ask questions about the values and to critically engage those we may disagree with. The goal is to gain more clarity about the values within our classroom community. We encourage reflection on the values, on their connection with previous experiences, on the power lines that structure classroom/workshop dynamics, and on points of tension. For example, often someone in the class will suggest that we should assume we all have good intentions. And yet others have had the experience of how people often defend themselves from accountability for harm by resorting to "innocence" of intention. We then turn to the importance of the value of accountability for impact, regardless of intention. As the class grapples with the different values offered and shares their stories of how classroom dynamics play out, it clarifies for students how often a default to "innocent" intentions often contributes to upholding the norms reflective of systemic power relations.

The values are guides for the community we are building with an understanding that the space is not assumed to be "safe" or without tensions. The value setting brings an awareness of the different bodies, minds, and hearts in the room. Recently, one of my classes got into a tension-filled conversation about the value of "gentleness." While some students thought it is important for us to be gentle with ourselves and others, others saw the value as problematic for its tone policing. As we went around the circle, different perspectives and experiences emerged. We eventually landed on the recognition that accountability may not be gentle and that rather than upholding gentleness, we embraced the values of compassion, of meeting people where they are. The conversation felt important to setting the ground for a collaborative learning space with the recognition that we are coming in with different knowledge and experience.

When I have not engaged in values setting at the beginning of a class, I have found that when tensions build, they are more difficult to address. Participants are less intentional about what they bring into the space, and there is little ground upon which to engage in conflict. This can create more polarized and divided learning communities. This happened in a class of mine several years ago. When a conflict erupted on the third night around white privilege and dominance, it was very difficult to recover. In the following class, with guidance from Misty, I created space for the class to work through the conflict by developing some shared values. Through a discussion of values, some of the tensions were aired but not fully resolved. Residues of anger and mistrust haunted the rest of the class. It reminded me of the importance of setting a groundwork of values early on in any given class. The goal, for me, is not to evade conflict nor to squelch disagreement; instead, it is to create a more intentional space in which such disagreements can be addressed in ways that deepen our understanding of the conflicts and their structural and social roots.

What's transgressive about our collaborative and embodied pedagogy is our attention to the ways all participants, including ourselves, are both implicated in and impacted by the issues, the power systems that produce them, and the dynamics created within a heterogeneous classroom. The potential for collaboration and community is possible when participants are able to talk about our differential relationships to structures of power and consciousness and to understand what it might mean to practice accountability in our efforts toward belonging and community in the classroom (Carillo Rowe). Such practices can lead us to a solidarity based in difference rather than a unity based in sameness. In her essay "'Pedagogies of the Broken-Hearted': Notes on a Pedagogy of Breakage, Women of Color Feminist Decolonial Movidas and Armed Love in the Classroom/Academy," Anne (Anna) Rios-Rojas writes, "Unity and assimilation are anchored in domination." In turning us toward a pedagogy of love and care as a grounding for solidarity, she writes:

> Solidarity springs from a deep desire to pursue the right to be fully human and from a real commitment to engage in that humanizing process with others we might construct as different—too culturally different, too foreign, too weird, too queer, too alien for us ever to feel as if their lives and dreams are wrapped up in ours. The challenge is to love in the way that Gloria Anzaldúa and other third world decolonial feminist thinkers have urged us to love—in a way that allows us to "world"-travel to see our face in the heartbreak of an/other. (167)

Cultivating Care

Misty: I find that the cultivation of care really sets in through the use of storytelling. Ann has had the single most influence on my understanding of the role of storytelling in the classroom, particularly its power in building communities, which may be ironic, given my years of training and experience as an actor and performance artist. Although as an actor I connected with the work of storytelling, and through my work as a performance artist I began to interrupt the barrier between artist and audience—as often associated with theater—it was not until I began working with Ann that I came to better understand how stories serve to connect participants to one another. Through sharing and *listening* to each other's stories, especially when centering the role of values that Ann writes about so meaningfully here, participants in the classroom begin to invest in one another's perspectives, experiences, and lives, and this allows for a cultivation of deep, critical care.

Alongside our ongoing analysis, then, it is crucial to think anecdotally, to evoke the work of personal narratives; otherwise the idea, the lessons, and the transformative possibilities become lodged in abstraction. In such cases the body disappears, is obscured. Accordingly, engaging in embodied listening or deep critical "presence-ing" when witnessing is the gravitational pull to cultivating care. That is, such modes of listening push against power-over dynamics like self-preservation, coercion, and competition and prompt groups toward heart-centered approaches to empathy, accountability, and sustainable collectivity.[4]

Ann: The practice of cultivating tenderness and care within the community of the classroom allows us to face conflicts and tensions with care as well as accountability to one another. Circle practices create a communal space rather than a group space that feels more individualized. They invite everyone to speak to whatever has been spoken or done. Each participant becomes accountable to the space and everyone in it. Accountability for addressing issues is not only on the teacher or the individuals immediately involved; it becomes the responsibility of the whole. This allows us to collectively name, process, and understand the dynamics between us and to work together to create paths toward deepening our relationships and community. As we hear the different responses and understandings to what was said or done, the possibilities for shifting, learning, and transforming arise. The tensions between specific individuals become communal tensions that we are sharing; the potential for repair and change increases because everyone in the circle participates rather than only one or two people. Polarized conversations shift into communal conversations that are collaborative and direct us to communal rather than individual understandings.

On the second day of a transformative justice class, in a conversation about the prison industrial complex (PIC), a student who identifies as a cisgendered white man with leftist politics stated that all police were fascists. I could feel the tension rise in the room. At first no one addressed his comment as we went around the circle with each student talking about the PIC. Then a cisgendered Latino student, dressed in army fatigues, shared that he was troubled by the student's statement because he felt it as an attack on his family, some of whom were police officers. He said that he did not condone the brutality of the police nor the prison system and that he wanted to learn. He felt that his family members were being unfairly categorized as fascists and that the class felt like a setup against him because of his relationship to the PIC. A Latina student shared her discomfort with the label of fascist as well, given that she had family members who were police officers. Other students began to weigh in as well. Some students thanked the Latinx students for sharing and some talked about their struggle of navigating a critique of the system without relegating all of those working in the system as evil. Some African American students shared their experiences, and those of their relatives, with police harassment and brutality. Most expressed the view that the police needed to be held accountable for their violence, including the Latinx students with relatives in law enforcement. As more people opened up, the complexities of the issues and our relationship to them deepened. When the circle came back around to the person who made the initial statement, he apologized to the students with police in their families for his statement. He explained that his comments came from a position of not having any relationships with individual police officers. He then clarified his position by saying his criticism was of the institution of policing and prisons, and he understood that not every individual worker was necessarily aligned with the institution's violence. With his acknowledgment, in conjunction with all that had been shared, a collective sense of relief could be felt by the time everyone had a chance to weigh in. This did not alleviate the tensions, and yet it prompted class members to be more thoughtful in how they approached the issues. The space of the circle as a place to examine and reflect on the source of the tensions and to share the complex and different relationships with these systems deepened the class's understanding of the issues at hand and our different stakes in them. As a group, we were able to stay connected and committed to one another around these differences in our effort to understand and struggle against these systems of oppression and violence.

Turning Toward Failure

Ann: The collaborative space we have created together to process our failures has been a generative space of healing, change, and accountability. I live with a very loud inner critic who zeroes in on my feelings of failure in relation to unresolved conflicts or escalated tensions and missed opportunities in my classes or workshops. I sometimes find it unbearable when harms and traumas occur within a class and we are not able to address them in a way that mends the harm, shifts the dynamics, or heals the relationships. I am often heartbroken by the underlying and unresolved tensions that simmer underneath classroom communities. Turning to Misty with these worries, concerns, and upsets has been invaluable. We have been able to create a space within our relationship where we can admit and wrestle with the challenges we face and the feelings of failure and inadequacy. It is a space where we can process without having to make it all better. bell hooks's *Teaching to Transgress* offers such wisdom here. She describes so well the reality that we are teaching against the grain and that it is hard not only in relation to the students but also within ourselves. For me, it is an inner struggle and one with those who inhabit the space. Each time that Misty and I share our struggles, we are able to stay in the hard work of excavating and shifting these dominant ways of knowing and relating across differences that are always tugging at our efforts to build a collaborative learning space. The potential for creating an accountable vibrant and engaged classroom community is always offset by these systems that are structured to undermine that very potential. Having a collaborator like Misty, who welcomes commiseration about uncertainty, failure, confusion, and disappointment, as well as experimentation, patience, and staying the course, has been a deep place of nourishment as we continue this difficult and complicated work of cultivating individual and social change.

Notes

1. For more reading on these concepts, see Foster; Lepecki; and Noland.

2. For more reading on these overall concepts, see Moraga and Anzaldúa.

3. To note, there are also instances where I set the room up such that the class walks into the space having been set. I find this is useful for smaller groups as the intimate activity of exchanging glances and falling into a new rhythm establishes a felt sense of common experiences that makes for a useful affect to engage from the start in building toward notions of community here.

4. For more reading on these concepts, see Morales.

Works Cited

Ahmed, Sara. *The Cultural Politics of Emotion.* Routledge, 2014.

Ahmed, Sara. *The Promise of Happiness.* Duke UP, 2010.

Ahmed, Sara. *Queer Phenomenology: Orientations, Objects, Others.* Duke UP, 2006.

Alexander, M. Jacqui. *Pedagogies of Crossing: Meditations on Feminism, Sexual Politics, Memory and the Sacred.* Duke UP, 2006.

Al-Saji, Alia. "A Phenomenology of Hesitation: Interrupting Racializing Ways of Seeing." *Living Alterities: Phenomenology, Embodiment, and Race,* edited by Emily S. Lee. State U of New York P, 2014, pp. 133–72.

brown, adrienne maree. *Emergent Strategy: Shaping Change, Changing Worlds.* A. K. Press, 2017.

Carillo Rowe, Aimee. *Power Lines: On the Subject of Feminist Alliances.* Duke UP, 2008.

DeBerry, Misty. "Milkweed." *Solo/Black/Woman: Scripts, Interviews, Essays,* edited by E. Patrick Johnson, Ramon Rivera-Sirvera. Northwestern UP, 2013, pp. 300–350.

Fellows, Mary Louise, and Sherene Razack. "The Race to Innocence: Confronting the Hierarchical Relations among Women." *Journal of Gender, Race, and Justice,* vol. 1, 1998, pp. 335–52.

Fleetwood, Nicole R. *Troubling Vision: Performance, Visuality, and Blackness.* U of Chicago P, 2011.

Foster, Susan. *Choreographing Empathy*. Routledge, 2010.

Gumbs, Alexis Pauline. *Spill: Scenes of Black Fugitivity*. Duke UP, 2016.

Haines, Staci. *The Politics of Trauma: Somatics, Healing, and Social Justice*. North Atlantic Books, 2019.

Haraway, Donna. Staying with the Trouble: Making Kin in the Chthulucene. Duke UP, 2016.

Hartman, Saidiya V. *Scenes of Subjection: Terror, Slavery, and Self-Making in Nineteenth-Century America*. Oxford UP, 1997.

hooks, bell. *Teaching Community: A Pedagogy of Hope*. Routledge, 2003.

hooks, bell. *Teaching to Transgress: Education as the Practice of Freedom*. Routledge, 1994.

Jones, Omi Osun Joni L. *Theatrical Jazz: Performance, Jazz, and the Power of the Present Moment*. Ohio State UP, 2015.

Lepecki, Andre. *Exhausting Dance: Performance and the Politics of Movement*. Routledge, 2006.

Lorde, Audre. *Sister Outsider: Essays and Speeches*. Crossing Press, 1994.

Moraga, Cherrie, and Gloria Anzaldúa, eds. *This Bridge Called My Back: Writings by Radical Women of Color*. Kitchen Table Press, 1981.

Morales, Aurora Levins. *Medicine Stories: Essays for Radicals*. Duke UP, 2019.

Muñoz, José Esteban. *Disidentifications: Queers of Color and the Performance of Politics*. New York UP, 1999.

Muñoz, José Esteban. "Feeling Brown, Feeling Down: Latina Affect, the Performativity of Race, and the Depressive Position." *Signs*, vol. 31, no. 3, 2006, pp. 657–88.

Noland, Carrie. *Agency and Embodiment: Performing Gestures/Producing Culture*. Harvard UP, 2009.

Pranis, Kay. *The Little Book of Circle Processes*. Good Books, 2005.

Razack, Sherene. *Looking White People in the Eye: Gender, Race, and Culture in Courtrooms and Classrooms*. U of Toronto P, 1998.

Rios-Rojas, Anne (Anna). "Pedagogies of the Broken-Hearted': Notes on a Pedagogy of Breakage, Women of Color Feminist Decolonial Movidas, and Armed Love in the Classroom/Academy." *Frontiers: A Journal of Women's Studies*, vol. 41, no. 1, 2020, pp. 161–78.

Russo, Ann. *Feminist Accountability: Disrupting Violence, Transforming Power*. New York UP, 2018.

Thompson, Becky. *Teaching with Tenderness: Toward an Embodied Practice*. U of Illinois P, 2017.

2

Critical Transnational Black Feminist Queer Praxis

Engendering Collaborative Pedagogy through Care and Community Building

ANDREA N. BALDWIN

In 2016 Kia Hall developed a transnational Black feminist framework that she describes as providing scholars, activists, and scholar-activists with the tools to advance the freedom struggle. Hall's framework engages both Black and transnational feminist traditions guided by the principles of "intersectionality, scholar-activism, solidarity building, and attention to borders/boundaries" (90–91). In 2010 Kristen Renn called for utilizing critical scholarship that queers the academy and its inner workings. Renn points out the necessity of doing so by asking, "What is more nonqueer than traditional . . . education or the tenure system?" (132). According to Renn, these systems create structural obstacles for those not situated in so-called pure disciplines. Renn's sentiment is echoed by Miller and Rodriguez, who state that an aim of queer scholarship is to interrogate and disrupt normative structures within academia (xvi). In this chapter, I build on Hall's guiding principles, joining these with the world-making possibilities espoused by queer theorist José Esteban Muñoz to espouse a critical transnational Black feminist queer praxis that centers an ethic of care, demonstrating how this praxis utilizes collaborative pedagogy to bring together those confined to the margins of the academy—those who are queer, Black, Brown, working class, and immigrant—to share and produce communal knowledge.

Herein, I examine the normalized ways in which knowledge is produced in the academy, how people who work within these Eurocentric institutions are positioned in relation to this production, and the marginalizing consequences. I show how even after feminists of color have exposed the structure of the academy as creating artificial, hierarchal, and peripheral boundaries, these structures remain wholly intact and work to keep certain constituencies based on their identities, job titles, and status within and outside the academy in their own separate "worlds" (Lugones), working to deter community by using a rhetoric of scarcity (Crawley). I demonstrate how existing in such a space can be very isolating and result in a constant struggle for survival for some who find themselves on the periphery.

Despite this struggle, however, I show, with a particular focus on collaborative pedagogy, how we can reimagine teaching as a knowledge exchange process that occurs with those inside and outside the classroom, among faculty, staff, students, and the community. Using my own collaborative pedagogy—with faculty, staff, and students in my courses and with participants in my Black women's writing group—as an example, I detail how those confined to isolated academic spaces can deliberately claim space and time by utilizing their teaching to re-spatialize academia through collaboration toward a goal of academic/educational justice. I show how a critical transnational Black feminist queer praxis has the potential to awaken spatiotemporal disidentificatory activist performances toward the co-creation of a world where we (re)discover the possibilities of connection, collaboration, and coalition.

Marginalization and Academic Injustice

In 2018 I joined the faculty of a Research 1 institution in the US South as an assistant professor. Located in a deeply Christian conservative community, it is a predominantly white institution (PWI). In my first semester there, I learned of a racist incident perpetrated by white women on the women's hockey team that summer, a freedom of speech claim by a white instructor who made racist remarks in his classroom the semester prior, and read the racist, ableist, transphobic remarks of a white parent who had attended orientation earlier that semester. I came to quickly understand the ways in which the funding model at the institution meant that the two programs in which I was appointed—Africana Studies and Gender Studies—had very tiny operating budgets. I witnessed how during the height of the COVID-19 pandemic these programs were unable to support many of the Black and Brown immigrant students experiencing disproportionate hardship with accessing funding as they negotiated the ever-changing visa requirements of the Trump administration, which sought to disqualify students from renewing visas if they accessed federal pandemic relief monies granted to educational institutions. My four years spent at this institution were ones of experiencing and observing the continual oppression of the marginalized and minoritized. In my search for community, I very quickly realized that it was up to me to build my own.

The university, according to Crawley, is a place of neoliberal capitalist logics and "a way to think antisociality as the grounds for relation" (6). This concept of antisociality is evident in how the university has been and remains a space of contention and imposed scarcity (6). This practice of scarcity, what Desai and Murphy refer to as "crisis mongering" (31), while useful for justifying and enforcing neoliberal norms in the university, has several negative consequences for those left out of the Enlightenment knowledge project—women, nonwhite, non-cis folks. Deprived of resources, they are forced to inhabit spaces of precarity, situated literally and figuratively at the academy's borders.

One consequence of the forced inhabitation of academic borders/borderlands is having to focus on the immediacy of individual survival, which can negatively impact collaboration and community building. Borderlands are "vague and undetermined place[s] created by the emotional residue of an unnatural boundary" (Anzaldúa 3), producing ecologies constructed on the fallacy of (un)belonging and the spatiotemporal logics of outside and inside in order to uphold white supremacist "epistemological limits" (Crawley 4). These artificial peripheral and hierarchical borders actively dissuade community and collaboration by reinforcing subjugation not only of faculty of color, who are largely concentrated in contingent positions and whose scholarship is often confined to the elective, the specialized, and the intervention, but also of staff of color—often labeled as incapable of producing knowledge and whose job it is to support those who do—and students of color, queer students, and women whose bodies are legible for doing and providing diversity.

The injustice that occurs from occupying/inhabiting the academy as women, queer, Black, and Brown bodies often requires a posture of survival via institutional legibility. In order to be institutionally legible, those occupying academic borderlands are too often "forced to either translate themselves into the institutional framework of their university . . . or remove themselves from their languages that defined their cultural hubs" (Moffett-Bateau 91–92). But in my four years at this Research 1 institution, I found that neither of these strategies worked to disrupt academic "enclosed . . . logics of the very possibility of universality, abstraction, stilling" (Crawley 11). As an unapologetically Black and proud Caribbean woman, I was already mostly illegible at this PWI, and cultural removal would result in even more isolation. I did not merely want to survive this academic space and certainly did not feel like I could do so alone.

Black and Caribbean feminist M. Jacqui Alexander writes that our focus should be on collaboratively reexamining and transforming inherited practices standing in the way of justice and on building community. Building community in rigid academic space requires a measure of indiscipline, a disruptive praxis focused on unlearning academia's "modes of sociality" (Stein 142), paying attention to the particular vantage points possessed by those confined to socially constructed margins (hooks, *Feminist Theory*). These vantage points provide a particular way of seeing reality, as well as room to contemplate the doings and possible undoings of the academy, its imperial logics, and how it structures the way people think of themselves and others (Myers). Understanding "how structures of domination work in one's own life, as one develops . . . critical consciousness" (hooks, *Yearning* 15) begets a sense of clarity.

My clarity came from an incident of refusal, an incident where, because of arbitrary academic rules, I and one of my students became "out of compliance." What does it even mean to be out of compliance as Black women who are already regarded as out of place? In this moment of clarity, I gave myself permission to be indisciplined and to look for spatiotemporal possibilities to work, think, be creative, be radical, and build transformative collaborative communities. Clarity allowed me to locate the fullness of my geographical, historical, and epistemological residences—inside, outside, and in the in-between spaces of the academy—and *see* those who also inhabit similar spaces toward the potential of working together to "territorialize . . . [our] own bodies" by refusing refusal, marginalization, and oppression (Hughes 166). Clarity provided the luxury of being my full self, not a self that is predetermined by academic disciplinarity but that confers "the privilege or the pleasure of being a historical subject" and therefore "the luxury of thinking about the future" and beyond the immediate needs of individual survival toward collective thriving (Muñoz 189). It provided the *vision* to invent "new, alternative habits of being, and resists from that marginal space of difference inwardly defined" (hooks, *Yearning* 15). Clarity afforded the audacity to grab hold of those who resided with me at the periphery with a vision of re-spatializing the academy to recreate a world for ourselves collectively, one that goes beyond surviving and existing only in struggle to oppose "dehumanization but as that movement which enables creative, expansive self-actualization" toward academic/educational justice, and this is exactly what I did (15).

Collective World-Making toward Academic Justice: A Critical Transnational Black Feminist-Queer Praxis

In the spring 2019 semester I set out to create a world in which I wanted to exist and to inhabit within the academy—a world built upon what I would come to call a critical transnational Black feminist queer pedagogical praxis. This was a world of co-mentoring, co-teaching, cowriting that stems from a very deliberate attempt to *see* and *recognize* those with whom we share space and to engage in a knowledge exchange process that is rigorous, experiential, and future focused. This world re-spatialized my classroom and my relationships with students, staff, faculty, and others.

In 1999 José Esteban Muñoz wrote about the possibilities of world-making through what he referred to as "disidentification." To disidentify, according to Muñoz, is to enact survival strategies as minority subjects "in order to negotiate a phobic majoritarian public sphere that continuously . . . punishes the existence of those subjects who do not conform to the illusion of normative citizenship" (270). While born out of a need to survive, disidentification, Muñoz writes, is also a "powerful and seductive site of self-creation" (4). When one enacts a disidentificatory strategy, one is "*not* content merely to survive, but instead to use the stuff of the 'real world' . . . and willful enactments . . . to continue disidentifying with this world until [one] achieve[s] new ones" (200). Minoritarian subjects who have difficulty finding safe spaces and individual mentors in hostile academic terrain have been forced to enact modes of survival based on maps that were already created for them to follow for too long. Merely surviving many have become lost, traumatized, exist in spatial isolation, or have been forced out of the academic landscape. For Muñoz, willful enactments that allow the minoritarian subject to map their body in ways they would like to are necessary acts. These enactments are especially critical in this time of performed academic scarcity, where available resources remain concentrated in the hands of few majoritarian bodies, creating even more unjust and uninhabitable academic spaces. As a matter of academic/education justice, these willful enactments refuse separation and isolation and invest in the collaborative creation and curation of a new or reconfigured space.

I conceptualize academic/educational justice much like we do reproductive, environmental, and social justice—not only as an issue of individual access to systems founded on "colonizing anti-Indigenous and antiblack racist *logics* and *logistics*" but, according to Crawley, also becoming antagonistic to this system's survival (10). The Enlightenment knowledge project that is the university was founded on the making of the normative modern subject based on a racist, imperialist understanding of this subject as white, cis, and male, and to continue to be trained in the established ways of the academy is to continue "learning *about* and being trained *in* colonizing and antiblack racialist logics . . . that . . . include the proliferation [and] practices of violence, violation, dispossession, displacement, and exclusion" (10). Gaining access to this system and hoping to survive once access is given is not a transformative strategy; it will not bring just results. By being attentive to how the structure works to construct some as noncitizens and then prevent them from being engaged as full citizens, working collectively toward and demanding fundamental change and a spatial reorganization that "account for the history of racial capitalist violence and exclusion . . . that cannot be easily folded into the logics of inclusion, diversity, and multiculturalism" (11), is to work toward achieving a new world and justice.

To imagine academic justice for Black and Brown bodies, free from the constraints of marginalization and where access is insufficient, is to imagine the making of a new academic world. To imagine it is the beginning of working toward developing and engaging in transformative collective experiential research and pedagogical methods, toward building community, even while still existing in academia's hostile environments. The way I set out to do this was through a transnational Black feminist queer praxis that is intersectional, focuses on scholar-activism, solidarity building, pays attention to borders/boundaries, and is disidentificatory.

This praxis as it unsettles, imagines, and enacts otherwise is a practice of self-creation, (re)naming, and community collaboration. It is based on a transnational feminist politics of reclaiming time and claiming space, using what is useful in the academy as well as from various communities seen as traditionally foreign or outside of the academy, combining these to disrupt normative academic barriers. It works toward erasing these barriers by being unapologetic about how the "lived experience of theorizing is fundamentally linked to processes of self-recovery, of collective liberation, [such that] no gap exists between theory and practice" but that there is a "reciprocal process wherein one enables the other" (hooks, *Teaching* 61). It builds solidarity through employing a Black feminist care ethic that, according to Black feminist Brittney Cooper, is profoundly queer because loving Black women in a world that hates us means transgressing boundaries and labels (22). Utilizing the fluidity of a transnational Black feminist queer approach, then, is to mess with/queer the academy because loving each other "deeply and unapologetically is queer as fuck. It is erotic in the way that Audre Lorde talks about eroticism. It's an opening up, a healing, a seeing and being seen" (20).

A critical transnational Black feminist queer praxis, therefore, is grounded in a love for marginalized communities—both within and outside the academy. Grounding transformative political scholar and activist work in a love for self and community is based in ancestral knowledge (Combahee River Collective) and pulls from genealogies of the past and the present by being attentive to the work that is being done in communities, by mentors and teachers, and collaborating pedagogically to impact how students can create their own present and future worlds. These palimpsestic knowledges—gathered from inside, outside, and beyond spatiotemporal academic logics is collective, lived, subjected, subjugated, oppositional, and produced over centuries of living and loving as oppressed peoples—are powerful (Collins). It is "through power and love we can produce a world in which . . . we're not vested in economies that are based on both scale and profit . . . that we're not reduced to human capital but human beings" (Hughes 170).

In 2019 I started to develop this praxis, which I had, without knowing, already begun years earlier at my first academic institution. I detail this in my first coauthored book chapter written about co-mentorship with one of my former undergraduate students (Baldwin and Johnson). In that chapter we examine why disidentifying with traditional mentorship strategies to achieve a counter-space and build community was crucial for Black women in the academy. That same year I began to create a class-space community through both curriculum and class engagement in my Black feminism graduate seminar. Intersectional; focused on theory, methods, activism, solidarity building; and paying attention to borders/boundaries, the curriculum centered those with marginalized identities and focused on global contemporary issues with which students could relate. I adopted a measure of fluidity, utilizing student suggestions, making decisions as a community, and also being attuned enough to sense how students felt, especially during major, deeply impactful occurrences resulting from state violence, the COVID-19 pandemic, and global tragedies, validating their feelings and frustrations. I advocated for students and celebrated their achievements publicly and engaged in appropriate and relevant anecdotal/experiential knowledge talking about our experiences as socially constructed people. I also held myself accountable to being honest with students, never pretending that I knew more than I did. As such, I regularly invited scholars and activists from around the globe to present to students. I invited students from that class whose research touched on topics addressed in my undergraduate classes to co-teach and share their work. I invited leaders of student affinity-based organizations, directors of student centers and the counseling center to discuss issues of identity-based discrimination, mental health, and self-care. I communicated with students that their concerns are relevant and worth talking, writing, and speaking about and, when they did so, supported their efforts by co-organizing events and attending forums to which I was invited; I also provided space to help them decompress and to dialogue. I shared opportunities with students for funding or internships, wrote letters, and facilitated relationships with colleagues who might be helpful.

From that class we started the Standpoints: Black Feminist Knowledges anthology series and have since published two volumes (2019; 2023). Important to a pedagogy based on a critical transnational Black feminist queer praxis is the focus on teaching students how to apply what they have learned in the class to their own research projects and how to turn those projects into publishable scholarship. Over the course of that first semester, I collaborated with colleagues—staff and faculty—across disciplinary and professional boundaries as coeditors and coauthors to work together with students as knowledge producers. This class project was fundamental to demonstrating to students how pedagogy and research are integral to each other. At the beginning of the semester, students in the class were required to respond to a call for proposals by submitting abstracts. Throughout the semester, we carved out time before each class to answer questions students had and to hear and validate their frustrations and uncertainty with their ability to create scholarship and the writing process. Throughout this process, I also shared my frustrations with my own writing as I, too, undertook to submit a chapter for the anthology about Black love and, in the spirit of care and collaboration, invited the director of the Black Cultural Center to coauthor it with me.

We set aside a few classes dedicated to writing as a community—faculty, staff, and student authors—and after the semester was over, we remained committed to the project. Outside of the classroom structure, students remained invested, met deadlines, and responded to feedback, moving the community project beyond the boundaries of the classroom. At the heart of this project was a collaborative pedagogy of community and care. We learned together from the publishers, who visited us to talk about copyright and licensing, and made the decision as a community on how we wanted to license the text. The coeditors were attentive and patient with getting students to a place where they could see the possibility of a world where they were authors who had something to write that people would want to read. As a group we poured our time and intellectual labor into this work, and the students challenged and pushed themselves to go beyond what any course should require. We laughed, talked, and cussed, and worked to produce scholarship that demanded we see Black women and their knowledge. What is more, these texts will continue to foment future community interactions as they are intellectual gifts to future Black feminism classes. In the spirit of Muñoz, I have passed on the editing responsibilities for the third and final volume in the series to two former students, now faculty, who took the class and wrote chapters for the anthologies. While editing is a difficult task, it provides them the opportunity to think about and work toward the future. We wrote these anthologies together to show that academic border logics are useless to the oppressed, and it is when we refuse to uphold these logics that we can create our own world to learn and thrive.

While working on this anthology series I also saw the need to create a regular space where Black women could write together in solidarity. In summer 2019 I received grant funding to pilot a writing group for Black women faculty and staff, graduate students, and community members for the 2019–2020 academic year, including funds for a writing coach. I called the group Solidarity. The purpose of the group was to provide encouragement and build a support network. As a group, we meet once a week for four to five hours. This group has since grown, continuing to thrive even after my departure from the institution, as Black women graduate students made it their own place by turning it into an officially funded student organization with elected officers and a weekly newsletter.

The above are examples of a critical transnational Black feminist queer pedagogical praxis at work. We created a space where we taught and learned with each other. We shared writing techniques, time management and coping skills, created a call for proposals, and organized conference panels. We celebrated successful dissertation defenses, completed qualifying exams, supported each other's events, and got T-shirts to match. It was while sitting in the writing group surrounded by these Black women that I received an email informing me that I had received tenure. They would be the first people I would tell, and they screamed with excitement and joy! Telling them a few weeks later that I was leaving would be hard, but the surprise party they would throw to celebrate me on a stormy Sunday afternoon made me feel glorious! When I started Solidarity, it was made up of faculty, staff, students, and community members who experience academia in very different ways, teaching and learning how to be in community together; now it has evolved into a space where Black women graduate students hold space for each other. These students have a space not dictated by their disciplinary "homes" but by community where they *see* each other as co-teachers and learners breaking down strict academic barriers, caring for each other and growing. Many of the original Solidarity members, myself included, still pop in via Zoom from time to time to be in community even from afar.

The work on percussive feminism by the Crunk Feminist Collective (a hip hop feminist scholar collective) illuminates "the tension between

competing and often contradictory political and cultural projects . . . that
. . . is both disruptive and generative" (Durham 724). A critical transnational Black feminist queer praxis is a disruptive and generative project. It
disrupts academic space as it generates community. Percussive instruments
like drums can generate beautiful sounds as tension is created when we hit
them (together). Tension, therefore, is not necessarily a bad thing. When
we hold in place modes of inquiry and ways of being "that might not traditionally fit" and smash them together—queer disidentificatory practices
and transnational Black feminist theory—to examine the academy, it is
possible to create the percussive beat and theoretical pulse of a collaborative world-making pedagogical praxis. Understanding, as Black feminist
anthropologist Irma McClaurin stated, that we are faced with the difficult
task of creating transformative activist scholarship in order to alleviate conditions of oppression requires the work of a percussive rhythm—"a poetics,
a practice, that unsettles, disorients, imagines [and amplifies] otherwise
possibility" (Crawley 11).

The rhythm of the critical transnational Black queer feminist praxis can
be found in the call and response of the collaborative pedagogy outlined
above. This type of pedagogy at work invokes what Perlow and her colleagues refer to as "perspectives that unbind pedagogy from the academy
and white supremacists' education, while simultaneously celebrating . . .
rich rebellious resistance" (3). It is a loving pedagogy, which centers the
"feminists' determination to generate alternative ways of knowing . . . [that]
disrupts traditional claims to power" (Barriteau 13).

Caring for myself and the other Black women with whom I created community during this period also meant that we held one another accountable.
There were times when interventions needed to be made for one reason or
another, and while sometimes this was taken as a blow that created tension
with the potential to disrupt our small community, we trusted each other,
and this made for some of the most generative discussions and closer forging of bonds in some of the tensest times. Trusting this community started
from trusting the students in my Black feminist class as capable knowledge
producers, trusting and allowing them to exist within spaces outside of
institutions—conference spaces as cowriters and presenters, activist spaces,
and campus community spaces as co-mentors and co-teachers. Trusting
them meant I would co-create a class space where, according to Lugones,
people learn to love "by travelling to each other's 'worlds'" (390). Once I
started trusting students in this way, I could begin to start doing so with
other academically marginalized and minoritized folks. This was another
percussive moment, as the tension between those on the faculty and staff
sides of the university—at least the one I was at—is palpable because of the

hierarchical logics of the university. While academics often write about how faculty of color are treated, rarely do they engage with how staff within the academic machinery (who are usually folks of color) are also marginalized by these same systems.

However, trusting and valuing the expertise of those traditionally seen as largely incapable of producing knowledge such as community organizers and partnering with staff to relocate the knowledge production site outside of an assigned classroom—in the community, outdoors, in community centers—and engaging with these partners as knowledge producers and subject matter experts was necessary for community building. To do this collaborative geospatial pedagogical work, I had to be reflexive of how even though I am marginalized in the academy, I also had a measure of privilege vis-à-vis those with whom I wanted to build community. I was conscious not to enact epistemic violence as I traveled across class and status borders within academia in my effort to work toward justice. I did not want "to perceive others arrogantly . . . fail to identify with them—fail to love them—in this particular deep way" (Lugones 391). By traveling and enlisting the voices, knowledges, and pedagogical practices of those similarly and differently marginalized to co-create, co-teach, and form coalition, my hope was to encourage these voices to bring with them from their various spatiotemporal locations the stuff necessary for radical collective social transformation.

Conclusion

According to bell hooks, "learning is a place where paradise can be created" (*Teaching* 207). This paradise looks like "a space that we must imagine to come together, to laugh in rather than smile politely within, to remake ecologies for racialized queer bodies, and to reimagine care not as individual self-care but as . . . radical care and healing [that] requires recognition of interdependence and collective response" (Desai and Murphy 39). For people of color, women, and queer folks who were constructed as outside of the academy, this may sometimes seem like an impossible vision. However, to realize the vision requires thinking outside of the spatiotemporal logics of the Enlightenment knowledge project, "reach[ing] back and consider[ing] epistemological foundations for the *space* and *place* of the university as a modality through which knowledge was presumed to be produced . . . [and] mov[ing] toward the end of a knowledge production that produces *as it is produced by* modern Man" (Crawley 11). It means not only resisting the marginalization of oneself and others in the academy but also blurring the borders through meaningful teaching/learning exchanges that are not limited to the classroom/academy, to formal education or formally trained academics. In fact, the belief that teaching should be bound to the classroom is oppressive (Freire) when one considers that access to these same classrooms was denied to folks of color. Therefore, enacting a pedagogy that queers the academy by first refusing and then disidentifying with its processes engages students as co-creators of knowledge and emphasizes the importance of looking inside and outside of the university space to find, connect, and create community. It results in the creation of spaces that bring our interest, experiences, scholarship, passions, and identities together, connecting threads of suffering that have the possibilities of disrupting discursive fields to discover the world-making properties found in the material.

Works Cited

Alexander, M. Jacqui. *Pedagogies of Crossing: Meditations on Feminism, Sexual Politics, Memory, and the Sacred*. Duke UP, 2005.

Anzaldúa, Gloria. *Borderlands/La Frontera: The New Mestiza*. Aunt Lute Books, 1987.

Baldwin, Andrea, and Raven Johnson. "Black Women's Co-Mentoring Relationships as Resistance to Marginalization at a PWI." *Black Women's Liberatory Pedagogies: Resistance, Transformation, and Healing Within and Beyond the Academy*, edited by Olivia N. Perlow, Durene I. Wheeler, Sharon L. Bethea, and Barbara M. Scott. Palgrave Macmillan, 2018, pp. 125–40.

Barriteau, Eudine. "Disruptions and Dangers: Destabilizing Caribbean Discourses on Gender, Love, and Power." *Love and Power: Caribbean Discourses on Gender*, edited by Eudine Barriteau. U of the West Indies P, 2012.

Collins, Patricia Hill. *Black Feminist Thought: Knowledge, Consciousness, and the Politics of Empowerment*, 2nd edition. Routledge, 2000.

Combahee River Collective. "The Combahee River Collective Statement." *Home Girls: A Black Feminist Anthology*, edited by Barbara Smith. Kitchen Table: Women of Color Press, 1983, pp. 264–74.

Cooper, Brittney. *Eloquent Rage: A Black Feminist Discovers Her Superpower*. St. Martin's Press, 2018.

Crawley, Ashon. "Introduction to the Academy and What Can Be Done?" *Journal of Critical Ethnic Studies Association*, vol. 4, no. 1, 2018, pp. 4–19.

Desai, Jign, and Kevin P. Murphy. "Subjunctively Inhabiting the University." *Journal of Critical Ethnic Studies Association*, vol. 4, no. 1, 2018, pp. 23–43.

Durham, Aisha, Brittney C. Cooper, and Susana M. Morris. "The Stage Hip-Hop Feminism Built: A New Directions Essay." *Signs*, vol. 38, no. 3, 2013, pp. 721–37.

Freire, Paulo. *Pedagogy of the Oppressed*. Herder and Herder, 1972.

Hall, Kia M. Q. "A Transnational Black Feminist Framework: Rooting in Feminist Scholarship, Framing Contemporary Black Activism." *Meridians: Feminism, Race, Transnationalism*, vol. 15, no. 1, 2016, pp. 86–105.

hooks, bell. *Feminist Theory from Margin to Center*. Routledge, 1984.

hooks, bell. *Teaching to Transgress: Education as the Practice of Freedom*. Routledge, 1994.

hooks, bell. *Yearning: Race, Gender, and Cultural Politics*. South End Press, 1990.

Hughes, LeKeisha, "Robin D. G. Kelley and Fred Moten in Conversation, Moderated by Afua Cooper and Rinaldo Walcott." *Journal of Critical Ethnic Studies Association*, vol. 4, no. 1, 2018, pp. 154–72.

Lorde, Audre. *Sister Outsider*. Random House, 1984.

Lugones, María. "Playfulness, 'World'-Travelling, and Loving Perception." *Making Face, Making Soul/Haciendo Caras: Creative and Critical Perspectives of Feminists of Color*, edited by Gloria Anzaldúa. Aunt Lute Books, 1990, pp. 390–402.

McClaurin, Irma. "Theorizing a Black Feminist Self in Anthropology: Toward an Autoethnographic Approach." *Black Feminist Anthropology: Theory, Politics, Praxis, and Poetics*, edited by Irma McClaurin, Rutgers UP, 2001, pp. 49–76.

Miller, sj, and Nelson M. Rodriguez. "Introduction: The Critical Praxis of Queer Memoirs in Education." *Educators Queering Academia: Critical Memoirs*, edited by sj Miller and Nelson M. Rodriguez, Peter Lang, 2016, pp. xv–xxiii.

Moffett-Bateau, Courtney. "American University Consensus and the Imaginative Power of Fiction." *Journal of Critical Ethnic Studies Association*, vol. 4, no. 1, 2018, pp. 84–106.

Muñoz, José. E. *Disidentifications: Queers of Color and the Performance of Politics*. U of Minnesota P, 1999.

Myers, Joshua. "The Order of Disciplinarity, the Terms of Silence." *Journal of Critical Ethnic Studies Association*, vol. 4, no. 1, 2018, pp. 107–129.

Perlow, Olivia N., et al. *Black Women's Liberatory Pedagogies: Resistance, Transformation, and Healing Within and Beyond the Academy*. Palgrave Macmillan, 2018.

Renn, Kristen A. "LGBT and Queer Research in Higher Education: The State and Status of the Field." *Educational Researcher*, vol. 39, no. 2, 2010, pp. 132–41.

Stein, Sharon. "Higher Education and the Im/possibility of Transformative Justice." *Journal of Critical Ethnic Studies Association*, vol. 4, no. 1, 2018, pp. 130–53.

3

Radical Feminist Transgressions in Teaching/Learning

LINH U. HUA and K. MELCHOR QUICK HALL

This joint project showcases the value of adjacency as an intentional politics of collaboration. Rather than work toward a static condition of "coherence," we embrace a process of "messy collaborations" to signal that we continue to work, teach, and learn together. As feminists of color, we recognize that we teach and learn better together, with our individual voices heard and our joint vision seen. Our "individual" voices come out of the birth and participation in the chosen communities that have nurtured us and, therefore, are not individual at all. We honor the words and work of our epistemic communities and our social and spiritual circles. With them, we commit once more to transgressive practices that challenge the boundaries of the academy.

Articulating a Liberatory, Feminist Andragogy

The way that capitalist hierarchy in the United States was formed required a lot of people at the bottom and a few wealthy, mostly white men at the top. A liberatory, feminist andragogy, or adult learning theory, requires a pivot to address the needs of the masses rather than the needs of a few elites and challenges different forms of domination that are present in the classroom. Especially as education, from kindergarten to college, becomes increasingly corporate-driven by neoliberal principles, teachers must clarify who we are—inside and outside the classroom—and how we intend to open spaces that serve to educate and free us all. Feminist educators have articulated the challenges: "We are critically aware of the dominant trends in corporate academia pushing us to build up hierarchies between teaching and research, and to separate and compartmentalize what we do/are:

teachers-educators-researchers-activists within learning communities" (Icaza and de Jong xxix–xxx). We must find ways to bring radical feminist transgressions to our classrooms, in approaches that open teaching and learning to the communities that surround us.

Formal educational institutions in the United States are, and have always been, inadequate for the masses. These systems were never intended for the general population: "Education serves the interests of those who own and control the economic resources of the country—the Establishment. . . . The founders of the great fortunes of the nation were not educators nor educated. They were enterprisers. Education for the laboring classes was inimical to their interests" (Katz 124). Exclusive and discriminatory practices were critical to the early histories of predominantly white colleges and universities in the United States. These oppressions persist in the academy today: "Racism and sexism in the academy are systemic, supported by the entire institutional structure and rendered invisible to many by the complex workings of the academic marketplace" (Duncan 178). Institutions of higher education were designed for elites and have not been redesigned or revolutionized to accommodate the broader population served in contemporary contexts.

Pedagogy, with the root word *ped*, is about the education of children, and much has been written about what children need. However, with increasing numbers of students who do not fit old norms related to the age and stage when people pursue university education, we should be thinking more broadly about what a liberatory, feminist *andragogy* (or adult teaching theory) can offer. Malcolm Knowles distinguished between pedagogy, the principles that inform the teaching of children, and andragogy, which is focused on teaching adults. Knowles and his colleagues acknowledged the age/maturity of the adult learner, taking into account the significant life experiences of the adult learner and how self-conceptualization impacts orientation and motivation to learning (3–4). Thus, we should be thinking about college and university education in ways that consider adult maturity and motivation.

If we are to focus on adult education for the masses, then we must also bear in mind the wide range of reasons why adults attend colleges and universities. Beyond that, we must think about why we teach. What is our commitment to the masses? How can we best serve a population that is diverse in terms of race, ethnicity, gender, and class? Paulo Freire's pedagogy—and we might extend this to an andragogy—of the oppressed connected education to freedom struggles beyond the classroom: "This pedagogy makes oppression and its causes objects of reflection by the oppressed, and from that reflection will come their necessary engagement in the struggle for

liberation. And in the struggle this pedagogy will be made and remade"
(30). In proposing a liberatory, feminist andragogy, we might consider both
what adults bring to an educational experience and what an engagement
of liberation struggles can bring to the teaching/learning environment.

Influenced by the work of Freire, Black feminist bell hooks reflected on
"the difference between education as the practice of freedom and education that merely strives to reinforce dominance" (*Teaching* 4). Education
as the practice of freedom requires a shift in focus from a powerful elite,
for whom educational systems were created, to the marginalized majority.
Xicana lesbian feminist Cherríe L. Moraga offered her insight about such
an education: "May we want an education which honors the bodies of the
margins—our own and that of our ancestors—as the repository of knowledges capable of transforming this benighted nation we still dare to name
'home'" (174). Claiming and transforming our educational system(s) into
a home for the masses is both political and andragogical work; it is also
liberation work. Following are five principles that we might use to guide
us in this scholarly and activist work.

Radical Multilingualism: *Invite multiple languages into the classroom, embracing the complexities of translation.*

That we can simply understand another person's lived experience based on
the words they choose is an illusion. When I am speaking in Spanish, a
second language, I do not provide the same level of nuance as when I am
communicating in my native English. In teaching mathematics, I am aware
that the numbers and symbols I use are imperfect approximations of the
phenomena I intend to capture. For these reasons, feminists should embrace
the ambiguities that present themselves when individuals in the classroom
speak in their native languages. Feminist educators should embrace a radical
multilingualism that challenges the idea that all knowledge must be, or even
can be, translated. In her writings, Moraga does not mark the difference
between English and Spanish words with italics because her undifferentiated reality is a bilingual one. As she explains, "Spanish words are neither
translated nor italicized (unless for emphasis) to reflect a bilingual Xicana
sensibility. No glossary is provided, since most readers, if they do not have
some basic knowledge of Spanish, will easily be able to find a Spanish
dictionary" (xxii).

When I write about my work in the Black Indigenous Garifuna villages
of Honduras, where I learned from women who make *ereba*, I use the Garifuna word for cassava bread because translation is not the point. Instead,

the goal is to create space for Black indigeneity, including the Garifuna language. When our students encounter words that are not native to them, we teach them that other worlds exist. We must also teach them that those worlds are not always (easily) accessible to them. Sometimes it takes years (of language learning) to access other worlds. By existing in a classroom that recognizes and welcomes multiple, incongruent worlds, feminist andragogy can engage in a transgressive borderland praxis.

Transgressive Borderland Praxis: *Create course activities that embody radical practices that engage lived liberatory aspirations.*

Like bell hooks, Moraga was inspired by the work of Freire. She has described her message to students as follows: "I urge my students que se aprovechen el momento of their college years; to look beyond conventional career-oriented concerns toward something deeper, toward the discomfort and wonder of real conciencia, which comes, as the educator Paulo Freire understood, through a self-determined, self-defined education" (Moraga 86). This respect for the adult learner's capacity to define and direct a meaningful educational experience is one of the key tenets of an andragogical approach that respects and responds to the maturity of adults. This means we should encourage our students to bring their very real and adult problems into the classroom.

We should understand the division between the academy and the rest of the world as a borderland, or "a vague and undetermined place created by the emotional residue of an unnatural boundary" (Anzaldúa 25). The radical feminist must boldly cross these unnatural boundaries and others that separate her from her comrades. The kind of disciplining that the university promotes has never sustained us. In fact, "borders are set up to define the places that are safe and unsafe, to distinguish *us* from *them*" (25). The way to challenge the academy's elitist practices is by inhabiting the Borderlands with a transgressive borderland praxis. When we think about who is inside the university and who is outside it, we must create classrooms that boldly and unapologetically fill the gap. A transgressive borderland praxis could share the use of a classroom with an organization looking for space to hold an event, allowing students to become part of the activity. It might also involve holding class at a town hall meeting, during which students are engaging in community challenges. Both examples close the gap between an individual's college or university education and a community's collective knowledge.

Collective and Communal Knowledge Traditions: *Model Indigenous practices of collective and shared knowing in the classroom.*

Indigenous scholar Leanne Betasamosake Simpson has shared some important insights about the collective nature of Indigenous knowledges, including that Michi Saagiig Nishnaabeg epistemology "takes place in the context of family, community, and relation" (Simpson 151). In other words, knowledge building is a relational practice. She explains: "It doesn't make sense for everyone to master the same body of factual information. Nishnaabeg society in its fullest realization requires a diversity of excellence to continue to produce an abundance of supportive relationships" (155). Honoring knowledge as a communal and collective practice, rather than a space for individuals to compete, changes how we understand classwork. What if all assignments were collaborative? Aren't we almost always working with other people to solve the most pressing issues of the day? What use is it to train competitive individuals when what we need is a community of people solving complex problems together?

Cultivating a community orientation to learning encourages students to consider the strengths and weaknesses of the members of a particular group working on a specific task. When we do not attend to individual contributions to the group, everyone competes to set the table for dinner only to find that no one has cooked any food. Why are we creating artificially competitive environments in the classroom? Instead, we should cultivate teamwork that recognizes and appreciates difference. This kind of diversity results in resilient communities that are able to rely on a range of specialized knowledge, perspective, and skill to problem-solve. Identifying problems and solving them as a community of individuals is critical to the survival and learning of the group. Relationships with one another are nurtured rather than weighed for their benefits. When engaging collective and communal knowledges, we will undoubtedly encounter oral traditions.

Oral Traditions: *Respect and accept oral forms of knowledge production.*

Engaging diverse cultures requires being open to different forms of recording and memory media. Our histories are not just written; much of what we need to learn from our past has been passed down through oral traditions. So we all must listen. Much of what I have learned from my African American community was shared with me through stories. Similarly, Moraga wrote about Xicanx spoken word traditions:

As Xicanas and Xicanos, one of our oldest written traditions resides on the indigenous ground of the spoken word, interpreted from the black marks of resin wept from trees onto a piece of amatl paper. MeXicanas and MeXicanos have always told stories aloud: as weapons against traíciones, as historical accounts and prophetic warnings, as preachers and teachers against wrongdoing, as songs of celebration, as exhalations of laughter, as prayer in the presence of the divine. And through this storytelling one's awareness of the world and its meanings grows and changes. There is no other common way, really, to explain an old way of using words; maybe even to justify it in the context of an unjust Western literary canon that extols the privately read, soundless word and abstract thought over the canto of cuento. (xvi)

As Moraga describes, much of our lives are heard; much more community interaction is spoken than written. Thus, any reasonable attempt to learn from the community that surrounds us must include attention to oral traditions. We exclude much community knowledge and elder wisdom if we fail to engage oral traditions in our classrooms. However, we should go beyond having oral presentations and move toward embracing oral forms of knowledge production (e.g., oral assignments). As we bring ever-diverse content into the classroom, some scholars will be tempted to appropriate and even lay claim to owning that knowledge, through unscrupulous citation practices (e.g., writing and publishing another community's folk songs). Therefore, we must consider counter-canonical citation practices.

Counter-Canonical Citation Practices: *Develop a curriculum that challenges dominant knowledges and centers perspectives from the world's majority, who have been excluded from texts that privilege a powerful minority.*

Sara Ahmed clearly articulated this point: "Feminism is at stake in how we generate knowledge; in how we write, in who we cite" (14). We must not bring community knowledge into our classrooms only to have it stolen. In a liberatory, feminist andragogy, educators cite works at the margins, on the edge, and out of the (mainstream) picture. We should encourage counter-canonical practices among students, who may be tempted to cite only the best-known or oft-mentioned scholars. This homage to disciplinary canons will only make our world smaller through citation convergence. Instead, we should invite native languages (*through a radical multilingualism*), inhabit the borderlands (*through a transgressive borderland praxis*), learn from our communities (*by respecting collective and communal knowledge traditions*), and listen to everything that is happening around us (*through oral traditions*) so that we can expand what is known in the academy through counter-canonical citation practices.

Especially in the context of adult learning theory, we should aim to create a classroom experience that increases life opportunities for our students and their communities. Feminist andragogy as liberatory practice requires "developing a radical ethic that challenges power and global hegemonies" (Alexander and Mohanty 41). We can only do that if we open our classroom to the world and give credit to the knowledge that existed before it entered. Otherwise, we are complicit in the kind of theft that has long marked university researchers, who often insist on "discovering" people who knew what they were doing well before any university researcher appeared.

Imprinting and Knowledge Economies: Material Impact of Citation Practices

It is not always clear when imprinting begins or ends or when or how an encounter is going to change us. This is as true of people as it is of events, song, taste, touch, and text. It is more likely true that the things that shape us most deeply or that stay with us most profoundly cannot be precisely traced. As an example, Melchor and I met in 2014 through the National Women's Studies Association's (NWSA) Women of Color Leadership Project. Several of us (all strangers at that point) connected to decide room-shares for a conference in San Juan, Puerto Rico; Melchor and I agreed to room together. We spoke on the phone for the first time soon after and arranged for her to stay with me before Puerto Rico to attend a conference in my city. I do not know if it was when I met her to help with luggage or if it was in our first phone conversation or email that bonds began to take root. I cannot pinpoint when our conversations are academic and when they are not; they are usually a little bit of both. Why do we pretend that knowledge formation and knowledge acquisition is any less nebulous and imprecise?

A new citation practice can feed and nourish our work and spirit and facilitate feminist transgressions through the principle of adjacency. Conventional citation practices reinforce an intellectual history that rigorously occludes our feminist teachers and community-based knowledge as important sources for medicine, song, and theories of love and subjectivity. Stolen knowledges become an individual's property rather than a society's treasure. We do not need to accept this tradition as natural or necessary. Citation as intentional adjacency foregrounds the politics of citation structures. It makes legible the logic of algorithms and the compulsory nature of citation practice in order to counteract them. Adjacency enables clarity in who we are talking to and sharing with, who and what draws our attention, and who we can build with. Adjacency moves us to reflect on whose name we call forth and why. Feminists of color have long decried the white worldview that informs women's US history. Contributions by women of color are classed as historical outliers rather than as representative of a multilingual, multiclassed, nonwhite global majority—a difference that makes Shirley Chisholm's historic 1972 run for US president "specialized" knowledge rather than general knowledge. Young boys and girls who know Chisholm's name are more likely to develop insightful analysis of the US political structure. This cannot be understated. Our intellectual genealogies, the names and ideas that imprint on our character and spirit, form long before we can name them.

A parallel challenge exists in writing instruction. Asao Inoue argues that language standards in the composition classroom amount to punitive measures rather than pedagogical tools, reproducing value judgments and power inequities with life-and-death consequences. Radical multilingualism is one way to intervene. Citation formats have expanded to include blogs, Ted Talks, and Twitter (now X) feeds, but the content that fills these categories follows a predictable gender, class, and linguistic pattern. A transgressive borderland praxis purposefully centers the languages, voices, and traditions that teach us at home, increasing everyone's knowledge potential exponentially. I incorporate these principles into my teaching by encouraging students to use non-English sources if they can. I benefit immensely from being able to access a non-English source through adjacency; my personal linguistic limitations do not limit our learning. Radical multilingualism requires that we educators let go of the need to be experts if it means controlling what information is legible. When students are free to harness their full potential, we also become free of a closed knowledge system. Even more, we model the preciousness of linguistic, cultural, and perspectival diversity for teaching and learning.

We learn from Safiya Umoja Noble in *Algorithms of Oppression* that technology not only reinforces but also instrumentalizes our biases through search engine algorithms. I often use Patricia Hill Collins's careful nuancing of *subjugated knowledge* to teach students about the assumptions we have about knowledge holders and creators. As an analysis of power, subjugated knowledge is articulated by Black women from the unique position of being multiply oppressed. "The difficulties these women face," writes Collins, "lie less in demonstrating that they have mastered white male epistemology than in resisting the hegemonic nature of these patterns of thought in order to see, value, and use existing alternative Afrocentric feminist ways of knowing" (267). Through this naming, Collins asserts the value of partial, situated knowledges to the work of liberation. Unfortunately, students who turn to the internet to supplement class notes are led to engage with the concept as it is articulated by Michel Foucault, quoting his words without awareness or concern. This elision of Collins, a leading Black feminist scholar, through computerized formulas reflects the gender, race, and geopolitical hierarchies that are inherent in citation practices. Not only does the elision erase Collins's contributions to antiracist thought, but the seamlessness of the elision makes way for the perpetuation of racist and misogynist media while uplifting white male perspectives as authoritative. Noble's warning is dire: "Search results reflect the values and norms of the search company's commercial partners and advertisers and often reflect our lowest and most demeaning beliefs, because these ideas circulate so freely and so often that they are normalized and extremely profitable" (35–36).

Other sites of academic ritual—namely, syllabus creation, conference presentations, and published scholarship—are areas where we can be accountable by applying a lesson from Afrocentric feminist thought: "The existence of Afrocentric feminist thought suggests that there is always choice, and power to act, no matter how bleak the situation may appear to be" (Collins 290). To align our citation practice with our values and objectives, we can dispense with current practice to build genealogies of knowledge more meaningfully. We now *over-cite* and teach students to do so (usually to deter plagiarism). We can conscientiously refuse the current system by challenging the presumption that citation numbers reflect a source's impact. Asking students to think seriously about how a source has changed their thinking may yield deeper reflection on how information gets in front of us. Was it on a syllabus? Was it on the first page of search results? We should aim to find and cite sources that we want to honor for a lifetime. Notably, choosing an alternative practice may risk charges of participation in what Iztok Fister Jr., Iztov Fister, and Matjaž Perc call "citation cartels," where "members cite each other in order to increase their own number of citations" (Introduction). The three authors observe troubling schemes that game the system, but their assertion that "in the past, the citation process was fair," pretends that disciplinary canons have not operated in similarly selective style, past and present (3). To the contrary, citation practices are heavily directed by disciplinary expectations, signaling disciplinary tradition more than intellectual engagement. Citation is compulsory practice, a way to show membership rather than to engage ideas. Carrie Mott and Daniel Cockayne argue that sources that are most often cited are, perhaps, the *least* often read and engaged (961). They point out that "citation is often a way of *not* talking about something or *not* engaging, a perfunctory act that assumes the reader is familiar with a set of assumptions about a text as the author" (965). Mindfully choosing a different citation practice moves us closer to "feminist treason," what bell hooks calls acts that disregard patriarchal approval (*Feminism* 14).

A deliberate citation practice is only one element in building a liberatory intellectual genealogy. Superficial citation often happens with works by women of color, as we learn from Audre Lorde's "Letter to Mary Daly." Moreover, citation of scholarship by or about Black women rarely translates to material transformation of institutional spaces or culture. Nikol G. Alexander-Floyd echoes concerns made by Ann duCille in "The Occult of Black Womanhood" when she bemoans hiring and research practices that reward attention to Black women's experiences but do little else to change the culture of academia. As universities tout antiracist agendas, they invest little in training, hiring, and promoting the very women whose experiences are written about. Alexander-Floyd calls for complete reassessment of the cultural and material capital that drives common undergraduate experiences at predominantly white institutions, most of which are premised on white cultural norms (820). She calls upon universities to implement intentional mentoring and professionalization structures at the undergraduate and graduate levels, and transform departmental culture and management to center Black intellectual production. Disciplinary scholarship on Black women and US politics, she asserts, should be accompanied by actual cultural and structural transformation of institutions (819).

Academic scholarship rarely affects cultural and structural systems, in large part because citation culture reinforces conformity. In 1984 Richard Delgado observed that scholarship on civil rights law written by scholars of color suffered from a tradition of citing established white scholars. He underscored the material consequences that this practice has for communities of color, even if traditions are reinforced "at the level of unconscious action and choice." Delgado writes, "Courts do cite law reviews . . . [and law reviews] are read and discussed by legislators, political scientists, and their students. They affect what goes on in courts, law classrooms, and legislative chambers. Ideologies—perspectives, ways of looking at the world—are powerful" (573). Ten years later, Cheryl Harris's publication of "Whiteness as Property" denounced the legal tensions that ultimately led to protections for white Americans. She argued that civil rights cases should not be adjudicated as an issue of individual rights (see Harris's footnote 312), an approach that can be made only if one acknowledges the racist and patriarchal histories of institutions such as schools, churches, and corporations. Similarly, the question of citation is not a neutral one. A decade after Delgado's original observations, reports on tenure and promotion provided by Delgado suggest that conditions had deteriorated rather than improved ("Revisited"). Compulsory citation practices accumulate to inform hiring patterns and tenure cases, thereby impacting job security, publication levels, and the perspectives that are taught and reinforced in the university system.

Published in 1990, Collins's *Black Feminist Thought* came on the heels of nearly two decades of scholarship by Black women aiming to recover their cultural, political, social, and intellectual contributions. Alice Walker's recovery of the life and work of novelist and anthropologist Zora Neale Hurston is a well-worn example. The conditions under which Hurston died brought with them sober recognition that economic and political power remain in the hands of white men unless we choose differently. Walker reveals that Hurston died of a stroke while rejections by publishers led to poverty and little access to health care. If the work and names of women of color such as Collins and Hurston can be so easily occluded, what does that mean for the class of emergent scholars of color and, moreover, for knowledges posed and refined through conversation, oration, and song? In the end, moving toward more ethical, intentional citation practices can make for messy and uncharted feminist collaborations, but the alternative is a structure that restricts our engagements and imaginations and pretends objectivity. Citation informed by antiracist and Black feminist theory recognizes the intellectual value of our day-to-day interactions and reveals to us the uncelebrated teachers whom we have elided as a matter of course. In recognizing these teachers, we engage in a transgressive practice that eschews canonical boundaries in order to move hearts and minds and engage those that truly move ours. Collective and communal knowledge traditions account for much more of what we know and how we survive, making group knowledge and the communities from which those groups come important sources for citation.

Messy Feminist Collaborations

Feminist collaborations rooted in community are transgressive and messy—they go against the grain and challenge norms. This is not to say that we do not have teachers or examples but that transgression is a continuous effort. We should always be questioning and learning. We are inspired by the words of bell hooks, who urges all of us to "open our minds and hearts so that we can know beyond the boundaries of what is acceptable, so that we can think and rethink, so that we can create new visions" (*Teaching* 12). Radical feminist transgressions make porous the boundaries that confine and restrict our teaching and learning. Sara Ahmed reminds us that "we have to bring feminist theory home because feminist theory has been too quickly understood as something that we do when we are away from home (as if feminist theory is what you learn when you go to school)" (7–8).

We have aimed in this collaboration to blur the boundaries between home and school, between student and teacher, between academic canons and community wisdom, between ideas and institutions. We have written through messiness, foregoing the need for "coherence" to embrace adjacency. Through adjacency we have enlarged our ideas by noticing connections and contrasts. We have retained our voices and allowed voices that are not ours alone. This is important because consensus works against a transgressive spirit. While many factors have had a hand in contributing to our individual intellectual genealogies—our ways of knowing, living, and leading—we are accountable for what we choose to add. Who we engage with and how we engage are political acts, making citation practices too valuable to be dictated by algorithms, left to chance, or worse, to the pressures of tenure. To find the thing (or things) that change us for the better, that stay with us for a lifetime, to find a place for them when they first do not "fit," and to watch them change us through the principle of adjacency is our journey in teaching and learning and in our practice of collaboration.

Works Cited

Ahmed, Sara. *Living a Feminist Life*. Duke UP, 2017.

Alexander, M. Jacqui, and Chandra Talpade Mohanty. "Cartographies of Knowledge and Power: Transnational Feminism as Radical Praxis." *Critical Transnational Praxis*, edited by Amanda Lock Swarr and Richa Nagar. State U of New York P, 2010, pp. 23–45.

Alexander-Floyd, Nikol G. "Written, published, cross-indexed, and footnoted": Producing Black Women PhDs and Black Women's and Gender Studies Scholarship in Political Science." *PS: Political Science and Politics*, vol. 10, no. 4, 2008, pp. 819–29.

Anzaldúa, Gloria. *Borderlands/La Frontera: The New Mestiza, 25th Anniversary Fourth Edition*. Aunt Lute Books, 2007.

Collins, Patricia Hill. *Black Feminist Thought: Knowledge, Consciousness, and the Politics of Empowerment*. Routledge, 2000.

Delgado, Richard. "The Imperial Scholar: Reflections on a Review of Civil Rights Literature." *University of Pennsylvania Law Review*, vol. 132, 1984, pp. 561–78.

Delgado, Richard. "The Imperial Scholar Revisited: How to Marginalize Outsider Writing, Ten Years Later." *University of Pennsylvania Law Review*, vol. 140, 1992, pp. 1349–72.

duCille, Ann. "The Occult of True Black Womanhood: Critical Demeanor and Black Feminist Studies." *Signs*, vol. 19, no. 3, 1994, pp. 591–629.

Duncan, Patti. "Hot Commodities, Cheap Labor: Women of Color in the Academy." *Are All the Women Still White? Rethinking Race, Expanding Feminisms*, edited by Janell Hobson. State U of New York P, 2016, pp. 177–203.

Fister Jr., Iztok, Iztock Fister, and Perc Matjaž. "Toward the Discovery of Citation Cartels in Citation Networks." *Frontiers in Physics*, Dec. 15, 2016. https://doi.org/10.3389/fphy.2016.00049.

Foucault, Michel. *The Archaeology of Knowledge*. Translated by A. M. Sheridan Smith. Pantheon, 1972.

Freire, Paulo. *Pedagogy of the Oppressed: New Revised 20th Anniversary Edition*. Translated by Myra Bergman Ramos, Continuum, 1998.

Harris, Cheryl I. "Whiteness as Property." *Harvard Law Review*, vol. 106, no. 8, 1993: 1707–791.

hooks, bell. *Feminism Is for Everybody*. South End Press, 2000.

hooks, bell. *Teaching to Transgress: Education as the Practice of Freedom*. Routledge, 1994.

Icaza, Rosalba, and Sara de Jong. "Introduction: Decolonization and Feminisms in Global Teaching and Learning—A Radical Space of Possibility." *Decolonial and Feminisms in Global Teaching and Learning*, edited by Sara de Jong, Rosalba Icaza, and Olivia U. Rutazibwa. Routledge, 2019, pp. xv–xxxiv.

Inoue, Asao B. "How Do We Language So That People Stop Killing Each Other, or What Do We Do about White Language Supremacy?" *College Composition and Communication*, vol. 71, no. 2, pp. 352–69.

Katz, Maude White. "End Racism in Education: A Concerned Parent Speaks." *The Black Women: An Anthology*, edited by Toni Cade Bambara. Penguin Books, 1970, pp. 124–31.

Knowles, Malcolm, Elwood F. Holton III, and Richard A. Swanson. *The Adult Learner: The Definitive Classic in Adult Education and Human Resource Development*, 5th edition. Butterworth-Heinemann, 1998.

Lorde, Audre. "Letter to Mary Daly." *Sister Outsider: Essays and Speeches*. Crossing Press, 2007.

Moraga, Cherríe L. *A Xicana Codex of Changing Consciousness: Writings, 2000–2010*. Duke UP, 2011.

Mott, Carrie, and Daniel Cockaynne. "Citation Matters: Mobilizing the Politics of Citation toward a Practice of Conscientious Engagement." *Gender, Place, and Culture*, vol. 24, no. 7, 2017, pp. 954–73.

Noble, Sofiya Umoja. *Algorithms of Oppression*. New York UP, 2018.

Simpson, Leanne Betasamosake. *As We Have Always Done: Indigenous Freedom through Radical Resistance*. U of Minnesota P, 2017.

Walker, Alice. "In Search of Zora Neale Hurston." *Ms. Magazine*, 1975.

4

Beyond Critique

Building a Feministqueerpublichealth Classroom

BARBARA L. SHAW and REBECCA DAWSON

In 2017 we started co-teaching a class titled "Sex and Health" that intentionally put into conversation the interdisciplinary humanities (women's, gender, and sexuality studies) and sciences (epidemiology/public health). It was experimental and we were both unsure of what would or could come of it. In fall 2023 we taught our third iteration of the course, and this collaborative space has grown into one of the most rewarding experiences in our teaching careers. Typically, Barbara offers classes in women's, gender, and sexuality studies (WGSS), global health, and public humanities and was trained in American studies, cultural studies, women's studies, and Caribbean diaspora studies. Becky, an epidemiologist with training in public health research and practice, teaches courses in global health and biology. Originally, we imagined our work providing a bridge between our two fields, especially as the humanities faced administrative erasure. Since then it has become clear that our collaborative work seeks to show the interdependence of WGSS and public health. For the last five years, our endeavors have meant we are consciously building something new, brick by brick, that names and works against hierarchies that exist between feminist-queer theory and public health while actively creating a classroom and research space that moves beyond facile critique and toward realized collaboration that offers new questions and perspectives for thinking about sex and health. From the outset, it is important to state that doing this work has renewed our joy in teaching and research. In this essay we lay out the genesis of our collaboration, what we do in the classroom, what we have learned along the way, and why and how we are thriving in a new interdisciplinary space of ambiguity.

In *Borderlands/La Frontera*, Gloria Anzaldúa theorizes the cultural spaces of in-between that create a new identity and writes, "On our way to a new consciousness, we will have to leave the opposite bank, the split between the two mortal combatants somehow healed so that we are on both shores at once . . . or perhaps we will decide to disengage from the dominant culture . . . and cross the border into a wholly new and separate territory" (78–79). To be sure, the borderland work that we are doing is not Anzaldúa's, which is located specifically within Latina/e-Chicana-Mexican American, Indigenous, feminist, lesbian communities in the Texas-Mexico borderlands. However, its insistence on the need to create new spaces from places of contradiction and connection outside of either/or thinking deeply informs our integrative work. Thinking of our collaboration as a cultural and academic borderland has allowed us to listen carefully to each other and to the different languages we use to discuss sex and health and, more broadly, our respective fields.

When we got started in 2017, we agreed that the best way we could imagine working collaboratively was to practice nonhierarchical thinking, learning, and research with each other, share it with our students, and then ask them to practice it with us and one another. In doing so, the emphasis in our class is on the *process* of blending feminist-queer and public health approaches to our topic. We have named this as "feministqueerpublichealth" praxis, and it is inspired by Angela Willey's reinvigoration of Donna Haraway's "naturecultural," or "a world beyond the nature culture binary" (Willey 17). In *Undoing Monogamy*, Willey reintroduces "naturecultural" as a method—a practice—that intervenes in how we think about feminism and biology:

> Key to this methodological intervention is the interruption of stories about a progression from *critique* (of politics) to *engagement* (with biology). Rather, it must be understood that nature and culture do not "belong" to science and feminism respectively. Disciplinary thinking re-roots what and how any given field thinks and this is neither reflexive or complete. [Instead,] nuanced and careful narratives about relationships between feminism, science, and the body enable the work of producing newly accountable knowledges. (22)

Understanding that fields need one another to see and do their work more holistically, accurately, and politically has been our anchor in our collaborations with each other and students. Aimee Knupsky and M. Soledad Caballero's framing of *ethical interdisciplinary collaboration*, a phrase they coined, best captures how we ground ourselves: "The model . . . places disciplines on equal footing, recognizes the limitations of any one disciplinary perspective, and creates an opportunity to address real-world, complex problems no discipline can solve on its own" (96). While WGSS and public health may be considered as coherent interdisciplinary fields, arguably, through their institutionalization they have become more disciplined or departmentalized, and scholars may envision their own theories and methods as enough to answer some of the most pressing contemporary issues. Ethical interdisciplinary collaboration, as Knupsky and Caballero put forth, is a "process [that] requires flexibility, open-mindedness, and a sense of curiosity to engage with others as scholars [across inter/disciplines] to think through how to name and then solve historically sticky problems" (96).

AnaLouise Keating's theorizing of post-oppositional thinking in *Transformation Now!* also underlies our efforts. In defining oppositional consciousness, she writes, it "represents binary either/or epistemology and praxis that structures our perceptions, politics, and actions through a resistant energy—a reaction against that which we seek to transform" (2). The humanities critique the sciences, the sciences eye humanistic evidence and feminist and queer theoretical frameworks with suspicion, and we become locked in a dance that feeds the erasure of one another, particularly the humanities and interdisciplinarity. In her book, Keating asks those interested in feminist praxis and pedagogies to think at the thresholds:

> Thresholds represent complex interconnections among a variety of sometimes contradictory worlds—points crossed by multiple intersecting possibilities, opportunities, and challenges. Like thresholds—that mark transitional, in-between spaces where new beginnings, and unexpected combinations can occur—threshold theories facilitate and enact movements "betwixt and between" divergent worlds, enabling us to establish fresh connections among distinct (and sometimes contradictory) perspectives, realities, peoples, theories, texts, and/or worldviews. (10)

Keating's work builds on the scholarship written by Black women and other women of color, reminding us that these theoretical interventions were enlivened by the many who contributed to *This Bridge Called My Back*, in which naming and feminist accountability open up space for intersectional approaches in feminist and queer thought. The disciplinary chasms that create hierarchies of knowledge are the riverbanks that Anzaldúa saw so clearly when writing *Borderlands/La Frontera*. So we began to ask, How are feminist-queer and public health approaches interdependent, connected, and in relationship to one another?

Eli Clare's work in *Brilliant Imperfection* guides us through this question. In thinking through a world built on sameness (in his case looking at people moving quickly and with relative ease through an airport), he reflects on the human creation of monocultures: "They move as if their body-minds are separate and independent from the others around them" (132) They are "ecosystems that have been stripped, through human intervention, of a multitude of interdependent beings and replaced by a single species" (132). In drawing a parallel within our natural environment, he continues: "I think of a wheat field with its orderly rows of one variety of grass, a clearcut forest replanted with one variety of tree" (132). People with seen and unseen disabilities live in a more interdependent world—sometimes forced and at other times intentionally sought to politically, economically, socially, and emotionally support one another. What if our worlds are more interdependent than we impose? What if what we know and how we know it would *benefit from* seeing our jigsaw pieces connect so that we can learn from and with one another and generously support each other in who we are and what we do? What if our learning communities expand to "choose this messy, imperfect work-in-progress called interdependence" and if our fierce independence is an illusion? (136).

From our corner of the world—teaching at Allegheny College, a small liberal arts college in the snow and rust belts—our question became, What could we build together that asked students to think differently about the topic and the fields? The process of making nonhierarchical, interdependent, and collaborative thinking a practice in our shared classroom began with recognizing that we share similar pedagogical approaches that value open environments for students to be curious, critical, and creative to construct new ways of thinking and being. We also said out loud what the assumptions were about each other's fields so that we could consciously disrupt discursive spaces of competition and institutional hierarchy. We agreed early on to use teaching tools—such as class discussions, group work, in-class writing, and project-based assignments—to engage students in the learning process to value and practice synthesis (both/and thinking) rather than delivering a content-driven syllabus siloed by our inter/disciplines.

Beginning the Process

Our partnership was made possible alongside the collaborative work done by Knupsky and Caballero. Their Great Lakes Colleges Association (GLCA) grant, Expanding Collaborations Initiative—Interdisciplinary Team Teaching across the Arts/Humanities and Sciences, provided the structural time and space to develop our co-taught course. We chose this starting point to flag the political economy of how some collaborations are built within departmentalized institutions. The goal of the larger initiative was to name and enact interdisciplinary teaching that fostered collaboration across the sciences and humanities through the development of courses taught by two faculty members. What it made clear is that it was not the sciences "saving" the humanities. The grant and its participants' subsequent work was to "ensure bi-directional and value-based equity" between fields. This pushes against what Knupsky and Caballero noticed when "scholars reading a book here and there, reading a few articles here and there and then appropriating that work for their own purposes and calling it interdisciplinary" (99).

We began our work together by reading an extensive bibliography related to sex and health in each other's fields; it is a simple step and the most crucial one. We spent a summer discussing the power of language in our fields, how scholars/teachers/practitioners/activists build arguments, what evidence has weight, and how and why theory and methodology are articulated in published works. For Rebecca, this meant learning how feminist-queer scholars build arguments using theory as frameworks to make sense of various types of qualitative evidence—such as personal narratives, ethnographic data, mediated images and other forms of visual culture, primary and secondary sources, and literary contributions. Barbara learned how quantitative evidence is compiled through survey data and arranged in graphs and tables in public health publications. During this multiyear process of reading together—some of which still appears on the syllabus—and building the course collaboratively, we worked to translate "feministqueerpublichealth" from our own praxis to a *class identity*. From the first day, we meta-teach that the course is based on moments of connection rather than resistance or inter/disciplinary antagonism. In the 2023 version of the course, we anticipated a literal split in the room where students who study WGSS or global health might congregate with one another. We have been pleasantly surprised by their own integration, and this particular group worked hard and in earnest to understand each other's academic and social backgrounds to build community and eventually their own advocacy and activist projects.

Building a class together with intentional approaches to disrupt hierarchies is time-intensive. We committed to weekly meetings nearly nine months before setting foot in a classroom. During these meetings we discussed articles and teaching/classroom philosophies, outlined a syllabus, drafted assignments, and began to compose questions for students about the language that structures our understanding of sex and health. Students can see what nonhierarchical thinking looks like on the syllabus as we purposefully paired one reading from WGSS and a related one in public health. Our weekly meetings continued throughout the semester when teaching the course. We devoted substantive time each week to planning our classes, designing in-class activities, incorporating current events and timely cultural references, and crafting questions that challenged students to pull together qualitative and quantitative information to ask new questions or view information about sex and health from a new perspective.

Building a class collaboratively with attention to field and classroom hierarchies also means we were willing to take intellectual risks by acknowledging the strengths and gaps in our training along with considering how these two very different research methodologies might work better together. For example, the field of public health is grounded in the science of epidemiology. As an epidemiologist, Rebecca's responsibility to her field is rooted in work that seeks to quantify the determinants and distributions of health, including what are known as the *social determinants of health*. Defined as the conditions in which people are born, grow, live, work, and age by the World Health Organization (https://www.who.int/social_determinants/ sdh_definition/en/), the social determinants of health are often operationalized in the work of epidemiologists as individual- or community-level variables. Epidemiologists are taught to group (using simple and often sophisticated statistics) these variables into a 2×2 table (see below).

An epidemiologist interested in teen pregnancy, for example, might ask the following research question about race and teen pregnancy: "Is there an association between race and teen pregnancy?" Our hypothesis could be: "Black teenagers are at greater risk of becoming pregnant compared to white teenagers." To answer this research question, a study will be designed to measure (count) the number of pregnancies among Black and white teenagers. Imagine that a group of one thousand teenagers in New York City are asked to complete a survey in which they are asked to identify their race and answer the question "Have you ever been pregnant?" Data from this survey will be organized by an epidemiologist like this:

Survey participants	Number who did report a pregnancy	Number who did not report a pregnancy	Total
Black teenagers	400	100	500
White teenagers	100	400	500

Using this table, epidemiologists can calculate the risk of experiencing a pregnancy among Black teenagers compared to white (risk = (400/500)/ (100/500) = 4). An epidemiological study seeking to understand the association between race and teen pregnancy would conclude that Black teenagers are four times more likely to experience a pregnancy (during their teens) compared to white teenagers. The goal of an epidemiologist's work is to quantify the risks associated with health behaviors and disease and use those numbers to propose interventions and public health programming to reduce risk or minimize disease. This way of thinking/knowing—illustrated through a 2×2 table—provides a systematic and repeatable method for researching and understanding risk as well as change over time.

Barbara's approach to the same question pushes on the edges of public health's collected data to ask about the methods for how data was collected for the survey (*Was there bias in its design and execution?*) as well as what the sociopolitical and historical reasons are such that Black teenagers are four times more likely to experience pregnancy compared to white teenagers. While the numbers reflect racial health disparities that require public health intervention, knowing the numbers is not enough to create a grounded intervention that will produce change that works and is good for and within Black communities. Instead, decolonial, antiracist, and anti-imperialist feminist-queer frameworks and analyses insist that we must understand the root of why this takes shape across generations and how this knowledge informs working in and with communities—indeed the situated knowledges of who can do this work and under what contexts. This requires theoretical and research work that clarifies racial, gendered, and socioeconomic histories that create and maintain contemporary structural inequities. We then name how institutions, such as public health, need to be grounded in these frameworks, or it is bound to repeat and perpetuate social inequities in approaching teen pregnancies.

Public health research does not allow for in-betweens, whereas WGSS approaches complexity as a rich theoretical and activist site to understand and change the formations of gender, race, class, sexuality, and nationality. For example, in public health, a study participant cannot be categorized as both Black and white or having sex with both men and women unless a new category is created. There is no space outside of the 2×2 table to deal with the real-life fluidity of human sexuality and gender or multiply-racialized people. Public health surveys and other practices often, and problematically, ask individuals to choose the "category that fits best." These distinctions allow practitioners to make comparisons between groups and quantify risk factors. Epidemiological research is done to identify inequalities and document patterns and distributions of health; however, epidemiologists are not seeking to understand why inequalities exist. Public health training allows for measuring health outcomes across space and time. Researchers are not taught to ask why inequity is happening, and current methodologists are ill-equipped to address questions of why differences in health exist across race, gender, sexualities, class, and nationalities.

In doing our reading together to prepare for the class, we had our first "ah-ha moment" when discussing "Understanding Racial HIV/STI

Disparities in Black and White Men Who Have Sex with Men: A Multilevel Approach." In this published epidemiological study, the authors write, "The reasons for these black/white disparities among MSM (men who have sex with men) in HIV prevalence and incidence are unclear" (Sullivan et al. 1). While epidemiological studies cannot provide clarity, an intersectional approach in WGSS offers, and requires bringing, sources together from history, literature, art, cultural geography, sociology, and religion. It became clear that our feministqueerpublichealth collaboration is about *the process of creating space* for us to imagine new approaches for asking how to quantify human behaviors and disease and how feminist-queer inquiry provides theoretical frameworks and research questions that contextualize findings and reroute versus re-root statistical information. By putting the two fields into conversation, the work regarding Black and white men and HIV/STI does not have to end with a statement about lack of clarity. Together we can begin to unpack the reasons that disparities/inequities exist between Black and white pregnant teens and Black men and HIV—and well beyond what we have outlined as examples here. We need to value each other's expertise to do this work.

The Class

Our North Star guiding principle in the classroom was engaging students with questions that emerge when we synthesize ideas. We wanted students to begin to understand how research done by epidemiologists informs the work done by researchers in women's, gender, and sexuality studies and vice versa. The foundation of this work rests on our shared conclusion that neither one of our disciplines has the sole ability to reduce the number of teenage pregnancies, sexually transmitted infections, coerced sterilizations or birth control, or to end sexual violence. We were not looking for answers to questions or to fix the issues. We were looking for ways to ask new questions that could provide avenues for intervening in disease and violence. What we learned in the first iteration of the class was that synthesizing needs to be built carefully. In our latest iteration, this has meant spending time learning how WGSS and public health address the issue separately and then designing in-class activities that walk students through what may be possible when we weave the two approaches.

Our collaborative work values generous thinking, process, and, specifically, teaching undergraduate students how to think across inter/disciplines by integrating quantitative methods and qualitative theories through the content of the course. To do this work, we draw on Kathleen Fitzpatrick's framework for thinking generously as a "mode of engagement that emphasizes listening over speaking, community over individualism, collaboration over competition, and lingering with the ideas that are in front of us rather than continually pressing forward to where we want to go" (4). In slowing down to do this work intentionally, it provides opportunities to name both the limitations of our disciplinary training and find value in asking new questions that require multiple/mixed methods to be explored and pursued. This type of work is messy; we were creating a new process to generate conversations between and among students of public health and feminist-queer inquiry. Not only did we struggle to understand and teach from this new space of collaboration, but students struggled, too. Many found it easy to find fault in their own sex education. Others wanted to "solve" problems or minimize health inequalities within the space we created. They sought quick solutions to problems that are seemingly intractable since they are anchored in power. We continuously recentered the students, reminding them that the work we were doing was to be generative and that our goal was to ask new questions about sex, health, and power. By our latest iteration, we learned that assigning less course material is necessary so that we can spend time processing and practicing what analysis and synthesis looks like. For instance, Rebecca might ask us to slow down and explain how theory plays a role in our example for the day. Alternatively, Barbara might slow things down by asking the class to explain how the statistical analysis is completed or if the data could have been collected in a different way. By the second iteration of the class, we reduced the number of individual writing assignments and increased the value of group work so that the assignments aligned with the philosophy of the class and our teaching.

When we started, the syllabus we created paired readings (one from WGSS and one from the public health literature). In the current iteration, we spend the first two weeks of class with one reading per day learning how to locate the argument, evidence, results, and conclusions in the public health and WGSS pieces so that students can see the similarities and differences in each before synthesizing. As we move through the foundational first weeks, we ask questions that pull in the ideas from the previous readings, practicing how we make connections. By the time students read one of each piece in preparation for class, the scaffolding is in place to have more robust conversations. Once everyone in the room understands what each author is arguing and what evidence there is to support that argument, we ask our students to think about how the articles are in conversation. We look for places where conclusions align or could inform one another, where disagreements exist, and where the conclusions from one article are further explained or expand upon the conclusions that have been made. For example, when we assigned the article by Sullivan and his colleagues (referenced above), we paired it with a selection from Patricia Hill Collins's *Black Feminist Thought*. We put these pieces together because we wanted students to understand that one field's approach may provide the raw materials (data) to create a snapshot of the differences between white men and Black men who have sex with men, while the other field's approach makes clear that systems of racism and controlling images shape the data and its interpretation.

Another pairing that has been effective in generating robust conversations and "ah-ha" moments is Sprecher and Treger's "Virgin College Students' Reasons for and Reactions to Their Abstinence from Sex: Results from a 23-Year Study at a Midwestern U.S. University" with Jessica Valenti's "The Cult of Virginity" from *The Purity Myth*. The first piece conducted a longitudinal study of how women and men in a particular class at a Midwestern university conceptualize virginity with many women and some men remaining virgins for fear of pregnancy and disease. When we paired that with Valenti's work, students immediately connected the dots and could talk through why the students responded the way they did on the survey. In teaching paired materials, students have their own moments pointedly referencing that public health researchers and practitioners need to have a better understanding of antiracist feminist and queer theory to do their work and make sense of the studies if their aim is social change and more equitable health outcomes.

The course assignments are synthesis papers where we specifically ask students to describe, analyze, and synthesize a series of articles and artifacts. An artifact might be a specific state policy, a database of information about sex education, or a movie or TV show with pop culture significance that teaches sex education without claiming to do so. The assignments require that all students incorporate evidence from at least one article from the field of public health and at least one from WGSS. Students are required to develop a strong thesis statement and are asked to use description judiciously—enough to make clear what they have consulted and why—and not necessarily to write about a solution to a problem. We ask them to think about how the pieces of evidence from various fields come together—are they telling a similar story in different ways? If so, what are the differences and how does that increase our understanding of a subject? We encourage them to think about what is being said and what is silent; what gaps exist in the literature in both fields, and might there be a way to ask new questions that bring together qualitative and quantitative methods now that we can see the gap. The assignments ask students to look for these moments and then to think and write about how the information is coming together and what new narrative or thesis is emerging.

Teaching interdependence can make us and our students uncomfortable—many of us have been taught to want concrete answers and a clear and correct pathway to "fix" the problem (e.g., pregnancy among teens that identify as LGBTQAI+, racial injustice, and HIV). Students whose backgrounds are in the sciences sometimes struggle to make sense of critical analyses that use feminist and queer theories and methods that ask us to understand pregnancy and HIV through an intersectional lens before writing and implementing health policy. Those trained in using statistical analyses of large populations do not always understand what is valuable about reading personal accounts or literature. WGSS students may be suspicious of the methods that collect data and may struggle with the public health literature that assumes not only that survey questions are objective but also that the reader understands statistical methods and how to read charts and tables of data. We push students from all disciplines to acknowledge this uncomfortableness, to sit in it and "take a pause," and then work through it in the class by nudging them to see how new questions can be asked. It is demanding and risky work for us as instructors, too, since the work is process-oriented while students learn the course content. We are doing the work with them and do not hold the answers to some of their questions because we, too, are learning how to reimagine feministqueerpublichealth. Instead, we intentionally model vulnerability and the joy in not knowing and exploring possibilities.

Our Collective *JoyStruggle*

By emphasizing the process, we free ourselves and the students from needing to feel like becoming an expert is the goal. As instructors, we experience the joy of learning on a weekly basis. Our example in the class is often to say, "Wait, slow down, I don't understand what you mean when you say 'evidence,' 'data,' 'theory,' or 'culture.'" We often ask each other to explain more and in the process role-model the phrase "We don't know, so let's see if we can piece something together." We pass along what curiosity looks like, sounds like, and requires from us. To return to Knupsky and Caballero's insights, "Engaging interdisciplinary collaborations is developmental. . . . The journey is inherently and unsurprisingly unpredictable because until faculty come together across disciplinary boundaries, they have no way to anticipate the integrations that are there to be found" (105). There is most certainly *joystruggle* in learning how to blend qualitative-quantitative methods as well as analytical-creative questions and seeing students conclude that both/and is more meaningful than either/or. Our excitement for the process and the subject matter translates into role-modeling how to rethink in nonhierarchical and post-oppositional ways.

The struggle—and it is a real struggle—was more profound at the institutional level. Both of us were untenured when we began our collaborative work. When we taught the course for the first time, Barbara had just completed her tenure review and Rebecca was in her third year in a tenure-track position. These kinds of collaborations are a form of choreography that is time-intensive, requiring ongoing conversations about how to be in the classroom, grade, respond to emails, and offer shared office hours. Despite institutional support for our team teaching through the grant and mentoring from Knupsky and Caballero, co-teaching this course was a risk for us moving through the tenure process, given the considerable weight of student evaluations at our institution. We made two strategic decisions to reduce these risks. First, we asked Knupsky and Caballero to observe our course and provide a formal evaluation of our collaborative classroom for our tenure files. Additionally, we were given permission by our provost to have one set of evaluations for the course. At our institution, team-taught courses traditionally have two sets of student evaluations for a course, one for each faculty member. We pushed against this practice and argued successfully for one set of evaluations that enabled us jointly to contextualize scores and comments to support each other rather than being pitted against one another. This did not necessarily take away the sting of evaluations— some students said we spent too much time on social justice approaches and WGSS, while others stated that they needed more time to critique why and how researchers quantify people's lives, and a few said it was "unorganized." These evaluative comments suggested that our post-oppositional approach may not have been as successful as we had hoped in the moment—and we both understand that unraveling oppositional thinking takes more than one semester if not a lifetime of intentionality. The positive evaluations have ensured that the endeavor is worthwhile because students spoke to how they learned to do challenging work across disciplinary boundaries with one another and appreciated spaces that are intentionally creative. We are now both tenured, and the course is officially housed in WGSS as a 300-level course and offered once every three years since it is dependent on our teaching commitments in departments that are stretched thin. This speaks volumes as to what is valued in institutional cultures. What is clear in retelling this story is that team teaching and interdisciplinary collaboration require flexibility and commitment within institutions and that the resistance to engage in collaborative work may be amplified for contingent and new faculty.

We are still in the process of learning what it means to live in ambiguity—to work in between differences, to see our points of connection, and, in doing so, to seek new interdependent questions so that social transformation may be realized. What we know and practice is that we collectively must teach our students to do more than "tolerate" one another because this is the language of disciplines, hierarchies, and oppositions built within institutions of higher learning that elevate the sciences and harm the humanities. Practicing Keating's insistence on creating a post-oppositional world requires an unlearning of solidified disciplinarity, including within interdisciplinary fields. It also invites us to pursue new ways of being and knowing—to think beyond critique and toward creativity—because it is in those spaces that we will be able to reach students, role-model and imagine what it could be otherwise, and build a new generation of change makers who understand how to strive toward transformation and social change through interdependence and collaboration.

Works Cited

Anzaldúa, Gloria. *Borderlands/La Frontera: The New Mestiza*. Aunt Lute Books, 1987.

Clare, Eli. *Brilliant Imperfection: Grappling with Cure*. Duke UP, 2017.

Collins, Patricia Hill. *Black Feminist Thought: Knowledge, Consciousness, and the Politics of Empowerment*. Routledge, 2008.

Fitzpatrick, Kathleen. *Generous Thinking: A Radical Approach to Saving the University*. Johns Hopkins UP, 2021.

Keating, AnaLouise. *Transformation Now!: Toward a Post-Oppositional Politics of Change*. U of Illinois P, 2013.

Knupsky, Aimee C., and M. Soledad Caballero. "Applying an Ethical Interdisciplinary, Collaborative Approach to the Scholarship of Teaching and Learning," *Ethics and the Scholarship of Teaching and Learning*, edited by Lisa M. Fedoruk. Springer, 2022, pp. 95–110.

Moraga, Cherríe, and Gloria Anzaldúa. *This Bridge Called My Back: Writings by Radical Women of Color*. State U of New York P, 2015.

Sprecher, Susan, and Stanislav Treger. "Virgin College Students' Reasons for and Reactions to Their Abstinence from Sex: Results From a 23-Year Study at a Midwestern U.S. University." *Journal of Sex Research*, vol. 52, no. 8, Oct. 2015, pp. 936–48.

Sullivan, Patrick S., John Peterson, and Eli S. Rosenberg, et al. "Understanding Racial HIV/STI Disparities in Black and White Men Who Have Sex with Men: A Multilevel Approach," *PLoS One*, vol. 9, no. 3, March 2014, pp. 1–11.

Valenti, Jessica. "The Cult of Virginity." *The Purity Myth: How America's Obsession with Virginity Is Hurting Young Women*. Seal Press, 2009, pp. 17–40.

Willey, Angela. *Undoing Monogamy: The Politics of Science and the Possibilities of Biology*. Duke UP, 2016.

5

Challenging Hierarchy

Feminist Praxis and Sustainable Community Collaboration

ARIELLA ROTRAMEL and KIMBERLY SANCHEZ

Community-engaged learning is a hallmark of women's, gender, sexuality, feminist, and queer studies (Luhmann et al. 1). In the 2010s the US National Women's Studies Association (NWSA) emphasized the role community engagement plays in the field's teaching and research (NWSA "Women's Studies as Civic Engagement"; NWSA "Women's Studies Scholarship"). This common practice reflects the field's investment in social justice, often pursued through *feminist praxis* (discussed in detail below). As faculty in the field recognize, community-engaged learning offers a unique opportunity for students to collectively engage in applied work. This approach seeks to produce a positive outcome for community partners and higher education institutions as students "practice [transformative] citizenship . . . [and learn] the values and skills associated with social justice activism" (Iverson and James 20). Despite the promise of community engagement, the reality is often that many "service learning proponents have decided what is best for the community, or have never gotten past the exploitative mind-set of using the community as a way to educate their students" (Stoecker and Tryon x). Community organization partners may find themselves shifting priorities and taking on additional labor commitments to accommodate students, draining rather than augmenting their work. Our work together in community-engaged learning illustrates how an approach that grapples with issues of hierarchy and power can support deeper collaborations intentionally over time.

Ariella Rotramel is the department chair and Vandana Shiva is associate professor of gender, sexuality, and intersectionality studies (GSIS), whose teaching portfolio includes multiple community-engaged GSIS courses and the gateway course for the Holleran Center for Community Action and Public Policy. Kimberly Sanchez is the former director of Community Partnerships and Holleran Center associate director of Engaged Scholarship and Community Learning. Within the former Community Partnerships office (part of the Holleran Center in 2019), Sanchez served in all existing roles within the office as a community learning coordinator, assistant director, associate director, and director. Together we worked for two years as faculty and community learning instructors for the Holleran Center's gateway course: the Foundations of Community Action seminar and the corresponding New London Community Practicum. In 2017 we brought together college colleagues to plan a long-term collaboration with the local nonprofit legal aid organization, Immigration Advocacy and Support Center (IASC). Rotramel's department became an anchor partner with IASC, and the trajectory of this collaboration serves as a case study for this chapter. Our extensive work together has allowed us to recognize our shared pedagogical values and build a strong level of rapport to pursue and critically reflect on our community-engaged work.

Recognizing and Responding to Power and Hierarchy

Issues of power and hierarchy permeate community-engaged learning. Thanks to feminist theory and practice, we have theoretical tools to explicitly work through these issues. Feminist philosopher Iris Marion Young emphasizes that modern power operates through structures, and "individuals daily contribute to maintaining and reproducing oppression, but those people are usually simply doing their jobs or living their lives, and do not understand themselves as agents of oppression" (41–42). Within our own work, we have to name and account for power dynamics that span the classroom, college, and community. While real resource and decision-making differences exist, from our team's graded assessment of student work to some students' financial and social privilege, we invite students not to take these realities for granted through class discussions and assignments. We make our teaching transparent, discussing how we have developed our relationships with community organizations and the existing stakes of these partnerships. We ask students to push themselves throughout the semester to identify and navigate dynamics that may be discomfiting—from the power a community site supervisor may have over clients as a gatekeeper of resources to a new recognition of their own status as people with high educational attainment.

We identify hierarchical, binary thinking as a key driver of the normalization of power dynamics that is too often ignored in community-engaged learning efforts. The critique of a dualistic hierarchy that establishes one identity as dominant and the opposing identity as other/negated is a cornerstone of our approach (Gaard 23). Women's, gender, sexuality, feminist, and queer studies not only questions definitive divides between identities but also explores continuums across social categories; studies the dynamic, historically specific creation and articulation of identities; and emphasizes how multiple identities and systems of oppression interact with each other. Despite this pronounced sensitivity to hierarchy and binaries, a casual "we're all friends here and any help is great!" attitude can permeate community-engaged learning. For many community organizations, once they open their doors to college members, they assume a positive contribution to their work and become cautious about critiquing these efforts. The result can be a failure to have open and honest reflection on the work being done and deeper accountability from college partners to meet the aims of the organizations they engage in. We believe it is our responsibility to proactively open up communication with organizations in a manner that emphasizes our desire for growth in the quality of our relationships. A cornerstone of this practice is being available and honestly naming historic or ongoing barriers to effective collaboration with an understanding that we will continue our relationship. For example, we have found it important to maintain ongoing communication to obtain critical feedback from partners about student engagement as there are often complicated or unhelpful elements to their presence. This approach accounts for the power tied to our affiliation with the college and seeks to support community partners in owning their right to determine how, when, and why they collaborate with us and our students.

Within our context, we have observed that the following binaries are often assumed and perpetuated in community-engaged learning as a hierarchy, with the term on the left privileged over the term on the right:

authority	non-professional, non-expert
formally educated	uneducated
helpful women	needy community members
predominantly white institution (PWI)	racialized community

These hierarchies can problematically permeate the development of a collaboration as well as the expectations and dynamics within a project. While we do work to unpack and destigmatize communities as discussed below, issues of bias and privilege still emerge frequently. For example, at a community location a college student was the target of racist language from a community participant. The student's classmates observed the incident but did nothing to address it then or later after they returned to campus.

When the student reported the incident to Sanchez, it was necessary to facilitate a conversation with the students about their failure to support each other in an uncomfortable moment and the need to find productive ways to intervene to mark such interactions as inappropriate. This instance was part of a broader set of concerns when working with students from diverse backgrounds who are uncomfortable with conflict and responding to the demands of solidarity work.

In our work together it has been important to resist the common faculty-staff hierarchy. Instead of Rotramel performing the "scholar-on-stage" as a professor, we have sought ways for Sanchez and other colleagues to share their expertise in the development of the course and in-class teaching. Rotramel participates in community work from discussions with partners to the execution of projects with Sanchez and colleagues. This approach contrasts with either waiting for a new semester to begin with a prepackaged community project created by Sanchez's colleagues that is ready to receive students or pursuing a community project that ignores any existing relationships between Connecticut College colleagues and the community partner. Our approach seeks to reject the assumption that staff members are at the beck and call of faculty to handle the distasteful logistics of community engagement at any point in the academic year. Instead, logistics and communication with community partners and among our college team are inherently part of the pedagogical process and made transparent to students.

From the development to assessment of community-engaged projects, we embrace an approach of "recognizing the community as a source of knowledge and expertise and sharing authority with community partners" (Engaged Scholarship Advisory Committee to Connecticut Campus Compact 94). Rather than approaching community partners with a set project, through dialogue we learn about their existing needs and develop projects that not only hold value for the partner but also can meet course learning goals. When campus representatives convey an attitude of openness at the outset of planning, community partners can articulate their own priorities, identify clear measures of success necessary for their organizational sustainability, and wield their expertise in the planning phase.

An often-forgotten component of community-engaged learning is determining whether students will engage directly with community members or only with the host community organizations' staff and volunteer membership. If an organization supports students interacting with general community members, students simultaneously represent the organization and their institution. If they are tabling an organizational event, unless they are wearing collegiate-logo clothing, they may first be perceived as organizational representatives by passersby. Through conversation, it may become clearer that they are students volunteering for the organization. As novices they might not have the appropriate training, language, and cultural competencies to make a significant contribution during these interactions. Both we and organization leaders have a responsibility to prepare students to consider how they engage community members as well as represent themselves, the organization, and our college. In particular, highlighting what the focus of an event is and challenging students to consider their own biases throughout their experience are important elements to consider.

Powerlessness is highlighted in these cases as community members are often assumed to be individuals with no technical expertise, and community organization staff commonly are not able to either provide training or criticize students' limitations (Young 56). Faculty are responsible to consider not only these challenges as students interact with community organizations but also how they themselves are perceived by community partners. For example, months after a student project had been completed, during an informal conversation with Rotramel a community partner offered important critical feedback about students' limited contributions and behavioral issues. Despite having been in communication before and during the project, the staff person was reluctant to criticize students who were offering some valuable assistance to their organization. The existing tensions between town and gown, particularly a perceived lack of openness to negative input from community partners based on a systemic assumption that privileges any "help" from a college as beneficial to a community, inhibited having this conversation earlier. It was apparent that the assumed relationship between a faculty member, their students, and a community partner places the students above the community partner and their needs. Moreover, the faculty member may solely want positive feedback about the work of their students and themselves, as community partners seek to ensure a future relationship that may benefit their organization rather than risking criticizing their collaborators. Overall, we have found that partners are uncomfortable providing direct feedback due to such concerns, including power dynamics, as well as limited time and energy. It is through ongoing engagement that one can build trust and an understanding that constructive criticism is a welcomed, valuable part of these efforts.

As we have described, under-addressed hierarchical dynamics make a core element of community-engaged learning—reciprocity—impossible. Reciprocity occurs when

> two or more parties that take collective action toward a common purpose and in the process the parties are transformed in a way that allows for

increased understanding of a full variety of life experiences, and over time works to alter rigid social systems. . . . Transformational partnerships are characterized by higher degrees of reciprocity because the parties are planning and acting together toward a common goal. (Petri 95–96)

Our work centers the feminist pedagogical value of reciprocal relationships, valuing all people involved in these learning experiences. We recognize that the basic components of our relationship shift—from community organization's needs and staffing to students' own experiences and expectations—and that we are not able to get outside of these hierarchies as some of them are deeply structural. In this chapter we attempt to recognize, articulate, and address our desire as co-teachers to build relationships that can move toward a more reciprocal relationship between ourselves and our institutions. Our approach to reciprocity is informed by the larger discourse of interdependence that emphasizes that we are tied together by our shared needs for sustenance, community, and care (Hamraie). We utilize an intersectional critique of identity, power, and hierarchy that emphasizes naming and understanding how structural dynamics play out in the lived experiences of our communities, both inside and outside the classroom. Thus, our approach to reciprocity is always in process and growing complexity rather than static.

Feminist Praxis

Feminist praxis is the dialectical relationship between practice/action and ideas/theory, and most powerfully includes reflection as part of this process (Luhmann et al. 1; Peterson 16; Crass 253). As feminist praxis includes the term "feminist," this form emphatically embraces a recognition of the importance of social justice issues, particularly those tied to ongoing identity-based struggles. bell hooks posits, "Feminism as a movement to end sexist oppression directs our attention to systems of domination and the inter-relatedness of sex, race, and class oppression. . . . It is a starting point indicating the direction of exploration and analysis" (33). As a "starting point" rather than a static perspective, feminism is well aligned with praxis because it centers the powerful relationship between concepts, values, and practices.

Feminist praxis mixes direct political involvement and the feminist valuing of identity- and experience-based knowledges (situated knowledges) (Naples and Dobson 117). Nancy A. Naples and Marnie Dobson argue that praxis must address "the many dimensions of power and inequalities of access and resources within and across different nation-states" and that this approach builds on a bevy of feminist activist skills (133). Feminist praxis is thus explicitly focused on naming and negotiating questions of power, difference, and social change. These elements align with typical higher education institutional values, as Connecticut College's Mission and Values statement demonstrates:

> The College promotes understanding by offering a variety of academic and social experiences and is committed to building greater access, opportunity, and equity. . . . [It] fosters civic responsibility and enhances academic excellence through a long tradition of community involvement and through courses that provide opportunities for service.

As the college's legacy includes community engagement, feminist praxis efforts simultaneously build on this tradition while deepening an understanding of the root causes of limited access, opportunity, and inequity that are inherent to higher education and beyond. Such work productively marks and struggles with the limits of institutionally based praxis, much as activists continue to face conflicts within the broader nonprofit industrial complex (Incite!). Students are often struck by how limited organizations' means are when they learn about budgeting and resources and about the pros and cons of developing funding relationships that may steer organizations from their mission. Another element of frustration can be the need to conduct fund-raising efforts rather than focusing energy toward the core organizational mission areas. For example, students often found themselves conflicted as they moved from direct-service support at a community shelter to organizing a fund-raiser that drew significant financial resources into the organization. Though an important organizational priority, the fund-raiser engaged the students in a manner that was not how they imagined activist work to be, and some of them became disappointed in such an effort being a priority for the organization.

Community engagement as a form of feminist praxis centers collaboration between higher education institutions and their surrounding community. This approach requires a sophisticated understanding of "the relationship between a politics of location and accountability, and the politics of knowledge production" (Alexander and Mohanty 26). There can be a false, assumed binary of a safe campus "bubble" (to use the common language of our college) and a real "elsewhere" of communities (Luhman et al. 18). A key element of our work is to deepen students' ability to critically investigate our campus culture and structures. Some students experience a strong feeling of being out of place as first-generation, people of color, or international students. We also confront imaginings of communities as deficient and simply needing interventions from those with educational and other social advantages. It is necessary to take an intersectional approach that acknowledges "the complex ways that all of us are positioned differently across a diverse range of communities, within and outside of the university, and how these communities are all sites of co-education, dialogue, and relationality, as well as tension and inequity" (Luhman et al. 18; Collins). Power differentials between faculty and staff are significant in this context, as well as racial, class, citizenship, and gender differences among all participants in community partnerships. We seek to intentionally and iteratively address inequities that structure our own roles and the dynamics within our community collaborations.

Students' negative perceptions of our New London community emerge not only out of peer conversations but also from uninformed, biased perspectives of some college faculty and staff. In our community engagement work, it is necessary to deploy critical thinking skills to unpack our relationships with, and assumptions about, the college and communities. Early on in our class, we ask students to reflect on what they have been told about New London and then their own experiences. Each semester we hold a retreat in New London to experience the downtown area firsthand as a group and reconsider what it is like to be part of our community. This approach aligns with the Asset-Based Community Development model that rejects a style of community-engaged learning in which "community wisdom and knowledge, networks of support, and talents, abilities, and assets amongst residents are denied existence rather than drawn upon to solve problems and mobilize for change" (Peterson 36). Students complete an asset map of New London, focusing on their particular areas of interest, such as food justice, health, language, and affinity groups. This assignment prompts them to understand overlapping areas of resources as well as needs and to reconsider their role in community-engaged work. Rather than perceive themselves as individual heroes, they consider the assets of the New London community as well as their own limitations and areas for growth as undergraduate students. Their work with community partners and classmates is foregrounded and mirrored by faculty and staff teamwork that attempts to counter hierarchical assumptions and ground our interactions in communication and reciprocity.

College-Community Context

Connecticut College is a residential private liberal arts college of 1,800 students in New London, Connecticut, on the shoreline of the Long Island Sound. As of 2017, New London's population is approximately 27,218 people and 91.9% are US citizens. The city is racially diverse: white residents

(47.3%), Latinx residents (32.2%), Black residents (13.8%), multiracial residents (4.42%), and Asian residents (1.94%). An estimated 28.3% of New Londoners live in poverty, a higher rate than the national average of 13.1% (Data USA). It is the human services, transportation, medical, and legal center for the southeastern Connecticut region. The presence of these services along with three higher education institutions (Coast Guard Academy, Connecticut College, and Mitchell College) results in 40% of New London's 5.54 square land miles being tax-exempt. Due to New London's economic realities and its position in a less populous part of Connecticut, while simultaneously being home to many services, our local social service and nonprofit sectors are stretched thin. As the city relies heavily on a limited tax base to fund its operations, there have been increasing calls for organizations like Connecticut College to make multiyear voluntary payments. Alongside financial contributions, New London's mix of service creates an opportunity for Connecticut College to make significant contributions with our community partners. It also requires a mindfulness about ongoing tensions within the city and the labor that community engagement requires from community partners.

Connecticut College was founded in 1911 in response to the removal of higher education access for the state's women. The college became coeducational in 1969 but continues to predominantly serve women students. During this same period, the expansion of I-95, the key Northeastern interstate highway, divided the college from New London's downtown area. This geographic split, along with limited public transportation and demographic differences, has resulted in a pronounced town/gown dynamic. Many students arrive at the college from racially homogenous towns. However, the student body is increasingly racially and ethnically diverse, and there is a wide range of socioeconomic status backgrounds. Despite these demographic shifts, it continues to be a predominantly white institution. Community engagement both in and outside of coursework necessarily requires attention to the dynamics within the college, differing students' sense of distance or connection to communities and the ongoing gaps between our institution and the town it calls home.

The Holleran Center connects more than forty community organizations in the local area with students, staff, and faculty. Many faculty members practice a traditional service-learning model that requires their students to engage with a community placement for a set total number of hours. Unfortunately, this individualistic, consumerist approach does not emphasize reciprocity or understanding the basics of the community organization's work. Instead, weekly journals and other reflective activities center the student's own experience and interpretation of the work rather than challenging students to think more deeply about structural issues and multiple perspectives (Jacoby 3). Students do not receive feedback, nor do they think with community partners about the outcomes of their projects. The lack of accountability created by this approach is based in a neoliberal consumer model that meets students where they are rather than challenging them to grow or understand themselves in relationship to others.

Without dialogue, these assignments risk reinforcing a deficit-based attitude or contributing negatively to the idea that power and knowledge live within the institution rather than have the ability to be co-constructed with community partners. As the field of community-engaged learning has developed, critiques of existing pedagogical practices that perpetuate a deficit-based model have driven the growth of collaborative, co-creative partnerships that emphasize relationality and direct communication (Post et al. 4). The Holleran Center has sought to support faculty and scholar-practitioners, particularly those who have often engaged with this more reciprocal pedagogical approach as undergraduate/graduate students themselves, in pursuing asset-based, community-engaged teaching (4). Important challenges that continue to be part of our work are addressing the intensity of preparation needed to successfully enact these values and some students' resistance to the demanding nature of this educational opportunity. Despite these barriers, Sanchez and her colleagues have built strong relationships with faculty seeking to create and continue reciprocal community-engaged teaching efforts, including our work with local immigrant rights groups.

Building Deeper Collaboration

The Immigration and Advocacy Support Center (IASC) in New London provides legal counsel and support to immigrants, including individuals who are navigating the citizenship process. It has a paid executive director/staff lawyer and an administrative legal assistant. Its office manager and other support staff are volunteers, and Connecticut College students frequently intern with the group. Founded in 2014, IASC built on community responses to a dearth of legal support for its immigrant community. Connecticut College community members' involvement with the organization has varied from serving on its board to community-engaged courses. It became evident early in this partnership that there was a lot of campus interest in supporting IASC; however, challenges of power and hierarchy were evident when enthusiasm did not always advance the primary organizational priorities of IASC. Campus colleagues demonstrated a preference for community learning projects that prioritized encounters with "the other" over organizational needs such as fund-raising or clerical work.

In fall 2017, Sanchez met with GSIS faculty to discuss how to address the fallout from President Trump's efforts to end the Deferred Action for Childhood Arrivals (DACA) program (Shear and Davis). While President Obama was named "deporter-in-chief" by immigrants' rights activists due to the three million noncitizens deported during his administration, more than presidents Clinton or Bush, the impact of his policies had not been as deeply felt in New London or Connecticut College (Hing 1). The threat to the DACA program directly impacted Connecticut College students and young people in the broader community because it threatened their ability to stay enrolled in education or focus on academics as they or their families were at risk for detention and deportation. Sanchez and college administrators had been working to ensure that undocumented students could have off-campus and study away experiences and be able to safely return to campus. Along with the executive order President Trump signed early in his presidency calling for deportations and stricter enforcement of illegal immigration policies, the climate had shifted in ways that not only threatened the possibilities for undocumented students to fully access educational opportunities but also raised concerns about the security of all non-US citizen students, staff, faculty, and broader community members.

At the same time that Sanchez and IASC were seeking to consolidate their collaboration, the GSIS department was re-envisioning its curricular plan as it was finally fully staffed. This convergence of an interest in sustainability created an opportunity to build experiential learning into the student curricular experience and to collaborate at the departmental level. To Sanchez it was evident that IASC's limited staff could not support the work needed to organize and supervise community volunteers by themselves. It was important to bring together colleagues to discuss how to best work with IASC over the long term. As a college, we needed to identify how to consistently place IASC's priority at the center of our engagement rather than bombard the organization with projects that solely emerged out of our own interests or class objectives. Sanchez brought college faculty together with IASC's founding executive director to discuss how our courses could contribute to the organization's work. GSIS identified a new course, Social Justice Praxis, to serve as the initial course to work with IASC. Other faculty were not able to make a commitment for their departments, but over time they have advocated for a similar approach in their courses as they recognize the importance of better-articulated community-engaged learning.

IASC's use for community-engaged projects has included support for citizenship clinics and legal translation. A more difficult area to obtain faculty investment has been fund-raising. In our initial discussion with

IASC, the immediate need for unrestricted financial resources to support new staff positions rose as a top priority. GSIS's Social Justice Praxis was able to integrate this organizational priority as it would introduce students to the realities of nonprofit organization and engage them with an immigration organization as they learned about the history of immigration and resulting social movement. Over the spring 2018 and fall 2019 iterations of the course, IASC's interests expanded from a focus on fund-raising events to identifying community resources for immigrants across their identities and creating media for fund-raising and grant application purposes. Rather than solely study scholarship or situate immigration as an issue of borders "elsewhere," students' participation in IASC's work taught them how funding drives organizational capacity and how immigration statuses differentially impact people based on their social location and policies.

In the Social Justice Praxis course, students were expected to gain a deeper awareness of the experiences of immigrants within the current political climate and positionality as it relates to a learner in social justice work and college student working with nonprofits. The community project was coupled with a seminar-teaching style that included student-led reading discussions. Students found that as their own agency was central to the course inside and outside the classroom, "[this format] made me take responsibility for my learning." At the end of each semester, most students reported that the course content and community engagement experience contributed positively to their academic experience, their own social and political positions, and their opinions of New London. One student reported finding the community-engaged course rewarding because it was both challenging and engaging as a "commitment class." It was clear that the engagement experience paired with related readings and class discussion encouraged students to assume ownership over their learning and resulted in some students feeling as if they improved their understanding of immigration in general. A number of students reported increasing capacities in a range of skills that they did not expect. This included better understanding of how to work in a team, division of labor, time management, interview techniques, and new software. Notably, these projects placed less emphasis on face-to-face work with immigrant community members beyond fund-raising events. This reflects both IASC's limited capacity to facilitate such interactions and an increasingly serious concern about legal service clients' privacy and time as they seek out services. Instead, students attended to less attractive elements of nonprofit life, such as filing and answering phones rather than organizing protests and rallies, and thought more broadly about the network of resources immigrants seek to utilize in their daily lives. This experience foregrounded the importance of understanding both the needs of community partners and the context of their work. Students across identities learned directly that IASC most needed from students dedicated office support to ensure that immigrants could gain reliable legal support. It also highlighted the need for deeper student skill sets, such as bilingual abilities in professional communication and translation.

Long-Term Impact

Feminist praxis' emphasis on a reflective, iterative process has shaped our understanding of community-engaged pedagogy. In particular, it has changed the ways Sanchez supports other Connecticut College faculty who are interested in practicing engaged scholarship. Through discussions of our work with IASC, we encourage faculty to understand these organizations as collaborators who can co-create engagement opportunities that reflect both community priorities and students' learning needs. Despite the unequal position as a staff member, Sanchez is prompting faculty to build reciprocal relationships with community organizations that take their needs seriously, respect their time and expertise, and incorporate dialogue. Sanchez uses the departmental level commitment that GSIS made with IASC to demonstrate another means by which relationships can challenge the power differential between entities.

As IASC gained a new executive director and board leadership, it reevaluated its focus and capacity. The political climate increased challenges for clients seeking citizenship, reinforcing the need to prioritize providing legal services. As a result, IASC communicated to Sanchez that individual interns with experience in community-based learning and with relevant language skills could most fully support their work. This change in itself reflects a deepening of our mutual understanding that the college's involvement with IASC is reciprocal and must serve their interests first. In tandem with this change, the Social Justice Praxis course is in its next iteration. Three organizations, an Indigenous education group, a youth education leadership organization, and a grassroots health collaborative, serve as new sites for students. The first group has worked with our dean of Institutional Equity and Inclusion division previously, while the other groups are long-term partners with the Holleran Center. This model is an opportunity to replicate engagement that challenges hierarchies and prioritizes the aims of each group. The ability to shift the course's organizational partners while maintaining relationships through Holleran as the college hub for community work underscores the value of being responsive and flexible as organizations' needs shift and new opportunities for collaboration emerge.

In conclusion, the practice of coauthoring this chapter is also a means of challenging hierarchy. Our account provides two perspectives on the creation and execution of community-engaged learning to offer a sense of how and why contesting hierarchies matters. Sanchez's expertise in this field has provided the basis for course-based projects that refuse to reproduce a charity-based model of community engagement. Her pedagogical approach models deep listening to students and community partners, supporting interactions that are productive even in difficult moments. Sanchez has provided the support necessary for Rotramel and other colleagues to pursue community-based learning that reflects the feminist values of their field. Students recognize that this style of learning, while demanding, holds great value for their own social justice praxis development. In particular, it has been important for students to be part of interactions between faculty, staff, and community partners that are respectful and collaborative. Our work together models the values of feminist praxis as we strive for continual improvement and refinement of our partnerships and practices.

Works Cited

Alexander, M. Jacqui, and Chandra Talpade Mohanty. "Cartographies of Knowledge and Power: Transnational Feminism as Radical Praxis." *Critical Transnational Feminist Praxis*, edited by Amanda Lock Swarr and Richa Nagar. State U of New York P, 2010, pp. 23–45.

Collins, Patricia Hill. "Intersectionality as Critical Inquiry." *Companion to Feminist Studies*, edited by Nancy A. Naples. John Wiley & Sons, 2021, pp. 105–128.

Connecticut College. "Mission & Values." Connecticut College, www.conncoll .edu/at-a-glance/mission—values/.

Crass, Chris. *Towards Collective Liberation: Anti-Racist Organizing, Feminist Praxis, and Movement Building Strategy*. PM Press, 2013.

DATAUSA. New London, CT. https://datausa.io/profile/geo/new-london-ct/.

Engaged Scholarship Advisory Committee. Community Partnerships. Holleran Center. Connecticut College. Connecticut College. N.d.

Gaard, Greta. "Toward a Queer Ecofeminism." *New Perspectives on Environmental Justice: Gender, Sexuality, and Activism*, edited by Rachel Stein. Rutgers UP, 2004, pp. 21–44.

Hamraie, Aimi. "Designing Collective Access: A Feminist Disability Theory of Universal Design." *Disability Studies Quarterly*, vol. 33, no. 4, 2013, https:// dsq-sds.org/article/view/3871/3411.

Hing, Bill Ong. *American Presidents, Deportations, and Human Rights Violations: From Carter to Trump*. Cambridge UP, 2018.

hooks, bell. *Feminist Theory: From Margin to Center*. 2nd edition. Pluto Press, 2000.

Incite! editors. *The Revolution Will Not Be Funded: Beyond the Non-Profit Industrial Complex*. South End Press, 2007.

Iverson, Susan Van Deventer, and Jennifer Hauver James. *Feminist Community Engagement: Achieving Praxis*. New York: Palgrave Macmillan, 2014.

Jacoby, Barbara. *Service-Learning Essentials: Questions, Answers, and Lessons Learned*. Jossey-Bass, 2015.

Luhmann, Susanne, et al. "Introduction: Learning Elsewhere? Critical Reflections on University-Community Engagement as Feminist Praxis." *Feminist Praxis Revisited: Critical Reflections on University-Community Engagement*, edited by Amber Dean et al. Wilfrid Laurier UP, 2019, pp. 1–20.

Naples, Nancy A., and Marnie Dobson. "Feminists and the Welfare State: Aboriginal Health Care Workers and U.S. Community Workers of Color." *NWSA Journal*, vol. 13, no. 3, 2001, pp. 116–37.

Orr. Catherine M. "Women's Studies as Civic Engagement: Research and Recommendations." A Teagle Foundation White Paper. Prepared on behalf of Teagle Foundation Working Group and National Women's Studies Association, Sept. 2011. https://teaglefoundation.org/Teagle/media/GlobalMediaLibrary/documents/resources/Womens_Studies_as_Civic_Engagement.pdf?ext=.pdf.

National Women's Studies Association Field Leadership Working Group. "Women's Studies Scholarship: A Statement by the National Women's Studies Association's Field Leadership Working Group, 2013," https://www.nwsa.org/news-events/reports.

Peterson, Tessa Hicks. *Student Development and Social Justice Critical Learning, Radical Healing, and Community Engagement*. Palgrave Macmillan, 2018.

Petri, Alexis. "Service-Learning from the Perspective of Community Organizations." *Journal of Public Scholarship in Higher Education* 5, 2015, pp. 93–110.

Post, Margaret A., et al., "Introducing Next Generation Engagement." *Publicly Engaged Scholars: Next-Generation Engagement and the Future of Higher Education*, edited by Margaret A. Post et al. Stylus Publishing, 2016, pp. 1–11.

Shear, Michael D., and Julie Hirschfield Davis. "Trump Moves to End DACA and Calls on Congress to Act." *New York Times*, Sept. 5, 2017, https://www.nytimes.com/2017/09/05/us/politics/trump-daca-dreamers-immigration.html.

Stoecker, Randy, and Elizabeth Tryon. "Preface." In *The Unheard Voices: Community Organizations and Service Learning*, edited by Randy Stoecker, Elizabeth A. Tryon, and Amy Hilgendorf, vii–xvi. Temple UP, 2009.

Young, Iris Marion. *Justice and the Politics of Difference*. Princeton UP, 1990.

PART II

Intersecting the Transnational

6

Teaching and Learning Intersectional and Transnational Feminisms through Digital Humanities

MARÍA CLAUDIA ANDRÉ

All of us in the academy and in the culture as
a whole are called to renew our minds if we
are to transform educational institutions—and
society—so that the way we live, teach, and
work can reflect our joy in cultural diversity, our
passion for justice, and our love of freedom
—bell hooks, *Teaching to Transgress*

Shifts and challenges in contemporary feminist theory have brought new epistemologies and theoretical perspectives to the fore, generating not only alternative ways to think about the complexities and nuances of gender experiences but also more accurate approaches to examine the diverse tapestry of cultural, racial, and sexual co-identities of women and minorities. Thanks to the significant contributions by Black, Hispanic, and non-Western scholars and writers, transnationality and intersectionality have emerged as two of the most significant feminist paradigms to interpret and challenge the dynamics of power and identity politics across geographical and cultural divides.

Addressing the urgency to challenge monolithic and arbitrary constructs regarding the issues that affect women in the third world, feminist academics are starting to realize that the most effective means to pave the road for social solidarity and mutual understanding is through transnational collaboration. Particularly at a time when the most basic human rights are being challenged by nationalist right-wing policies and when femicide and violence against women are on the rise, feminist transnational alliances are key to promoting the level of activism necessary to push back against heteronormative and patriarchal agendas at a larger scale. With the advancement of social media, global communication networks, and digital technology, feminist academics worldwide may now not only easily collaborate with community leaders and nongovernmental organization (NGO) agencies but also, through them, engage in transformative educational experiences that will impact their students' lives and the lives of women in their respective communities. If, as feminists and scholars, we aim to debunk the status of the academic researcher as "the True intellectual thinker" (Alexander and Mohanty 8) and expand the boundaries of knowledge production beyond the elitist frame of Western academia, we must teach our students alternative ways to establish collaborative dialogues and close relationships across geographical, social, and cultural divides. As Richa Nagar and Amanda Swarr assert, "Collaboration across multiple institutional sites and social economic locations and in multiple languages and genres can play a critical role in undoing and remaking various layers that constitute transnational politics of knowledge production, and in interrogating and expanding the notions of skills and expertise in intellectual productions" (101).

This chapter examines the uses and applications of digital technology as a means to foster transnational and interdisciplinary collaboration, bridge theory into practice, and mobilize knowledge-making through alternative channels of production and dissemination. I begin my discussion with a brief overview of M. Jacqui Alexander's, Chandra Talpade Mohanty's, and bell hooks's writings on decolonial intersectionality and transnationalism. Together their frameworks and critiques share similar objectives: on the one hand, to demystify the academy as the only privileged location of knowledge production and dissemination, and on the other, to decolonize and liberate knowledge-making through collaborative work and pedagogical practices unrestricted by any institution, class, gender, or any social and political boundaries. Next, based on my interdisciplinary and transnational collaboration with faculty and students from Skidmore College and the Universidad San Francisco de Quito, I discuss effective methodologies and provide examples of how to teach transnationality and intersectionality through digital humanities projects.

Theoretical Considerations

In "Under Western Eyes: Feminist Scholarship and Colonial Discourses," Mohanty presents a compelling argument against the dangers of establishing a normative point of view as a primary referent for the development of feminism and feminist ideology. Monolithic preconceptions and arbitrary representations of women in underdeveloped countries as ahistorical subjects, according to Mohanty, reduce their economic, social, and ethnic differences to a single construct and a coherent group with matching interests and needs. It is in this process of labeling third world women as a powerless and oppressed group that "western feminisms appropriate and colonize the constitutive complexities which characterize the lives of women in these countries" (63).

An ethnocentric and reductionist interpretation of the problems, interests, and goals among women worldwide—instead of bringing us to a closer understanding of the institutional policies and power structures and practices that impact women's lives within a particular local context—"limits the female subject to gender identity, completely bypassing social class and ethnic identities" (72). To this end, Mohanty has challenged scholars and educators to acknowledge the material conditions and spaces that perpetuate discriminatory power dynamics and practices in Western academia.

Her essay "Cartographies of Knowledge and Power," coauthored with Alexander, speaks of the need to demystify the ideological postulate that anoints the academy both as the exclusive site for the production of knowledge as well as the strategies of governance that legitimize the ways of knowing and the kind of scholarship deserving recognition (28). The social and hierarchical structures of place and knowledge, according to Alexander and Mohanty, "permit the binary to operate as a verb, demarcating the spurious divide between academy and community while at the same time masking the creation of the divide" (28). The decolonization of hierarchies of space and position that limits the production of knowledge only to those at the top, as they point out, requires interdisciplinary and cross-cultural collaboration with multiple sites, locations, and sources where knowledge is produced but also the openness to alternative ways of thinking along with the realization that certain kinds of knowledge may emerge only within these contexts and locations (27). Community activists, private and public entities, NGOs, as well as other institutions that work together in different capacities with underprivileged women on a daily basis, are significant sources of knowledge that deserve to be duly legitimized and recognized by academic discourses. Alexander and Mohanty emphasize the importance of a critical tradition premised on the freedom of knowledge-making detached from a particular institution, regime, class, or gender, serving only the aspirations and interests of ordinary people: "If we take seriously the mandate to do collaborative work in and outside the academy, the kind of work that would demystify the borders between inside and outside and thereby render them porous rather than mystically fixed, it is imperative that the academy not be the only location that determines our research and pedagogical work" (27). While the writings of Mohanty and Alexander are essential to the understanding of the limitations of Western feminism, as a movement that advocates for gender equality and equal access to public life, they fail to provide hands-on methodologies or empirical examples of how to encourage students and the larger community to pursue the active praxis of feminism and social solidarity. Faculty-student research, experiential learning, oral history narratives, and feminist digital humanities, as I will later examine, not only have the potential of significantly impacting how students acquire empirical knowledge but also awaken their motivation to engage in community activism and social change.

In *Teaching to Transgress: Education as the Practice of Freedom* (1994), bell hooks addresses the inclusionary and exclusionary practices of the power/knowledge matrix as it operates in and through higher learning institutions, another academic space that replicates institutionalized structures of hierarchical privilege. hooks advocates an educational system that promotes social consciousness, encourages peer and community engagement, and embraces alternative ways of teaching and knowing across intersecting systems of domination and privilege. She argues in favor of an "education as the practice of freedom," a revolutionary pedagogy of resistance that teaches students to transgress social categorizations through collaboration, participation, and inclusion, embracing a diversity of experience and acknowledging the value of everyone's voice (30). The American social critic and activist also challenges the idea of the classroom as a "safe space," promoting instead an educational environment, where both the teaching content and methodologies are interrogated and where it is "assumed that the knowledge offered students would empower them to be better scholars, to live more fully in the world beyond academe" (6). Her groundbreaking work has shed light on the relevance of the classroom as a site where feminism and agency are taught and, more importantly, as a micro-cosmos of the world, where students may question entrenched power structures and turn knowledge into praxis through peer and student-faculty collaboration.

Although conceptualizations of knowledge production applied to the academic curricula calls for the development of practices that are more democratic, when thinking about course design, feminist theory generally tends to take precedence over practice, and traditional approaches rule over innovative teaching practices. Indeed, the production of tools and instructional materials with which to teach and engage students in the kind of meaningful collaboration and activism that Alexander, Mohanty, and hooks write about is sparse in relation to the number of publications focusing on feminist theory and academic scholarship. For hooks, this is so because it is not considered legitimate research and rigorous scholarship. As she argues, "Talking about pedagogy, thinking about it critically, is not the intellectual work that most folks think is hip and cool" (203).

Recent advancements in instructional technology are not only changing how we teach, collaborate, and conduct research but also how we produce, publish, and disseminate knowledge inside and outside of our institutions. To this end, merging the humanities and social sciences, digital feminist scholars are beginning to implement best practices to address issues of class, race, gender, and sexuality through digital visualization tools and applications, thus making it possible to interact with the discipline's data and theoretical content in more exciting ways. *Bodies of Information: Intersectional Feminism and Digital Humanities* by Elizabeth Losh and Jacqueline Wernimont is the first collection of essays from various scholars to examine from multiple viewpoints and arguments "the foundational role that intersectional issues related to gender and sexuality play in the formation of new media and digital tools" (Ruberg et al. 118). This publication is a valuable contribution to feminist scholarship as it draws facts and information from existing digital humanities projects to build a case for the application of intersectionality in the women and gender studies programs, academia, and the community. Yet, again, most of the essays focus on the challenges, ethical considerations, and theoretical underpinnings of digital humanities obtained from research projects and archives rather than illustrate the practical use of tools and applications of technology to advance the feminist curricula. Therefore, I hope that the examples, resources, and introductory pedagogies shared in what follows will result in enriching educational experiences that are conducive to building a solid women and gender studies curriculum as well as a community of lifelong learners and activists who are committed to do advocacy work concerning the issues that affect women daily.

From Theory to Practice

Let me begin by pointing out that my teaching strategies closely align with hooks's vision of an education for freedom and principles of intersectional pedagogy such as engaging and acknowledging students' intersecting identities and lived experiences through self-reflective activities and class discussions; transforming theory to praxis by promoting social action and fostering collaboration among students, faculty, and community US-based and international organizations; and facilitating students' understanding and conceptualization of intersectionality from interdisciplinary, comparative, and transnational approaches. My research agenda, and the courses I have taught for the past years for the Women's and Gender Studies (WGS) program at my institution, are shaped by my academic and field experience in Latin American studies and women's and gender studies.

As most of the student body at my institution is predominantly white of Midwestern Dutch heritage, I seek to incorporate diversity through enriching learning experiences and stimulating research projects that help them build intercultural bridges with people of ethnicities, beliefs, and social backgrounds that are different from their own. Diversity, as Naomi M. Hall remarks, is empowering but also essential for the acquisition and transfer of knowledge in all areas of study. "Faculty must dedicate themselves to creating opportunities for students to learn and experience diversity. With more inclusion comes more integration of critical identities into the curriculum and subsequent courses" (155).

Data-driven research in the humanities and social sciences through transnational and interdisciplinary collaboration has granted me the opportunity to travel abroad with students and to engage with local women, grassroots organizations, and focus groups. In May 2018, Dr. Viviana Rangil (Skidmore College) and I teamed up with three of our WGS majors to develop "Indigenous Markets in Latin America: Knowledge and Empowerment for Women," a bilingual website, showcasing oral narratives by artisan women selling their handicrafts at Indigenous markets in Peru, Ecuador, Mexico, and Guatemala. The marketplace, since pre-Columbian times, has remained a site of economic, cultural, and social exchange. For many Indigenous communities, this is still the main venue at which to sell goods, socialize, gain exposure, and interact with tourists but also a point of cross-cultural engagement where community members may engage in social exchange with outsiders and learn of technological and scientific advances. In recent years, Indigenous markets have become a popular tourist attraction and one of the main income sources for their respective communities; however, despite their growing popularity, little is known about the significant role women play in the production, distribution, and marketing of traditional handicrafts.

The main objective of our study was to elucidate how women from different Indigenous communities and ethnicities (Mayans in Guatemala, Quechuas in Peru, Otavalos in Ecuador, and Zapotecs and Mixtecs in Mexico) learn, develop, and run their business undertakings. Through our interaction with the interviewees, we hoped to gain a deeper insight on how handicraft making is transmitted and preserved across generations; which identity factors prevent or promote women's advancement inside and outside their localities; what the direct impact of globalization, capitalism, migration, and open market economies in the production of handicrafts is; and how women balance their household responsibilities and handicraft production.

Working as a faculty-student team, we first started by discussing the project's focus, the questionnaire, the interview process, and the website's content. Ascribing to hooks's educational paradigms, previously outlined, we envisioned this research opportunity as a fully interactive and transformational learning experience that would equally integrate faculty, students, and interviewees as partners and collaborators in the knowledge-making process. We opted for the *speaking with* model engagement, allowing Indigenous women artisans to freely guide the conversation, relating to us and the questionnaire in their own terms. By taking this standpoint, we hoped to position women as experts of their trade in their own right, acting and sharing their experiences as producers of culture across the borders of their own countries and communities. To avoid the limitations or biased constructs of an academic point of view, we opted to write brief accounts of our experiences at the marketplace, mostly to contextualize the women's working and living environments. Allowing the narratives and narrators to speak for themselves freed listeners to personally relate to the stories as a unique autobiographical piece, each one as a line in a map leading to the understanding of the complex dynamics of race, gender, class, and identity.

The oral narratives were introduced as a springboard for discussion in my women's and gender studies course, Women and Social Movements in Latin America. After students had grasped the key concepts of intersectionality and transnationality through readings, lectures, research, and technology-driven activities, they were given an assignment. Students listened to three stories of women from each of the different countries and, drawing from the narratives and the course content, wrote a commentary on how race and class became significant factors that shaped the women's identities, lives, and self-representation. Working in small groups at first gave students the opportunity to share their impressions; later, in shared class discussions, our conversations centered on the mechanisms of oppression and privilege that either enhanced or prevented women's access to equal labor rights and economic opportunities. Examining the interviewees' stories through the lens of intersectionality encouraged students to self-reflect on their privileged positioning and to identify how social categorizations of identity affected their perceptions and behaviors toward others. For instance, a Mexican American student shared her traumatic experience with cross-cultural discrimination—in Mexico, for her American background and citizenship, and in the United States, for her Hispanic heritage and ethnicity. The student's story drove our conversation to the differences and commonalities of identity labels and stereotypes as perceived in both cultures as well as the abiding mechanisms that perpetuate inequality, discrimination, and social injustice. Blending theory with practice, students not only learned to empathize, listen, and be open to other people's life experiences, but they also realized that feminist praxis begins, as hooks points out, by building solidarity and establishing relationships with their peers and community members.

Recently, I have designed and taught Gender Politics: Women's Agency and Activism in Latin America, an advanced course conducted in Spanish and mostly oriented for double majors in Spanish language and the social sciences. In addition to exploring a series of topics related to the history of feminist thought, theory, and praxis—such as reproductive rights, health disparities, feminist theology, feminist movements, environmental feminisms, domestic violence, and femicide—the main objective of the course is to raise students' awareness about the institutions and power structures that shape the identities and social experiences of women in the Americas. To widen the scope of the field of inquiry and emphasize the interaction between transnationality and interdisciplinary collaboration, the class shared lectures, discussed academic essays, and completed a series of assignments with students enrolled in Gender and Society, taught by social science instructor Dr. Cheryl Martens at the Universidad San Francisco de Quito in Ecuador. Dr. Martens and I became acquainted in June 2019 through our participation in the Great Lakes College Association's Global Course Connections Workshop, a one-week summer seminar geared to fostering intercultural and interdisciplinary connections and course development among faculty from partnering consortium institutions worldwide. During the seminar, and over the summer, we selected course readings and created a bibliography, cowrote a common syllabus, and developed a series of students' assignments, including a set of personal questions and cultural activities to facilitate student cross-cultural interaction. We wanted students to feel comfortable collaborating with their partners, so we asked them to briefly answer a few questions about their families, their hobbies, and their student life along with a paragraph describing their respective towns and countries. Students were then paired according to their mutual interests, likes, and dislikes.

Throughout the semester, and paired in small groups, students conducted research and created posters for presentations on specific topics; shared their personal opinions on contemporary issues in a blog and through a Facebook group; and cowrote short reaction essays to films and documentaries. They also collaborated on an oral history project developing a set of questions to interview Indigenous women artisans from the Quijo community in the Ecuadorian Amazon region. Unfortunately, due to heavy rains and poor internet service in the Amazon, US-based students were unable to participate in the interviewing process; however, they continued to collaborate with their South American peers in the transcription and translation of the interviews. First, students transcribed the original interviews in Spanish and then translated them into English. In this process, they not only gained a deeper insight of the lives and experiences of Indigenous women artisans, but they also enhanced their cultural and linguistic abilities. The interviews were uploaded in OHMS (Oral History Metadata Synchronizer)—a web application designed to facilitate online viewing and preserve oral data—and showcased in the OHLA (Oral History Liberal Arts) repository for public access. (Interviews may be accessed at https://ohla.info/indigenous-markets-womens-knowledge-and-cultural-production/.)

Before closing this section, I would like to add a few comments on transnational activism, feminist academic praxis, and collaboration. In my experience, and as Linda Peake and Karen de Souza examine, when engaging in cross-cultural collaboration, "one can never 'stand well clear' of racialized, classed, gendered and transnational power relations" (105). Indeed, transnational collaboration across sociocultural and geographical divides takes self-reflexivity, serious commitment, and humility to listen; it also takes the acknowledgment of the existence of alternative sources of knowledge production different from those of our discipline, or even of Western academia as a whole. Moreover, according to Peake and de Souza, transnational feminist praxis requires questioning and thinking more deeply about how the research process itself, as well as its results, are reproducing the same kind of divisive boundaries or hierarchies against which we are seeking to work (113). The success of transnational collaborative endeavors depends on not only the participants' ability to establish an open dialogue about the nature, the overall process, expectations, and the objectives of the research but also the willingness to interrogate the academic practices in their own fields, departments, and institutions. I draw once again on Alexander and Mohanty's call to challenge the narcissistic attitude and continued dominance of Euro-American academia and build instead a transformative practice of feminism that leads to the development of strong feminist coalitions and women's empowerment regardless of their race, class, and social status.

Digital Humanities in the Women and Gender Studies Curriculum

To acquire a deeper sense of the practices and pedagogical uses of instructional technology, I benefited greatly from attending annual digital humanities or technology-focused workshops and conferences, like HASTAC (Humanities, Arts, Science, and Technology Alliance and Collaboratory), ADHO (Alliance for Digital Humanities Organizations), THATcamp (The Humanities and Technology Camp), DLA 101 (Digital Liberal Arts), and HILT (Humanities Intensive Learning and Teaching). All of these associations offer intensive training on digital pedagogy for faculty, students, librarians, and administrators, but, additionally, they provide invaluable resources and collaborative opportunities.

Gaining a sense of the various digital tools used for teaching and research will render an insight of the many ways in which technology may be introduced in a course—as a practical resource to enhance students' analytical, writing, and digital literacy skills or as data-driven research. Open source content management systems (Omeka, Wordpress, and Scalar), mapping (Esri:GIS, Neatline, Mapme, and Mapstory), data visualization (Tableau Public, Google Data Studio, and Palladio), streaming media (YouTube, Vimeo, and Kaltura) and text analysis systems (Wordle, Voyant, and Textal) are free, easy-access tools that allow users to combine archival documents, text, images, charts, and video in creative ways that are easily accessible to the general public. In addition, infographic applications (Piktochart, Canva, and Google Slides) and video editing software applications (iMovie, Filmora, and Windows Movie Maker) are simpler and effective media to enhance students' research and visual design skills.

Small group activities, such as posters, blogs, and podcasts, ease the transition into more advanced assignments, like digital archiving, mapping, or data visualization. When starting a new project, begin by conceptualizing its content, production, and design, keeping in mind that digital technology is only a means to an end; therefore, select the tools and applications that will be most appropriate to help students achieve the established learning goals. For instance, to analyze intersectionality and transnationalism at a global scale, a map focusing on the origins and mission of some of the most relevant feminist social media movements (#MeToo, #Niunamenos, #WomensMarch, #SayHerName) may help students grasp the importance of "empowerment of activism," a feminist praxis that "underscores the significance of community and the availability of safe spaces . . . in which individuals can critically reflect on their experiences and political strategies in dialogue with others" (Naples 661). Similarly, an archive connecting maps, writings, and autobiographical accounts on the lives of anarchist women or political activists from different countries and different periods may challenge students to look at the power structures that shaped women's lives as they interfaced with gender, class, and race categorizations at a specific time in history. A collection of posters examining the working conditions of women and children in sweatshops and *maquiladoras* could spark a blog conversation or an in-class debate on the effect of capitalism, neoliberalism, and globalization in different regions of the world, thus highlighting the multiple layers of oppression in place and the systems that perpetuate them. Data visualization tools, such as charts, diagrams, and timelines, focusing on students' personal life experiences may facilitate the comprehension and discussion of how their own social identities and positionalities have intersected and fluctuated during their life span.

An easier alternative is to build educational activities around feminist digital projects or digital communities already available on the web, such as *BlogHer*; *FemTechNet*; *Feminist Online Spaces: Building and Linking Principled Sites in Collaboration*; *Feminist Websites, Blogs, and Resources*; *F-Word*; *Black Girl Dangerous*; *Everydaysexism*; *Crunk Feminist Collective*; *Bust*; *Artisteras*; *Chicanas por mi raza*; *Fat Ugly or Slutty*; and *The Latina History Project*. For example, as a class assignment, students could choose an article or a piece of news from *Feministing*, an online feminist collective site, and write a comment identifying the interconnectedness between social identity (like gender, race, and religious beliefs) and identity politics (the organizational strategies undertaken to defend the group's interests), from both a privileged and a marginalized positioning. They could also address how their own intersecting identities and positioning affect how they interpret and relate to the issue brought forth in the article. Some websites or digital projects allow students to expand the content of a data collection already accessible to the public. Having students write Wikipedia entries is also an exciting way to introduce them as active contributors to the knowledge-building community while developing their research, writing, and information literacy skills.

Final Considerations

Due to its interdisciplinary scope and ability to travel across borders and institutional boundaries, social science and humanities projects that incorporate digital technology appeal to a wide range of scholars, educators, and students, attracting the financial support of higher learning institutions, administrators, as well as state and federal granting agencies. As an example, of the eleven students who joined me as co-collaborators in various digital humanities projects, two were accepted into the Fulbright teaching program in Spain; one had just graduated from the Sorbonne in Paris; one initiated the Undergraduate Network for Research in the Humanities; and another was an intern at the Feminist Majority Foundation, a nonprofit organization focused on women's empowerment, equality, and economic development. Students' response to such unique learning opportunities has been extremely positive. Carolyn Wetzel, one of my student co-researchers and collaborators in the Indigenous women's market project, notes:

> Oral history is an incredible asset for decolonizing knowledge and learning spaces. Having the opportunity to learn about oral history as a methodology and then actually practice it and speak to indigenous women helped shape the trajectory of my learning experience as a feminist as well as my career aspirations. The project prepared me for my internship at a feminist advocacy organization not only by giving me several digital tools as well as improving my Spanish, but also through teaching me to value all types of knowledge and all kinds of lived experiences. My passion for women's issues only grew, and the importance of transnational solidarity and collaboration to organizations, especially in the United States, is immeasurable.

Our digital humanities projects have been presented at the National Conference of Undergraduate Research, MASAL (Michigan Academy of Science, Arts, and Letters), Asociación de Estudios de Género y Sexualidades, Hope's Conference of Undergraduate Research, the Midwest Latin American Studies Association, and the Alliance Institute Transnational Feminism(s), among others.

Transnational and interdisciplinary digital humanities projects that engage with women's issues and document their life stories offer students an insight into the various social factors at work, which perpetuate the structures of oppression and discrimination. By the same token, they are not only effective means to creatively visualize and capture the human experience from multiple perspectives but also effective global platforms to showcase the coalitions, movements, and networks that women forge to resist patriarchal systems and institutions in their own communities. Lastly, the inclusion of best practices for collaborative action across the disciplines broadens the potential of digital humanities as a field of inquiry and as a practical tool to engage students in the actual practice of feminism and community action.

An integral and holistic approach to education that facilitates co-creative learning spaces, exploring different styles and teaching methodologies, helps create an "epistemic community" of learners based on common political and social values as the unifying factors that "shape access to knowledge collectively rather than individually" (hooks 51). Regardless of how the individualized manner in which authorship is claimed, as Nagar and Swarr remind us, all academic production is necessarily collaborative, and the undergraduate classroom is one of the most significant collaborative spaces "through which academics create knowledges and learn to speak to various communities inside and outside of academia" (1). For those of us who are committed to teaching the younger generations to be critical thinkers and take an active role in bettering the world through the implementation of collective endeavors and community-building strategies, feminist digital humanities are, in this regard, one of the most effective tools to make it happen.

Works Cited

Alexander, Jacqui M., and Chandra Talpade Mohanty. "Cartographies of Knowledge and Power: Transnational Feminism as Radical Praxis." *Critical Transnational Feminist* Praxis, edited by Amanda Lock Swarr and Richa Nagar. State U of New York P, 2010, pp. 23–45.

Hall, Naomi M. "Quotes, Blogs, Diagrams, and Counter-Storytelling: Teaching Intersectionality at a Minority-Serving Institution." *Intersectional Pedagogy: Complicating Identity and Social Justice*, Routledge, 2016, pp. 150–67.

hooks, bell. *Teaching to Transgress: Education as the Practice of Freedom.* Routledge, 1994.

Losh, Elizabeth, and Jacqueline Wernimont. *Bodies of Information: Intersectional Feminism and the Digital Humanities.* U of Minnesota P, 2018.

Mohanty, Chandra Talpade. "Under Western Eyes: Feminist Scholarship and Colonial Discourses." *Feminist Review*, vol. 30, 1988, pp. 61–88.

Nagar, Richa, and Swar Amanda. "Theorizing Transnational Feminist Praxis." *Critical Transnational Feminist Praxis*, edited by Amanda Swarr and Richa Nagar. State U of New York P, 2010, pp. 1–20.

Naples, Nancy A. "Pedagogical Practice and Teaching Intersectionality." *Intersectional Pedagogy: Complicating Identity and Social Justice*, Routledge, 2016, pp. 110–28.

Peak, Linda, and Karen de Souza. "Feminist Academic and Activist Praxis in Service of the Transnational." *Critical Transnational Feminist Praxis,* State U of New York P, 2010, pp. 105–123.

Ruberg, Bonnie, Jason Boyd, and James Howe. "Toward a Queer Digital Humanities." *Bodies of Information: Intersectional Feminism and Digital Humanities*, edited by Elizabeth Losh and Jacqueline Wernimont. U of Minnesota P, 2018, pp. 108–130.

7

Engaged Global Pedagogy

Moving from Study Abroad to Transnational Scholar-Activism

LUISA BIERI

Social movements, like the flow of capital and information, increasingly operate on a global scale. Issues of environmental degradation, economic exclusion, and gender violence are not confined to national boundaries, even as local impact is unequally distributed and exacerbated across various regional, social, and economic landscapes. Rather than view each as unique, Chandra Mohanty's lens of transnationalism invites an understanding of how we are implicated and impacted across bordered spaces ("Under Western Eyes" 514, 518). This vision often contrasts with study abroad pedagogy in the United States that focuses on a singular destination country for learning a foreign language and culture. The programs are often financially accessible to only an elite few and typically reaffirm the nation-state as discrete, without emphasis on historical, economic, and political interconnections and impact (Mohanty, "Transnational" 970–71; Gristwood and Woolf 12; Rizvi). Others embrace neoliberal narratives of "global citizenship" that commodify notions of multiculturalism (Mohanty, "Under Western Eyes" 505; Alexander and Mohanty 23, 34). Both approaches are unsettling.

As an educator in US international education, I suggest that our pedagogies adopt a transnational feminist approach to counter efforts that center the nation and often reify stereotypes and nationalist tropes (Mohanty, "Under Western Eyes" 518–19). In "Cartographies of Knowledge and Power: Transnational Feminism as Radical Praxis," M. Jacqui Alexander and Chandra Mohanty define the transnational feminist lens as incorporating an antiracist, postcolonial, and anticapitalist critical analysis of teaching and learning that is too often absent in study abroad pedagogy. Without critical analysis, asymmetrical power relations reassert the centrality of the white,

Western, "first world" scholar and the world being consumed, interpreted, and understood through her gaze (Mohanty, "Transnational" 971–72). Even if most study abroad programs are not framed within the field of gender studies, the transnational feminist lens is increasingly critical to understand and apply to all areas of "internationalization" of the curricula in US higher education.

In the following pages, I analyze three lenses of global teaching and learning defined by Mohanty in "Under Western Eyes Revisited: Feminist Solidarity through Anticapitalist Struggles": feminist as tourist, feminist as explorer, and feminist solidarity (518–24). I focus on three pedagogical principles to understand and reshape these frameworks: reflexivity, reciprocity, and connectivity. Each principle operates within a critical praxis that highlights experiential, engaged learning within transnational feminist pedagogy. Through this lens, I reflect on my own pedagogical practices at Antioch College, a small, private, liberal arts college in Ohio. I use Antioch's Cooperative Education model for socially engaged global learning as a case study of pedagogical praxis. Finally, I invite a renewed understanding and commitment to scholar-activism within study abroad as we work to align our efforts toward a "feminist solidarity" pedagogical approach (Mohanty "Transnational"; "Under Western Eyes" 509, 523).

Before diving in, I call our attention as teachers and learners to the "acute ethical attentiveness" that Alexander and Mohanty remind us this work requires (26). I would like to emphasize the uncertain messiness of wading into transnational feminist pedagogy, where even our terms and definitions are continuously shifting to include new perspectives or sharpen old ones. Breny Mendoza cautions feminist scholars to be wary of transnational feminisms as a new "buzzword" that may merely be reinforcing an old false trope of "global sisterhood," critiqued by Mendoza, bell hooks, and others as requiring assimilation, flattening of differences, and supporting the academy's claims of "multiculturalism" while racism remains entrenched (Mendoza 295–96; hooks, "Sisterhood"). I agree that it is critical to remain wary of the language used in our discourse and theoretical notions that deny differences, reinforcing inequalities of privilege and power. I stay convinced, however, that the risks required to authentically engage in this work are necessary.

bell hooks invites feminist educators to step up to the challenges and not conform to status quo efforts in the academy or as scholar-activists within broader social movements. In our commitment to "further the development of a more inclusive feminist theory and practice," hooks reminds us that "withdrawal is not the answer" ("Holding" 105). To ignore these theoretical imperatives and "withdraw" would repeat the pattern of placing the burden of antiracist, postcolonial work primarily on colleagues of color. Succumbing to the fears of "doing it wrong"—a hallmark of white supremacist thinking, Kenneth Jones and Tema Okun assert—is an excuse to abandon our efforts altogether. The impulse of white feminists to retreat into isolation, silence, despair, and paralysis only reifies cycles of centering our own white fragility (DiAngelo). I embrace the challenges and mistake making of teaching transnationally yet the urgency—particularly as a white feminist educator—to move toward a new paradigm.

As Sara Ahmed points out in "Close Encounters: Feminism and/in 'The Globe,'" to be silent ignores our already deeply implicated relationships within the structures of globalization. We cannot assume that encounters are not taking place if they are not mediated by teachers and learners. Ahmed explains, "Women in different nation spaces within a globalized economy of difference, cannot not encounter each other, what is at stake is how, rather than whether the encounters take place" (167). Thus, I invite us to consider how we can develop transnational feminist encounters through reflexive, reciprocal, and connective pedagogies.

The Reflexive Turn Away from "Feminist as Tourist"

In "Cartographies of Knowledge and Power," Alexander and Mohanty articulate the ethical pitfalls of many study abroad models from a transnational feminist standpoint. They assert that the neoliberal academy reinforces neocolonialist, capitalist structures and knowledge frameworks and argue that transnational feminism should by definition centralize antiracist and anticapitalist critique (24). Given the demographic of study abroad students in the United States as 77% white and a primarily economically privileged group of students, the global relationships within much of study abroad reflect "imperial legacies" (Stebleton, Soria, and Cherney 17; Talburt 106–109). As we consider Mohanty's framework of "feminist as tourist," we begin to unpack the ways in which the academy has often reinforced problematic neocolonialist, capitalist, racist, and nationalist paradigms through international programming ("Under Western Eyes" 518–19).

Transnational feminist scholars have rejected the notion that simply moving the teaching and learning space to an international location— "elsewhere"—results in a pedagogical model that is transnational. This type of "add and stir method" of international pedagogy has been critiqued by Alexander and Mohanty as being insufficient to uproot racist, neocolonialist, capitalist, and patriarchal structures of learning within the academy, as transnationalism requires (32–35; Mohanty, "Under Western Eyes" 522).

There also continues to be criticism around study abroad programs' frequent emphasis on the nation-state as a monolithic and homogenous cultural and ethnic territory. Anthony Gristwood and Michael Woolf argue that focusing on study abroad in a singular destination country reinforces nationalist discourse and ignores a critical understanding of colonial exploitation as well as struggles for sovereignty and migration (12–18). Karen Rodriguez of the School for International Studies agrees that study abroad often reifies a homogenous, essentialized identity of the national subject (34). Within this framework, the gendered and racialized consequences of nationalist discourses and the "white, western gaze" are left unexamined, to which feminist scholars Alexander, Mohanty, Cynthia Enloe, and Anne McClintock, among others, have brought a wealth of critical analysis (Alexander and Mohanty 41).

Within a "feminist as tourist" uncritical approach, students may walk away from a global learning experience with reinforced US hegemonic, imperialist, white supremacist formative claims, including the "fetishism" of the Other (Rodriguez 36; Talburt 104–109). Often, study abroad models reflect the "feminist as tourist" model by emphasizing travel as a thrilling, exotic experience whereby teaching and learning take on a primarily capitalist consumer form ("Under Western Eyes" 518–19). It is the structural and pedagogical result of an "academy [that] fetishizes these elsewheres in the service of its own identity formation" (Alexander and Mohanty 41). In this sense, one's identity is forming around their problematic relationship to the Other rather than inviting the focus on a principal tenet in feminist pedagogy, reflexivity.

A reflexive approach turns one's gaze inward to focus on one's own positionality within the larger global structures of power and privilege. Reflexivity is often absent even within global feminist discourse, as Elora Chowdhury explains:

> US-centric global feminism . . . fits into the mission of the US imperial nation. This is a moment that has brought about a surge of interest and activism on behalf of oppressed women around the world but without a parallel examination of historical and geopolitical machinations by the US that has exacerbated oppressive situations world over. It also deflects attention away from domestic fractures and impact of structural inequality on various minority communities. (298)

Understanding reflexivity as a US American abroad is the topic of Adrienne Rich's influential 1984 article "Notes Towards a Politics of Location." Rich describes the turn of a critical gaze inward as a white, US American feminist and how her search to understand the impacts of US policies abroad—catapulted by a trip to Central America—brought new, reflexive awareness. Examining the impact of one's own position within global political and economic structures was viewed as groundbreaking at the time, yet it was characterized by Rich's underexamined whiteness and relationship to Western hegemonic logic. As Caren Kaplan explains, Rich did not make this turn in a vacuum, or only in the moment of travel, but rather through sustained dialogue with US Black and Indigenous feminists, such as Audre Lorde, Barbara Smith, and Michelle Cliff (139–41). Kaplan appropriately identifies how feminist theorists of color were foregrounding the critical importance of antiracist, anticapitalist, postcolonial analysis that now is considered a hallmark of transnational feminist theory.

With this understanding, certain pedagogical imperatives become clear. First, a process of self-reflexive thinking is critical to begin to uproot the internalized attitudes and assumptions of Western hegemony and white supremacy. Bringing our attention to our own "politics of location," we consider the implications of colonial, capitalist, and patriarchal oppressions in our own lives, society, and nation. Although, like Adrienne Rich, many scholars and students identify the experience of leaving one's country as the impetus for understanding their own positionality, Kaplan points to the crucial link. It is within authentic, sustained dialogue with feminists of color in the United States that Rich begins to develop a critical awareness that may be described as "transnational" (140–41).

Thus, it is a transnational feminist pedagogical imperative to be in sustained dialogue—which I define as staying at the table to generatively work through conflict and learn from differences—with our Black, brown, and Indigenous colleagues, students, and community members. Rather than placing the burden on people of color to teach these skills, we must make a commitment to teaching antiracism within our institutions and model reflexive dialogue as a transformative space for learning. We can create teaching and learning spaces that are accountable to these relationships and engage with differences, recognizing crucially distinct perspectives within the academy.

At Antioch we revised our general education curriculum to require all students to take at least one course in critical race and ethnicity studies and one in gender and sexuality studies. We also collaboratively designed a required first-year seminar titled Dialogue Across Difference. A diverse group of faculty and staff have taught the course across multiple areas of disciplinary expertise. The course offers a unique opportunity to deepen our pedagogical engagement with feminist and antiracist methodologies as well as practices of reflexivity within our community. The approach includes practicing mindfulness, deep listening, and nonviolent communication, among other strategies of dialogue. In an admittedly messy and insightful process, we are slowly and intentionally attempting to build a culture of inclusion and belonging from the ground up.

Repeatedly, the class was met with resistance from some administrators, faculty, and students alike. A significant number of faculty have said that they are unprepared to teach the class, while some question the value of the learning it espouses, asserting that it has been "disruptive." The class has invited action-based learning, resulting at one point in student activism targeting institutional flaws. Even in a social justice–centered institution like Antioch, the class continues to expose the deep discomfort and rejection in the academy of antiracist teaching and learning as well as the lack of practice in sustained reflexive dialogue across differences.

"Feminist as Explorer" and the Reciprocal Turn

In a "feminist as explorer" pedagogical model, Mohanty challenges gender studies curricula to reexamine the viewpoint that a "distance from 'home' is fundamental." Thus, international area studies courses are "viewed as entirely separate from the intellectual project of US race and ethnic studies" ("Under Western Eyes" 520). This not only alienates our teaching and learning from reflexivity but also lacks acknowledgment of knowledge formation in communities located "elsewhere" that have been historically and systematically excluded from the academy. As Alexander and Mohanty point out:

> It is imperative that the academy *not* be the only location that determines our research and pedagogical work; that we recognize those hierarchies of place within the multiple sites and locations in which knowledge is produced. . . . This mandate in turn requires the recognition that knowledge is produced by activist and community-based political work—that some knowledges can only emerge within these contexts and locations. (27)

The radical praxis encountered within community activist–led spaces often reflects the inequalities and differences between our campuses and nearby working-class neighborhoods, which may be just as stark as between our campuses and communities abroad. In this way, pedagogies that travel across these boundaries, whether locally or globally, invite an engagement with transnational feminist praxis and similar principles apply.

Reciprocity invites an ethical awareness of how power affects the relationship of teaching and learning and calls inequalities into question. Patricia Hill Collins notes that "most relationships across difference are squarely rooted in relations of domination and subordination." A shifting framework is required to analyze the relations of power as we seek to build equitable relationships across these differences (459). Tania Mitchell, in her analysis of service learning in higher education, agrees that our pedagogical emphasis must "focus on developing authentic relationships, relationships based on connection" (103). To build equitable relationships toward reciprocity, our pedagogy must deeply value the contributions and knowledge of local practitioners, centering their expertise within the teaching and learning experience. For communities that are willing to engage with academic learners, tangible results are sought that directly impact their lived experiences through material or other gains. Additionally, reciprocity seeks sustainability, which maintains relationships and projects for lasting impact over time.

The Cooperative Education Program at Antioch—known as "Co-op"—invites our students to participate in community engagement locally, nationally, and internationally. Through participatory action and reflection on experiential learning, reflexivity and reciprocity are intentionally built into the program. We build relationships with programmatic partners to be sustained over time through shared goals, dialogue, and mutual benefit. When an interested student is invited to engage with one of our partners, they actively contribute to a current project full-time for an eleven-week immersive academic term, earning twelve credits. By taking reciprocity seriously, we are in continued dialogue with our partners, who "set the agenda" (Mendoza 305). The community partners decide if they have the capacity and need for a student at that time, and they train our students toward effective impact. In this way our partners set the terms for engagement, and our students learn to prioritize and value the community's knowledge—from how the work is being done to why it is important.

In online coursework, co-op faculty invite continued reflection with each student while affirming that the primary teaching and learning is occurring with our community partners. We aim to acknowledge their expertise as they lead critical efforts in an area of practice that often aligns with students' area of study. This praxis allows students to see the critical connections between the liberal arts and the change work happening in communities at home and abroad. Students may amplify the partners' efforts through social media campaigns, website enhancements, grant writing, data collection in research projects, community outreach strategies, or other focused initiatives. I invite students to consider reciprocity as a form of accountability. It is an awareness shifting away from an individualist perspective and toward thinking through impact with our partners. Working together, they become invested in pedagogy that supports community-led action.

One such co-op partner is the Tandana Foundation, which works "to support the achievement of community goals and address global inequities" (https://tandanafoundation.org/). In 2016 an Antioch student joined Tandana's team in Otavalo, Ecuador, after hearing about a particular dilemma. The foundation had received a large donation of computers and tech equipment to outfit two rural schools with computer labs. The teachers, however, needed more training and tech support to operate these classes with full capacity. Our student was studying Spanish, while also working with the information technology department on campus.

By the end of our student's co-op term, three months later, the computer labs in the schools of Otavalo were fully functioning and he had trained the teachers in the software and basic troubleshooting. Tandana founder, Anna Taft, also noted that the student set up a local network each day in a new location for the mobile rural health clinics run by Tandana volunteers to support their online medical records system. Upon returning to Antioch, the student was near completion of his Spanish-language capstone project, having increased his language and cultural proficiency abroad. Since that time, we have had several more students contribute to Tandana's efforts in areas of public health and sustainable agriculture, assisting in multiple community garden projects at various rural schools and health centers.

In 2022 two Antioch faculty joined Tandana's volunteer efforts alongside a different co-op student to plant a new garden in the Otavalo highlands aimed to support local efforts of Indigenous foodways. Faculty member Beth Bridgeman engaged in a meaningful exchange regarding seed sovereignty with members of the Union of Peasant and Indigenous Organizations of Cotacachi (http://unorcac.nativeweb.org/english). Bridgeman has taught courses on this topic to enhance students' learning as they work on Antioch College's micro-farm producing seasonal food for our campus kitchens. Over the years as our dialogue and exchange continues, the exploration of new projects is generative and reciprocal in both design and implementation.

The Connective Turn Toward Feminist Solidarity

The understanding of how we are linked, implicated, and mutually responsible for our futures emerges within transnational thinking and flows from a reflexive and reciprocal framework. As Mohanty explains, the "feminist solidarity" model invites an understanding of the co-implication of our lived experiences and relationships as interconnected through both differences and commonalities:

> The local and the global are not defined in terms of physical geography or territory but exist simultaneously and constitute each other. It is then

the links, the relationships, between the local and the global that are fore-grounded, and these links are conceptual, material, temporal, contextual and so on. . . . Differences and commonalities thus exist in relation and tension with each other in all contexts. What is emphasized are relations of mutuality, coresponsibility, and common interests, anchoring the idea of feminist solidarity. ("Under Western Eyes" 521)

Numerous transnational feminist theorists agree that pedagogical alli-ances centered on authentic and reciprocal relationships make space for the possibility to move into action together. Kaplan refers to a "model of coali-tion" (139), while Nira Yuval-Davis refers to both "coalition" and "solidarity politics" (185). Elora Chowdhury cites the work of Chela Sandoval as mov-ing toward a "differential coalitional consciousness" (301). In "Pedagogies of Invitation," AnaLouise Keating describes the importance of redesigning the pedagogical encounter as a shift "from 'me' to 'we' consciousness" (175). She argues that the hyper-individualism of the capitalist project denies an acknowledgment of interconnectedness and interdependency on how our actions impact each other (171–76). Keating coins "pedagogies of invitation" that "employ relational, connectionist thinking" and invite the teacher as learner and learner as teacher (182–83). Acknowledging our interconnec-tions with "'we' consciousness" is what allows for the possibility of "working together for compassionate social change" (173).

It is with these ethics in mind that the turn toward connectivity invites a pedagogy of solidarity in action. The challenge is to do this without ignoring or erasing differences, interrogating the power and privileges of our diverse positions. As Rubén Gaztambide-Fernández reminds us in "Decolonization and the Pedagogy of Solidarity," it is critical to anchor our pedagogy in "an unapologetic commitment to antiracist and decolonizing aims" (51). He asserts that "educators are called upon to play a central role in constructing the conditions for a different kind of encounter, an encounter that both opposes ongoing colonization and that seeks to heal the social, cultural, and spiritual ravages of colonial history" (42). To do this, he engages the think-ing of Paolo Freire to affirm that solidarity is "a term of engagement"—"a praxis"—not simply a feeling toward others but "an action that also affects or modifies the one who acts" (54). Jill Steans, in "Negotiating the Politics of Difference in the Project of Feminist Solidarity," agrees: "The meaning and the possibility of solidarity has to be worked out in the course of practice. Feminist solidarity is not a sentiment based on an abstract idea or ideal, nor is solidarity a commitment born of 'women's common interests'" (743).

Mohanty explains that within a "feminist solidarity" pedagogical model, the possibility—and perhaps priority—of collective action emerges: "I think feminist pedagogy should not simply expose students to a particularized academic scholarship but that it should also envision the possibility of activism and struggle outside the academy" ("Under Western Eyes" 523). To do this from a place of equity, Yuval-Davis provides clues as to how one may stay grounded in an authentic relationship while moving into action together. In "Beyond Differences: Women, Empowerment, and Coalition Politics," she analyzes the Italian feminist movement Women in Black, which has developed a helpful framework to consider:

> The idea is that each participant brings with her the rooting in her own membership and identity, but at the same time tries to shift in order to put herself in a situation of exchange with women who have different membership and identity. . . . It is vital in any form of coalition and solidarity politics to keep one's own perspective on things while empathizing with and respecting others. (184–85)

Thus, we "root" to deepen a reflexive understanding of our own positionalities, but we also learn to "shift" toward an understanding of the historic, social, economic, and cultural realities of others. As I have outlined, self-reflexivity, sustained dialogue, and building reciprocal relationships that connect across differences are all required to move into collective action.

The Cooperative Education partnership with Mujeres de Artes Tomar (MAT), or Women Taking up Art, an Argentine feminist theater troupe, is a case study of developing a pedagogical praxis toward transnational scholar activism. The partnership with MAT began with student and faculty interest in performance and gender studies, while social movements to eliminate gender violence were on the rise. Before the Say Her Name and Me Too movements gained momentum in the United States, Ni Una Menos (Not One Less) surged across Latin America, demanding an end to gender violence and femicide from the domestic sphere to the disappearance and trafficking of women, LGBTQ+ people and girls (niunamenos.org.ar). MAT, founded by Claudia Quiroga and Sandra Posadino, developed a hybrid of performance and protest aimed to empower women through story, song, and movement in addition to street actions in Buenos Aires. From national women's strikes to protests for reproductive rights legislation, the artists, performers, student activists, teachers, mothers, and retirees who form MAT have been part of this substantial movement. They call their work *"artivismo"*—melding arts activism through "rebellious joy, freedom, autonomy, fulfillment, for the exercise of our rights and the enjoyment of our lives, for a society in equity and free of all violence" (mujeresdeartestomarcomar. wordpress.com/english/us/).

At Antioch our students care deeply about participating in cultural shifts toward the elimination of sexual assault, harassment, and violence. As Katherine Rosman noted in 2018 in the *New York Times*, it was nearly thirty years earlier at Antioch that students crafted the Sexual Offense Prevention Policy, first of its kind in the country calling for consent-based practices on and off campus. Students who have chosen to co-op with MAT do so because of a shared commitment to these principles and the invitation of transforming art into action. Our collaboration has included leading action during an International Women's Day strike and hosting MAT at Antioch for an arts residency held virtually due to the pandemic, Her Voice Rises (https://antiochcollege.edu/her-voice-rises/). Reciprocity in the form of compensation for the artists was possible through grants I had written, while participation of over 150 people in the activities led to our work's greater impact.

Quiroga, co-founder of MAT, agrees that meaningful transnational connectivity begins "in active dialogue with social organizations with converging interests. . . . [Antioch] students deployed a strong commitment to gender. One could recognize an expansive training, full of curiosity" and willingness to move "ideas into action." While on co-op, students assisted in website development, grant writing, and research in English and Spanish to expand MAT's international reach. The sense of connection was palpable following students' participation in MAT's empowerment circles and public actions. Students and leaders of MAT expressed feelings of mutual appreciation, gratitude, and respect. One student said, "What I learned from MAT about joy and celebration I brought back with me in my thinking about social justice actions and organizing in the United States" (Craig).

While student engagement with MAT deepened an understanding of a larger transnational movement, the co-op students' commitment to scholar-activist praxis spanned their time in Argentina. This was demonstrated through senior capstones and projects reflecting transnational feminist practice that they completed upon their return. In her senior capstone project titled "Malas Palabras," one student examined the ways that language impacts attitudes of misogyny, from which gender violence emerges (Navarette). Another student created simultaneous site-specific performances with women in Arabic, English, and Spanish around the globe (Craig). Through their pedagogical praxis on co-op in Argentina, students learned new methodologies toward feminist solidarity and connected directly to transnational communities of practice.

Increasingly, Antioch students are returning from co-op with a commitment of engaged praxis that reflects transnational feminist solidarity frameworks. As we build an intentional design of transnational pedagogy, it is critical to consider how these objectives are being integrated across the curriculum. The more we establish engaged global learning as an extension of efforts to teach and learn reflexivity, antiracism, and intercultural dialogue in our classrooms, the less likely it is to be an isolated "tourist" experience—disconnected from a commitment toward shared responsibility and reciprocity with community members. I encourage the creation of engaged transnational programs that emerge from sustained reciprocal relationships of scholar-activists. A likely starting place is faculty commitment to developing these relationships and implicating our scholarship within transnational feminist activism. As we model the dialogic teaching and learning that occurs through this praxis, we can invite our students to make direct contributions as scholar-activists and pivot our pedagogy toward sustained transnational movement building.

Works Cited

Ahmed, Sara. "Close Encounters: Feminism and/in 'The Globe.'" *Strange Encounters: Embodied Others in Post-Coloniality*. Routledge, 2000, pp. 161–81.

Alexander, M. Jacqui, and Chandra Talpade Mohanty. "Cartographies of Knowledge and Power: Transnational Feminism as Radical Praxis," *Critical Transnational Feminist Praxis*, edited by A. L. Swarr and R. Nagar. State U of New York P, 2010, pp. 23–45.

Bridgeman, Beth. Personal interview. Feb. 28, 2023.

Chowdhury, Elora Halim. "Global Feminism: Feminist Theory's Cul-de-sac." *Human Architecture: Journal of the Sociology of Self-Knowledge*, vol. 4, no. 3, article 27, 2006, pp. 291–302.

Collins, Patricia Hill. "Toward a New Vision: Race, Class, and Gender as Categories of Analysis and Connection." *Readings for Diversity and Social Justice: An Anthology on Racism, Sexism, Heterosexism, Ableism, and Classism*, edited by M. Adams et al. Routledge, 2000, pp. 457–62.

Craig, Hannah. "Re: questions for an article I'm writing." Emails received by Luisa Bieri, June 15, 2019, and June 24, 2019.

DiAngelo, Robin. "White Fragility." *International Journal of Critical Pedagogy*, vol. 3, 2011, pp. 54–70.

Enloe, Cynthia. *Bananas, Beaches and Bases: Making Feminist Sense of International Politics*. U of California P, 2003.

Freire, Paolo. *Pedagogy of the Oppressed*. Continuum, 2005.

Gaztambide-Fernández, Rubén. "Decolonization and the Pedagogy of Solidarity." *Decolonization: Indigeneity, Education & Society*, vol. 1, no. 1, 2012, pp. 41–67.

Gristwood, Anthony, and Michael Woolf. "Introduction: Questioning Nationhood, Memory, and Culture." *Woven by Memory: The Idea of Nation in Education Abroad*, edited by A. Gristwood and M. Woolf. CAPA International Education, no. 3, 2014, pp. 12–20.

"Her Voice Rises: A Transnational Arts Exchange at Antioch College." https:// antiochcollege.edu/her-voice-rises/.

hooks, bell. "Sisterhood: Political Solidarity among Women." *Feminist Theory: From Margin to Center*. Routledge, 1984, pp. 43–67.

hooks, bell. "Holding My Sister's Hand: Feminist Solidarity." *Teaching to Transgress: Education as the Practice of Freedom*. Routledge, 1994, pp. 93–110.

Jones, Kenneth, and Tema Okun. "The Characteristics of White Supremacy Culture." ChangeWork, 2001, http://www.cwsworkshop.org/PARC_site_B/ dr-culture.html.

Kaplan, Caren. "The Politics of Location as Transnational Feminist Critical Practice." *Scattered Hegemonies*, edited by Caren Kaplan and Inderpal Grewal. U of Minnesota P, 1994, pp. 137–52.

Keating, AnaLouise. "Chapter Six: Pedagogies of Invitation." *Transformation Now! Toward a Post-Oppositional Politics of Change*. U of Illinois P, 2013, pp. 167–88.

McClintock, Anne. "'No Longer in a Future Heaven': Gender, Race, and Nationalism." *Dangerous Liaisons: Gender, Nation & Postcolonial Perspectives*, edited by Anne McClintock et al. U of Minnesota P, 1997, pp. 89–112.

Mendoza, Breny. "Transnational Feminisms in Question." *Feminist Theory*, SAGE Publications, vol. 3, 2002, pp. 295–314.

Mitchell, Tania. "Critical Service-Learning as Social Justice Education: A Case Study of the Citizen Scholars Program." *Equity & Excellence in Education*, 40, University of Massachusetts Amherst School of Education, 2007, pp. 101–112.

Mohanty, Chandra Talpade. "'Under Western Eyes' Revisited: Feminist Solidarity through Anticapitalist Struggles." *Signs*, vol. 28, no. 2, Winter 2003, pp. 499–535.

Mohanty, Chandra Talpade. "Transnational Feminist Crossings: On Neoliberalism and Radical Critique." *Signs*, vol. 38, no. 4, Summer 2013, pp. 967–91.

Mujeres de Artes Tomar. mujeresdeartestomarcomar.wordpress.com/english/ us/. Accessed Feb. 27, 2019.

Navarette, Alyssa. "Malas Palabras." Colloquia 2019, June 21, 2019, Antioch College, Yellow Springs, OH. Installation Presentation.

Ni Una Menos. niunamenos.org.ar/. Accessed June 30, 2019.

Rich, Adrienne. "Notes Towards a Politics of Location." *Blood, Bread, and Poetry: Selected Prose 1979–1985*. Little Brown, 1984, pp. 210–31.

Rizvi, Fazal. "International Education and the Production of Cosmopolitan Identities." *RIHE International Publication Series*, 9, 2005, n.p.

Rodríguez, Karen. "Taking More of the World In: Expanded Subjectivities and the Productive Destabilization of National Identity in Education Abroad." *Woven by Memory: The Idea of Nation in Education Abroad*, edited by A. Gristwood and M. Woolf CAPA International Education, no. 3, 2014, pp. 34–42.

Rosman, Katherine. "The Reinvention of Consent." *New York Times*, Feb. 24, 2018, www.nytimes.com/2018/02/24/style/antioch-college-sexual-offense -prevention-policy.html.

Quiroga, Claudia. "Re: preguntas para una investigación." Email received by Luisa Bieri, May 26, 2019.

Steans, Jill. "Negotiating the Politics of Difference in the Project of Feminist Solidarity." *Review of International Studies*, 33, 2007, pp. 729–43.

Stebleton, J. Michael, Krista M. Soria, and Blythe T. Cheney. "High Impact of Education Abroad: College Students' Engagement in International Experiences and the Development of Intercultural Competencies." *Frontiers: The Interdisciplinary Journal of Study Abroad*, vol. 22, Winter/Spring 2013, edited by Brian Whalen, pp. 1–24.

Taft, Anna. "Re: article." Email received by Luisa Bieri, March 13, 2023.

Talburt, Susan. "International Travel and Implication." *Journal of Curriculum Theorizing*, vol. 25, no. 3, 2009, pp. 104–118.

Tandana Foundation. https://tandanafoundation.org/.

Union of Peasant and Indigenous Organizations of Cotacachi. http://unorcac.nativeweb.org/english.html.

Yuval-Davis, Nira. "Beyond Differences: Women, Empowerment and Coalition Politics." *Gender, Ethnicity, and Political Ideologies*, edited by Nickie Charles and Helen Hintjens. Routledge, 1998, pp. 168–89.

8

Teaching Feminist China

The Dream and the Real

MERYL ALTMAN and SHARON R. WESOKY

How to make political coalitions based on material
conditions rather than mystified fantasies?
—Caren Kaplan, *Questions of Travel: Postmodern
Discourses of Displacement*

It is an error to judge China as though things were stopped.
—Simone de Beauvoir, *The Long March: A Book on China*

Only the imagination and promise of an alternative future
allow historical and present suffering to emerge and speak.
—Dai Jinhua, *After the Post-Cold War: The Future of
Chinese History*

Nearly fifty years after feminism stormed the US academy, our libraries and
journals contain strong, specialized bodies of scholarly work about women
and gender in seemingly every imaginable time and place. Meanwhile, the
field of women's, gender, and sexuality studies (hereinafter WGSS[1]) has
developed a core pedagogy for undergraduate teaching, with a recognizable set of canonized texts and "habits of practice" for syllabus building
and classroom dynamics. But how do these two traditions of feminist
knowledge production intersect, and what is the best way to bring them
together? At its origin, the hope was that women's studies (as it was then
called) would be "the academic arm of the women's movement." We might
not use that language now, but the underlying thought—that the point of
studying the lifeworlds of the gender system is to change them—is still what
brings students into our classrooms. How are we mobilizing what feminist
scholarship "knows" to share it for the next generation of feminists to use?

The two of us began working together at a 2017 GLCA Curriculum Institute on "Teaching Transnational Feminisms" because we had both (separately) noticed that China does not figure as fully as one might expect on syllabi for feminist theory and other WGSS core courses, including our own. This marginality is surprising when we remember how important an idealized understanding of the Maoist project was to the second-wave origins that still ground our field. It also felt embarrassing, given the increasing numbers of Chinese and Chinese American students who take our classes now. Finally, it struck us as a missed opportunity because China's complicated socialist feminist history, as well as the challenges facing feminism in its transition to a free-market economy, can provide important lessons for transnational socialist-feminist praxis.

So we began a project to investigate the roots of this situation and to address it pragmatically by developing a set of course materials that we and others could use. We hope to enable readers who are not Asia specialists to bring a nuanced, well-informed view of China into their classrooms and to encourage them to see why it would be valuable to do so.

Though our institutions are quite similar—both of us have worked for many years at small Midwestern liberal arts colleges—we have moved through the academy in different ways. Meryl, whose PhD is in American literature, now describes herself as "post-disciplinary," or simply undisciplined. While developing and directing DePauw's women's studies program (starting in 1990), her teaching went in many directions, from Women in Classical Antiquity to Political Economy of Women, and her 2020 book about Simone de Beauvoir borrows from as many disciplines as *The Second Sex* did. Sharon, on the other hand, is trained as a political scientist and works at the meeting point of Chinese politics and feminist praxis; she has written on women's nongovernmental organizations (NGOs) in Beijing and on Chinese rural women's organizing. We have both taught WGSS core courses for many years, and despite our different backgrounds, both of us are committed to an approach that would not see feminist ideas in abstract isolation from material and historical conditions and would not reduce "feminism" to its American and European manifestations. The Women's Studies Committee of the Great Lakes College Association (GLCA), with its forty-year tradition of collaboration among those doing feminist work and its ethical commitment to workshops that are genuine learning communities, provided the ideal environment to incubate our work.

• • •

Meryl: For me, this began in fall 2013. My first-year seminar, Women and Work, was reading Annelise Orleck's *Common Sense and a Little Fire*, which deals with the activism of Jewish immigrant women in the garment trades of early twentieth-century New York. Orleck's book shows how socialist and feminist movements sometimes collaborated and sometimes competed and how different women resolved the conflicting loyalties that resulted. I often start class by asking students to write down questions they have about the reading, both to gather their thoughts for discussion and to alert me to what I should clarify, and that day a student from mainland China, who had been in the United States for less than a month, wrote down: "The socialism that the women talk about in the book, is it the same as Chairman Mao?" It seemed urgent to answer her, and I had no clue how to even begin. I just did not know enough about China. *How humiliating.* There were three students in the class from mainland China, and they all knew the basic outline of American history better than most of the students who had gone to US high schools. Also, I was unsure, and anxious, about what the concrete stakes of the answer to that question might be for *her.*

In the short term, I told my student, "I don't know how to answer the question about Mao, but I can tell you what socialism means to the women in Orleck's book, and what it means to me, since I see myself as their descendant," and I went on from there. But I also felt obliged to address my own ignorance. As Mao himself said, in the rather different context of a 1930 talk titled "Oppose Book Worship," "No investigation, no right to speak."

As a result of my collaboration with Sharon, I would now answer Chen's question by saying, "Well, yes and no." *Yes,* because the idea that workers should share the fruits of their labor is the same everywhere and always. *No,* because social movements *are* what social movements *do,* and the core ideas of socialism have had many different local versions and outcomes, ranging from the Scandinavian and British models of the welfare state, to the different models called by that name at different times in China (and the Soviet Union), to what Bernie Sanders was calling for when he proudly reclaimed the term in his 2016 presidential campaign. Ideas matter, but they do not matter everywhere in the same way. But (then again) *Yes,* because socialism (like feminism) was an international movement, where ideas traveled contemporaneously across borders in many directions. And also *Yes,* because Chinese feminists throughout the twentieth century have confronted the same question that faced those Jewish women on the Lower East Side: how a commitment to socialism, to feeding the hungry and enabling those who work to share the fruits of their labor, can be reconciled with a commitment to the rights and needs of women *as women*; and how sometimes, rather than trying to paper over the contradictions, it is necessary to acknowledge that class justice and gender justice are in tension with each other, and to continue one's work, regardless.

Sharon: My story begins when Meryl asked if we could work together to approach more self-consciously including Chinese feminisms in more general feminist theory courses. And therein lies my own embarrassment: I had not engaged in any systematic fashion to bring together my teaching/research on gender questions and activism in China with my teaching in WGSS. While I teach a course in Transnational Feminisms, and in a previous version as Globalization and Gender, I only ever included *one* case study of *one* Chinese feminist thinker or of China as a location among networks of global factories. My own episteme separated political science from WGSS from area studies, despite my own simultaneous claims to work in an interdisciplinary fashion.

And, yet, further back, my work on gender in China began because I longed to approach it from questions that felt meaningful to me and allowed for exploration of alternative forms of sociopolitical organization in a country that, when I began graduate studies, had just experienced the trauma of the Tiananmen Square massacre and was thus not heading down a recognizably "democratic" path. My research situated women's organizations in 1990s Beijing within a mainstream field, studies of the Chinese political system, but I also wanted to understand the agency available to women interested in pursuing social justice, due at least partly to historical and ideological legacies of revolution and party-state-supported women's liberation. But my late arrival to feminist theory per se has led to the bifurcation of my thinking and teaching about China and about feminist praxis more generally.

• • •

We tell these stories because we think our situations may not be unusual. While it feels dangerous to generalize, conversations with colleagues suggest that many people working in WGSS feel less well-informed about developments in China than about, for instance, Latin America, even if that is not their area of specialization either. To be sure, when one feels underprepared, or under- or mis-educated, it is often better to hold back than to foolishly rush in. Yet insofar as teaching about China requires "background" that many of us do not have, it is no different from many other places (and indeed from many social locations within the United States). Assuming the idea of "transnational feminisms" is a good one, collaborations like ours, along with the right resources, should be able to address this problem. This sort of collaboration, among other benefits, demonstrates that "transnational feminist theory" originates in many locations beyond the "West" and can provide an example of the process of "decolonizing feminism," which Linda Alcoff asserts "requires contextualizing feminism itself in order to be able to discern the particular, context-based ways in which gender is understood, and progress is imagined, from any given location" (33).

One thing a survey of syllabi and anthologies (e.g., Cudd and Andreasen; Kolmar and Bartkowski; McCann and Kim) suggests to us is that as the field has moved away from a country-by-country approach to more thematic or topical rubrics under the "transnational" banner, China qua China has become less visible. There were good reasons for moving beyond the country-by-country or area studies approach, which could mask larger configurations of cultural and economic power, and obscure interconnections in an increasingly global system (see Mohanty, "Under Western Eyes Revisited"). But a quick survey suggests that often when people do teach about China now, it comes up as part of *something else*—for example, global commodity chains (where was your shirt made?), "women in the global factory," sex work in the Asian diaspora, or "model minorities" within the United States. None of this is inaccurate, but there is more to know, especially if we seek to comprehend the "scattered hegemonies" that Inderpal Grewal and Caren Kaplan so rightly assert to be central to understanding transnational feminist practices (17).

We do not mean to suggest that there is something "wrong" with a thematic approach—these books and syllabi are excellent in other respects. But students will find more, and deeper, material about China in, for instance, several collections edited by Amrita Basu, *The Challenge of Local Feminisms* (first published in 1995) and *Women's Movements in the Global Era: The Power of Local Feminisms* (first published in 2010 and revised in 2016). In a sense, this is still "area studies" because these collections take a systematic country-by-country approach, and new editions provide updated entries to tell students what is happening there "now," even if they are much more sensitive to the multiplicity of feminisms that can be found in different locations at different historical moments than, say, Robin Morgan's *Sisterhood Is Global* (1984) was. The problem with a more thematic approach, though, is that some of the "themes" currently preoccupying WGSS are simply not a very good fit for China, and others, such as critiques of NGO-ization and cultural appropriation, can distract from or even distort the lived realities of Chinese women, historically and today, which is why we are suggesting that students in general feminist theory classes read works specific to China.

We encountered an ironic example of the difficulties of "placing China" when presenting an early version of our work at the National Women

Studies Association (NWSA) Conference in 2018. We had submitted under sub-theme five: "Revolutions and utopian projects: sustained, incomplete and derailed." But when our acceptance came through, we found ourselves on a panel labeled "Feminist Epistemologies from the Global South: From Revolutionary to Decolonial to Cosmopolitan." Without wishing to seem ungrateful for the chance to present, this seems wrong to us on several levels, in ways that may be symptomatic of what has happened to China within WGSS now. For one thing, to put it bluntly, China is not the "Global South." Parts of rural China could perhaps be characterized using that term, but only in the sense that it also applies to, say, parts of Appalachia—or Detroit. The label "postcolonialism" does not really capture either China's particular history or its position as a global economic power in the world today. The idea of an indigenous Chinese epistemology is also neither accurate nor helpful. Beauvoir already pointed out in the 1950s that it was *Westerners* who always wanted China to be, and to remain, "different" and who thus nostalgically deplored the gains of Mao's modernizations, including such effects as the abolition of prostitution and the disappearance of picturesque slums (see Beauvoir, *La longue marche*; Altman). Does it really make sense now to talk about "epistemologies from the Global South" in a situation that is fully globalized from an economic point of view, and where feminist discourses have been internationally intertwined, with the currents of influence running in both directions, from the early twentieth century until today? Our main contention is this: It is impossible to teach about China responsibly without teaching it historically and contextually. In particular, putting the Mao era, and indeed the Cold War, under erasure reinforces the idea that There Is No Alternative (Fisher) to globalized neoliberal capitalism. As Caren Kaplan observes, "Putting history back into our considerations of 'difference' neither erases nor simplifies our ambivalent relationship to the economic systems that we live with, by, and in spite of" (15).

• • •

Meryl: When I started to think about "adding" China to my feminist theory course, one thing I realized was that China, or a version of China, was already there, in texts I teach as documents of feminist history in the United States. As Robin Morgan reminds us in the introduction to *Sisterhood Is Powerful* (1970), the practice of "consciousness-raising," developed by radical groups around 1967, was directly derived from the Chinese practice called "Speak Pains to Recall Pains." This seems especially worth signposting because the feminist pedagogy most of us still practice had its roots in that practice. For instance, Carol Hanisch has summarized the broader connection between the women's liberation movement and the Chinese Revolution, describing what her group, New York Radical Women, "took" from Mao, including his ideas of "self-reliance," the need to build a grassroots movement, and sending intellectuals to the countryside to learn from the people, which she compares to Freedom Summer. And on the level of "theory," she writes, "We considered sexism and racism more than just a tradition or a bad habit. Being materialists (in the Marxist sense), we asked, 'Who benefits?'" (1–2). Now, what Hanisch describes belongs to a phenomenon Judy Tzu-Chun Wu has labeled "radical orientalism": Eager to form alliances with women in North Vietnam and China, US activists often romanticized or simply misread their Asian "sisters," and it is not difficult to uncover tropes of the mysterious East in much of this work. But seen as a whole, Wu's book describes a movement animated first and foremost by political solidarity—a commitment to support the struggles of women around the world—and by a desire to learn from those struggles.

Our professional field was being born around the same time, and there, too, the influence of China was palpable. In 1975 the journal *Signs* began publishing, and the next year their third issue ever was a special, multidisciplinary issue dedicated to China, with the editors explaining, "For if there is a subject that seems of the utmost pertinence to those concerned with women, culture, and society, that subject is China" (vi). Their approach is optimistic but not blindly uncritical, and articles pay attention to how various changes had different concrete results for different groups of women within the People's Republic of China. Overall, much 1970s feminist interest in China was animated by the hopeful view of alternatives to capitalism and to Western bourgeois feminine subjectivity but also by sensible research questions—in particular, to what extent was women's increasing entrance into work outside the household the solution to women's subordination? If we take *Signs* as the "journal of record," a careful perusal of that record from 1975 through today shows interdisciplinary feminist scholarship keeping up with that initial understanding of China's centrality—including a series of symposia, a commitment to hearing from Chinese scholars and those from the diaspora, and to making strong connections between scholarship and activism. But there has been a real divergence between scholarship and pedagogy. Not many of these excellent articles have made it onto syllabi. This seems like a missed opportunity.

The point we want to underscore is that second-wave feminists from Europe and the United States went to China, not "bringing theory" but *looking* for theory and looking for practice, for signs that theory could *work*. So, yes, there was an orientalizing uptake of China, but there was also something better: materialism, practice, history, hope. And China seemed like a crucial part of any feminist story. Such attention contributes to "reversing transnationalism" and moves "the discourse of global feminism away from its universalistic tendency" (Chowdhury 8). Building on that, the question we might ask (and want our students to ask) could be framed as, What can we learn about feminism *from* China, which has had a long and complex feminist history?

Sharon: Considering Chinese experience in relation to feminist theory takes us beyond questions as they have been asked before, beyond the 1970s optimistic vein—"How did Maoist socialism liberate women?"—but also past the 1980s and "How did Maoism socialism *not* liberate women?" (see, for instance, Andors; see also Stacey), moving toward a much more complex tale of the nature of gender, class, and socialism in China's "long twentieth century" and into the present. As Meryl notes, numerous themes from Chinese experience have infused "Western" feminism, and there are similarly abundant entry points to include Chinese feminist thinking to inform theory and praxis on central questions in contemporary transnational feminist thought. Here are a few examples of such entry points, which could get students thinking in new ways.

In the New Culture Movement of the 1920s, both male and female intellectuals put women's liberation at the center of their conceptions of "modernity" in China (see Wang, *Women in the Chinese Enlightenment*). But even before the fall of the Qing Dynasty, Chinese anarcho-feminist He-Yin Zhen fostered new ways of thinking that anticipated "intersectionality" almost a century before this concept entered Western discourse. In her 1907 essay "On the Question of Women's Liberation," He-Yin integrates race (by critiquing rich, white women-dominated suffrage movements in Europe and America), class (by advocating for "common property" and gender as well as decrying poverty), and gender (by regarding *nannü youbie*, the "differentiation between man and woman," as the basic, originary social distinction) into a comprehensive plea for the liberation of men *and* women (64–69, 70). She also examined transnational capitalism ("On the Question of Women's Labor") and the anticolonial implications of antimilitarism ("On Feminist Antimilitarism"). He-Yin demonstrated the value of situated, locational, and yet transnational feminist imaginaries from the standpoint of a China still ruled by a "foreign" dynasty yet also semi-colonized by Western "treaty ports" and mired in extreme poverty.

Subsequently, the Mao years of 1949–1976 offer a historical case study of "actually existing socialism," with its attendant failings but some successes for gender liberation. The recent work of Wang Zheng, in particular, offers a multifaceted picture of women's fate under Maoist communism that locates spaces for agency and strategies for fighting "multiple systems of oppression" in the often-inhospitable circumstances of Maoist authoritarianism while also finding that the work of state feminists in the Mao era "inscribed mainstream ideology with deep feminist implications" (*Finding Women in the State* 6, 17–18). Wang's treatment is itself an important retrieval of diverse visions of "socialism," and the vital place of gender politics within it, at a time when our students seem more open to "socialism" than in previous decades but lack nuanced treatments of its historical formations. Meanwhile, *Some of Us* (Zhong et al.), a collection of autobiographical reflections from Chinese feminists, including Wang Zheng, who lived through the excesses of the Cultural Revolution, provides a needed reminder that cultural change is filtered through individual subjectivity. *Some of Us* also provides another example of a more nuanced treatment of the Mao era than, for instance, the much-taught autobiography *Wild Swans: Three Daughters of China* (Chang).

As the dismantlement of China's socialist system began under "reform and opening" in the 1980s and 1990s, Chinese thinkers already anticipated more recent Western discussions about compatibilities between neoliberalism and versions of liberal or "choice" feminism (for instance, the analysis of Nancy Fraser). As Li Xiaojiang, the foremother of post-Mao women's studies in China, argued ("From 'Modernization' to 'Globalization'") for greater individual subjectivity as a necessary salve to the state-mandated gender sameness of the Mao era, film critic Dai Jinhua ("Class and Gender") argued for continuing attention to socialist and Marxist approaches, to capitalism *and* patriarchy. Dai has written more recently about how China's marketization has led to a shift from "collective" to "state" forms of ownership and thus to greater inequality (*After the Post–Cold War* 10); her approach allows for more nuanced theorizations of socialism and its institutional and social manifestations.

While China's hosting of the 1995 United Nations Fourth World Conference on Women was meant to highlight the progress being made on women's equality in the People's Republic, it also provided opportunities for women to organize in NGO formations, albeit ones with "Chinese characteristics," and to begin to engage in processes of *jiegui* ("connecting with the international tracks"; see Min for more on this concept) but also *bentuhua* ("indigenization") of transnational feminist theoretical concepts, including "gender" (see Xu). While many Chinese feminists translated the latter term as *shehui xingbie*, or "social gender," conversations surrounding this concept themselves demonstrated the process of *bentuhua* due to debates regarding whether Chinese notions of "sex" already inherently included the notion of the social (see Spakowski, "Gender Trouble" 34–35;

see also Song, "History's Inner Horizon" 126–27). Some of the sources we cite here allow students to see how Chinese thinkers thought about the relationship between Chinese and transnational feminist praxes and debated that relationship among themselves.

Such locating of China *in* the world, rather than as separate and apart from it, is also present in many other contemporary thinkers. Notably, Petrus Liu places China and Taiwan, "two Chinas," firmly within their historical and geopolitical contexts and employs a purposefully "transnational and transcultural" approach to theory, fiction, and human rights discourses in order to formulate "a Chinese materialist queer theory that sets it apart from its Euro-American counterparts" by examining systemic power relations as well as notions of substantive equality and social transformation in an increasingly neoliberal China (5, 6). Renmin University scholar Song Shaopeng has also asserted the need for a continued Marxist framework, drawing inspiration from Nancy Fraser but also situating her thought in the legacies of Chinese socialist feminism as well as the unique conjuncture of Chinese neoliberalization (see Song, "Capitalism, Socialism, and Women"; see also Spakowski, "Socialist Feminism in Postsocialist China," and Li, "Equality and Gender Equality with Chinese Characteristics"). Both Liu and Song specifically address the quandaries that arise from wanting to emphasize particular issues that affect women *as women* during neoliberalist times, when important issues of class are increasingly and problematically neglected; both use resources from Chinese history as well as present-day theories to integrate gender, sexuality, and class concerns. Including readings like these in a feminist theory survey course, particularly if introduced early in the semester, could deepen and complicate students' understanding of socialist feminist legacies and show why they are still relevant. Even more valuable, perhaps in a course fully configured around transnational feminisms, would be a series of case studies.

For instance, the strange circumstances of contemporary Chinese feminists, seeking forms of existence in a putatively socialist but actually neoliberal and authoritarian context allows for focused feminist engagement in environments that remain inhospitable to overt feminist activism and identification. The emergence in the 1980s and 1990s of "women's studies" and NGO activism featured forms of thinking and organizing that allowed for novel thinking but within constraints imposed by the party-state. One of these was "doing projects (*xiangmu*)" (see Wang and Zhang, "Global Concepts"), many of which connected urban, educated women with rural and migrant Chinese women. This pragmatic, activist approach even among academics shows one way that activism can contribute to forms of solidarity that cross often-great distances of class, life experience, and geography. Such notions of solidarity are perhaps especially challenged as "new" generations of young feminists organize in China, creating a new #MeToo movement that is both vitally necessary but also disconnected from both its earlier post-Mao foremothers as well as rural organizing (see Fincher; Wesoky). At the same time, while some younger feminists seek to engage with the fragile independent Chinese labor movement, giving them connections to class considerations, a number of them have been forced into exile, making the movement quite literally transnational in nature at the present moment (Shen). The emergence and reemergences of various forms of feminist thought and activism in China poignantly illustrate Dai Jinhua's view that "the resources of diverse histories" are necessary for "the imagination of an alternative future" (*After the Post–Cold War* 21–22).

As Tani Barlow notes in her analysis of the various meanings of "woman" in Chinese feminist thought, "Feminist theory is an embedded form of historical reflexivity or self-conscious thinking about perceived social crises. It is the evidence of thought" (66). Our work together has shown us that Chinese feminist thought has always been *strategic* in relation to both domestic political circumstances and transnational forces, reminding us that "national," "global," "Western," and "Indigenous" are always ideological counters in local games and cannot be understood without attention to context. Also, if as Saba Mahmoud has powerfully and influentially argued, conceptualizing feminism simply as "resistance" is a problem, conceptualizing it merely as resistance to the *state* is a particularly pernicious form of the problem. Chinese history shows that "state feminism" is not an oxymoron—that important and authentically feminist gains have been achieved by feminists working within and through the apparatus of government. This may be applicable in contexts well beyond China; the ways feminists in many countries have worked in partnership with the state to create policies benefiting wide groups of women should not be discounted or dismissed.

We hope we have demonstrated here the twin dangers of overemphasizing and underemphasizing China's difference from the rest of the world, the need always to attend to the multifarious differences *within* "China," as well as the central importance of always locating China *in* the world. If we wish to follow Grewal and Kaplan's call to see "the transnational" in its true heterogeneity, we need to look beyond one-dimensional caricatures of both "the second-wave feminist" and "that monster Mao," to excavate the histories of feminism in the United States and recuperate more complex understandings of "actually existing socialism." The complex and detailed literature on Chinese feminisms allows students of feminist theory to transcend what Dai Jinhua terms "the global trend of post–Cold War amnesia"

(*After the Post–Cold War* 41) without falling into the trap of nostalgia. Chinese feminisms also allow students to situate their frequent critiques of neoliberal capitalism within a complex history of socialism and postsocialism, various forms of feminist solidarity, and a deeper comprehension of the multidirectional ways that transnationalism operates in complex historical, social, and political circumstances.

Concluding Thoughts: On Collaboration

What does it mean to work together, locally or globally, in or out of the academy? The risks of getting things wrong are many, but if the alternative is to remain in one's safe and comfortable bubble, those risks must be faced. The nature of our collaboration was quite straightforward. Sharon had an expertise in something Meryl wanted to learn more about. Meryl wanted to be given "the right things" to read and wanted Sharon's authority to allay her anxiety about what she might be getting wrong. Sharon wanted Meryl's expertise in Western feminist theory and history to better inform her own understandings of transnational connections. Stepping back, we realize that this, too, mirrors the second-wave founding moment of many interdisciplinary women's studies programs at colleges like ours, when colleagues who were trained in various traditional disciplines simply sat down together, pooled what they knew, and began to ask the questions that their graduate training had not encouraged. Perhaps collaborations like ours were more common, and simpler, at a time when no one could lay superior claim to a central episteme or core, everyone was excited about learning more, and the state of the professional "game" made the professional risks of academic feminism more salient than its rewards.

So much has been gained, institutionally and intellectually, for WGSS in the intervening decades, that it seems almost churlish to point out that something has also been lost. While we were less able to work face-to-face than we would have liked, our own collaboration was undoubtedly made much easier, and more productive in a deeply satisfying way, by the fact that since both of us are long past promotion, we were working "off the grid" of competition over "turf" and relatively free from professional anxieties brought by the commodification of intellectual work, including academic feminism. We also felt more able to edge our way around a thematic, theory-driven approach to "transnational feminisms" that sometimes almost begins to feel like an orthodox paradigm, with obligatory denunciations of "Western feminism" and ritualized citation from a small set of authorities. The value of that approach is undeniable, but our wish for our students, and for the colleagues who will carry on this work in the years to come, is to hang on to the thirst for more information about the world and to what a long-ago survey of our field called "The Courage to Question" (Musil).

Notes

The authors wish to express our gratitude to colleagues who participated in the GLCA Curriculum Institute on "Teaching Transnational Feminisms" (Ann Arbor, May 22–24, 2017) and especially to the organizers, Isis Nusair, Barbara Shaw, and Marta Sierra. We also thank the GLCA for funding that gathering and our subsequent work together. We thank those who attended our panel at the National Women's Studies Association (NWSA) Conference, Atlanta, November 2018, for helpful comments.

Meryl further acknowledges a Mellon grant to Wabash and DePauw for faculty development in Asian studies, which funded two weeks of intensive study at the East-West Center in Honolulu (summer 2014) followed by a trip to China (summer 2015). She thanks her colleague Sherry Mou for leading that trip, and the scholars at the East-West Center, especially Shana Brown and Peter Herschock.

1. We've adopted "WGSS" as shorthand for work that is done under a range of titles in a range of US institutions, simply because that is the term used at the colleges where we have worked. Some years ago, at a time when academic feminist programs around the country were roiled by acrimonious discussions about name changes, our GLCA colleague Laurie Finke observed (during a program review) that "what matters is not what you call the program; what matters is what you are actually *doing*." That still strikes us as a healthy observation.

Works Cited

Alcoff, Linda Martin. "Decolonizing Feminist Philosophy." *Decolonizing Feminism: Transnational Feminism and Globalization*, edited by Margaret A. McLaren. Rowman & Littlefield, 2017.

Altman, Meryl. *Beauvoir in Time*. Brill, 2020.

Andors, Phyllis. *The Unfinished Liberation of Chinese Women, 1949–1980*. Indiana UP, 1983.

Barlow, Tani. *The Question of Women in Chinese Feminism*. Duke UP, 2004.

Basu, Amrita, editor. *The Challenge of Local Feminisms: Women's Movements in Global Perspective*. Westview Press, 1995.

Basu, Amrita, editor. *Women's Movements in the Global Era: The Power of Local Feminisms*. 1st edition. Westview Press, 2010.

Basu, Amrita, editor. *Women's Movements in the Global Era: The Power of Local Feminisms*. 2nd edition. Westview Press, 2016.

Beauvoir, Simone de. *La longue marche: essai sur la Chine*. Gallimard, 1957.

Beauvoir, Simone de. *The Long March: A Book on China*. Translated by Austryn Wainhouse. World Publishing, 1958.

Chang, Jung. *Wild Swans: Three Daughters of China*. HarperCollins, 1991.

Chowdhury, Elora Halim. *Transnationalism Reversed: Women Organizing against Gendered Violence in Bangladesh*. State U of New York P, 2011.

Cudd, Ann, and Robin Andreasen, editors. *Feminist Theory: A Philosophical Anthology*. Wiley-Blackwell, 2005.

Dai, Jinhua. *After the Post–Cold War: The Future of Chinese History*. Edited by Lisa Rofel. Duke UP, 2018.

Dai, Jinhua. "Class and Gender in Contemporary Chinese Women's Literature." *Holding up Half the Sky: Chinese Women Past, Present, and Future*, edited by Jie Tao, Bijun Zheng, and Shirley L. Mow. Feminist Press at the City University of New York, 2004, pp. 289–302.

Fincher, Leta Hong. *Betraying Big Brother: The Feminist Awakening in China*. Verso, 2018.

Fisher, Mark. *Capitalist Realism: Is There No Alternative?* Zero Books, 2009.

Fraser, Nancy. *Fortunes of Feminism: From State-Managed Capitalism to Neoliberal Crisis*. Verso Books, 2013.

Grewal, Inderpal, and Caren Kaplan. "Introduction: Transnational Feminist Practices and Questions of Postmodernity." *Scattered Hegemonies: Postmodernity and Transnational Feminist Practices*, edited by Inderpal Grewal and Caren Kaplan. U of Minnesota P, 1994, pp. 1–35.

Hanisch, Carol. "Impact of the Chinese Cultural Revolution on the Women's Liberation Movement." Presented at the 30th Anniversary Symposium on "China's Great Proletarian Cultural Revolution," New School for Social Research, New York, Dec. 14, 1996, http://www.carolhanisch.org/Speeches/ChinaWLMSpeech/ChinaWLspeech.html.

He-Yin, Zhen. "On Feminist Antimilitarism." *The Birth of Chinese Feminism: Essential Texts in Transnational Theory*, edited by Lydia H. Liu, Rebecca E. Karl, and Dorothy Ko. Columbia UP, 2013, pp. 169–78.

He-Yin, Zhen. "On the Question of Women's Labor." *The Birth of Chinese Feminism: Essential Texts in Transnational Theory*, edited by Lydia H. Liu, Rebecca E. Karl, and Dorothy Ko. Columbia UP, 2013, pp. 72–91.

He-Yin, Zhen. "On the Question of Women's Liberation." *The Birth of Chinese Feminism: Essential Texts in Transnational Theory*, edited by Lydia H. Liu, Rebecca E. Karl, and Dorothy Ko. Columbia UP, 2013, pp. 53–71.

Kaplan, Caren. *Questions of Travel: Postmodern Discourses of Displacement*. Duke UP, 1996.

Kolmar, Wendy, and Frances Bartkowski, editors. *Feminist Theory: A Reader*. 4th edition. McGraw-Hill Education, 2013.

Li, Xiaojiang. "Equality and Gender Equality with Chinese Characteristics." *Feminisms with Chinese Characteristics*, edited by Ping Zhu and Hui Faye Xiao. Syracuse UP, 2021, pp. 65–75.

Li, Xiaojiang. "From 'Modernization' to 'Globalization': Where Are Chinese Women?" *Signs*, vol. 26, no. 4, 2001, pp. 1274–78.

Liu, Petrus. *Queer Marxism in Two Chinas*. Duke UP, 2015.

Mahmoud, Saba. *Politics of Piety: The Islamic Revival and the Feminist Subject*. Princeton UP, 2011.

McCann, Carole, and Seung-kyung Kim, editors. *Feminist Theory Reader*. 4th edition. Routledge, 2016.

Min, Dongchao. *Translation and Travelling Theory: Feminist Theory and Praxis in China*. Routledge, 2016.

Mohanty, Chandra. "Under Western Eyes Revisited: Feminist Solidarity through Anticapitalist Struggles." *Signs*, vol. 28, no. 2, Winter 2003, pp. 499–535.

Morgan, Robin, editor. *Sisterhood Is Global: The International Women's Movement Anthology*. Feminist Press at the City University of New York, 1984.

Morgan, Robin, editor. *Sisterhood Is Powerful: An Anthology of Writings from the Women's Liberation Movement*. Random House, 1970.

Musil, Caryn McTighe, ed. *The Courage to Question: Women's Studies and Student Learning*. Association of American Colleges and National Women's Studies Association, 1992.

Orleck, Annelise. *Common Sense and a Little Fire: Women and Working-Class Politics in the United States, 1900–1985*. U of North Carolina P, 1995.

Shen, Lu. "Thwarted at Home, Can China's Feminists Rebuild a Movement Abroad?" ChinaFile, Aug. 28, 2019, http://www.chinafile.com/reporting-opinion/postcard/thwarted-home-can-chinas-feminists-rebuild-movement-abroad.

Signs. "Editorial." *Signs*, vol. 2, no. 1, 1976.

Song, Shaopeng. "Capitalism, Socialism, and Women: Why Does China Need to Rebuild Marxist Feminism?" *Chinese Modernity and Socialist Feminist Theory*, edited by Sharon R. Wesoky. Routledge, 2023, pp. 148–67.

Song, Shaopeng. "History's Inner Horizon: Investigating the Intellectual History of Chinese 'Women's/Gender Studies,'" *Chinese Modernity and Socialist Feminist Theory*, edited by Sharon R. Wesoky. Routledge, 2023, pp. 115–47.

Spakowski, Nicola. "'Gender' Trouble: Feminism in China under the Impact of Western Theory and the Spatialization of Identity." *Positions: Asia Critique*, vol. 19, no. 1, 2011, pp. 31–54.

Spakowski, Nicola. "Socialist Feminism in Postsocialist China." *Positions: Asia Critique*, vol. 26, no. 4, 2018, pp. 561–92.

Stacey, Judith. *Patriarchy and Socialist Revolution in China*. U of California P, 1983.

Wang, Zheng. *Finding Women in the State: A Socialist Feminist Revolution in the People's Republic of China, 1949–1964*. U of California P, 2016.

Wang, Zheng. *Women in the Chinese Enlightenment: Oral and Textual Histories*. U of California P, 1999.

Wang, Zheng, and Ying Zhang. "Global Concepts, Local Practices: Chinese Feminism since the Fourth UN Conference on Women." *Feminist Studies*, vol. 36, no. 1, 2010, pp. 40–70.

Wesoky, Sharon R. "(Dis)Continuities in Chinese Feminisms: Navigating Local and Global." WAGIC: Women and Gender in China, Sept. 18, 2017, https://

www.wagic.org/blank-2/2017/08/29/Discontinuities-in-Chinese-Feminisms
-Navigating-Local-and-Global.

Wu, Judy Tzu-Chun. *Radicals on the Road: Internationalism, Orientalism, and Feminism during the Vietnam Era*. Cornell UP, 2013.

Xu, Feng. "Chinese Feminisms Encounter International Feminisms." *International Feminist Journal of Politics*, vol. 11, no. 2, 2009, pp. 196–215.

Zhong, Xueping, Zheng Wang, and Di Bai, editors. *Some of Us: Chinese Women Growing Up in the Mao Era*. Rutgers UP, 2001.

9

Unpack *Here*

Challenging Privilege, Increasing Empathy, and Building Solidarity through Collaborative Feminist Pedagogy

DANIELLE M. DEMUTH and AYANA K. WEEKLEY

Are we going to be staying in huts? . . . Will I be safe? . . . Can I drink the water? . . . Everything is so dirty. . . . The food just doesn't taste right. . . . They just don't care about their children. . . . The children are so behind in school. They should know this stuff by now. . . . These children just need therapy. . . . These people ride in the back of pickup trucks; don't they care about their safety? . . . I just feel safer if I use Uber. . . . Why make up names for things that already have names? . . . Why is there gender oppression? How did it start? . . . My privilege hit me hard. . . . Why did we have to go all the way to Africa to see the inequalities and oppression in our own zip codes? . . . This trip will change you; South Africa will humble you. . . . I have to bring what I have learned into my life back at home. . . . If we can stand in solidarity, we can finally start to make social change.

These opening words reflect students' sentiments regarding their growth from pre-departure anxiety, culture shock, and curiosity to a shift in focus as they engage with broader issues of globalization, connect experiences and analyses across locations, confront their privileges in a myriad of difficult and multilayered ways, and begin to translate what this knowledge will mean for their futures as a result of our feminist pedagogy. The variety of statements also illustrates that study abroad is by no means a benign endeavor; it is challenging to students' established sense of their place in the world. A feminist pedagogy that emphasizes praxis—the connection between theory and practice—is necessary in order to trouble apolitical models of study abroad.

As universities respond to global pressures to recruit students internationally and to train students to be global workers who are marketable across the boundaries of nation-states, coursework, semesters away, and study abroad have increasingly come under the rubric of internationalization. As Ryuko Kubota found in an analysis of the ways universities market the benefits of study abroad, the following trends emerged: "These benefits can be broadly categorized as (1) developing language skills, (2) fostering cultural understanding and intercultural competence, (3) enhancing personal growth and identity and (4) increasing career opportunities" (349). The benefits of study abroad, promoted to Western students in highly industrialized countries of the Global North, are rarely contextualized within histories of colonialism, imperialism, and globalization, a context that privileges students from the Global North and makes global mobility possible for them. Internationalization emphasizes short-term projects and experiences that are easily transferred to resumés to illustrate the students' skills. The emphasis is not on establishing collaborative and sustainable relationships across these borders.

Similarly, universities have sought to promote service-learning to students as a way to build their resumés in preparation for future employment. Feminist scholars have problematized service-learning as uncontextualized volunteerism that often reifies the very structures of power and privilege that feminists seek to challenge (see Costa and Leong). Service-learning is often depoliticized and does not promote solidarity, which is a goal of our feminist work. Unless students examine and interrogate the context of service-learning, the structures of power and privilege remain invisible to them. Invisible privilege is a barrier to feminist collaboration and social change. In short, many approaches to both service-learning and study abroad programs deemphasize, and thus reify, structures of privilege and power, which is antithetical to our feminist pedagogy and our goal of collaborative social change.

Despite the neoliberal agenda that shapes service-learning and study abroad, we remain committed to the possibilities that may be realized when these two elements of education are structured according to feminist theories and methods of positionality, reflexivity, and critical transnational praxis as theorized by Richa Nagar and Amanda Lock Swarr in *Critical Transnational Feminist Praxis*. When study abroad and service-learning are developed in collaboration with local communities and partners in ways that are mutually beneficial, incorporating dialogue, empathy building, and problem solving, they can provide opportunities for critical engagement beyond the classroom. In this chapter, we will discuss a specific example of service-learning during a study abroad program. The example is a collaboration with the Students' Health and Welfare Centres Organisations (SHAWCO) at the University of Cape Town, a student-run activist organization that partners with local townships to provide education and health services. This model provides a particularly impactful experience for students who often find working with a nonprofit/social justice organization in an international context to be where the proverbial "rubber hits the road." Here, students are able to engage more directly with transnational feminist praxis, including principles of empathy and solidarity. It is through study abroad service-learning that many of their feminist assumptions are challenged even more deeply than when the students are engaged in similar work in their home contexts.

We argue that this program, including intentional design within a larger feminist curricular context and ongoing and in-the-moment pedagogical praxis, is a model for challenging privilege, increasing empathy, and building solidarity for students. First, we describe the structure of our program; second, we explore our feminist pedagogical praxis and strategies used to model collaboration; and, in conclusion, we discuss strategies to sustain intentionally collaborative work that can be applied to other courses and service-learning programs.

WGS South Africa Study Abroad: Program Design and History

This program was conceived as a collaborative effort between multiple entities including the women, gender, and sexuality (WGS) studies department; the Women's Center at Grand Valley State University (GVSU) in Allendale, Michigan; and SHAWCO at the University of Cape Town (UCT). SHAWCO is a nongovernmental organization (NGO) with more than sixty years' experience engaging approximately eight hundred student volunteers annually in six centers in marginalized communities in the Cape Town area. Through SHAWCO we support their educational program in Manenberg Township by tutoring approximately twenty sixth-grade learners in math, English, and social studies for six weeks. We developed the initial proposal for the trip and conducted a site visit in 2011. Our study abroad program has run five times, and, thus far, there are eighty-one alumni of the trip. Over the course of the eight years of this study abroad program, the structure of the faculty/staff collaboration has shifted. However, as staff changed, we realized collaboration is not about the people but about the partnership.

Collaboration requires a sustained commitment to the partnership and to goals of the program.

What Does Collaborative Feminist Pedagogical Praxis Look Like?

At the core of this program is an emphasis on social justice education, transnational feminist praxis, and destabilizing assumptions undergirding service-learning and citizenship; it is by design an example of collaborative, transnational, civic engagement, and teaching that challenges often-accepted concepts of feminism, service, citizenship, and the notion of "doing good." Through this study abroad program, we developed a pedagogical praxis that emphasizes what Chandra Mohanty calls "The Feminist Solidarity or Comparative Feminist Studies Model," described in *Feminism without Borders*:

> This curricular strategy is based on the premise that the local and global are not defined in terms of physical geography or territory but exist simultaneously and constitute each other. . . . Differences and commonalities thus exist in relation and tension with each other in all contexts. What is emphasized are relations of mutuality, co-responsibility, and common interests, anchoring the idea of feminist solidarity. (242)

Through readings, excursions, discussions, and service-learning, we show the interconnectedness of here and there, between South Africa and the United States, not only in terms of the global economy and shifting international alliances but also in terms of histories of white supremacy.

The students are enrolled in two courses: a course on the topics of history and activism in South Africa and a service-learning course. The program is designed so that academic lectures and excursions on the social history of gender and race in South Africa complement the experience of service-learning because that history explains the area's current political and social context. Lectures by local instructors, politicians, and activists introduce students to contemporary issues and current social and political debates for women and gender in South Africa, the relevant historical context leading to these debates, and the impact of these issues on feminist activism. These topics are developed in collaboration with a course convener at UCT and have included the women's movement, gender-based violence, HIV/AIDS, women's health and reproductive issues, environmental issues, history, education, women and labor, women's participation in government, and NGOs in South Africa.

We prepare students for excursions through readings on the history of apartheid and its legacy and the history of resistance against it. These excursions include the Apartheid Museum, the District Six Museum, Robben Island, St. George's Cathedral, and the Iziko Slave Lodge. In order to learn about local activist work, students engage with UCT student leaders and women in various local nonprofit/social justice organizations. From these leaders, students learn about the possibilities and challenges of transnational collaborations shaped by governmental, economic, and educational structures that institutionalize power imbalances between people, institutions, and nation-states.

Their second course is part service-learning and part lecture/discussion led by GVSU faculty. We spend time in class discussing the connection between the two courses, interrogating service work, civic engagement, their motives for taking part in this study abroad program, and the role of students' positionality in this work. It is in this class that we begin to unpack privilege by asking students to identify and examine their "location" in the United States and as students visiting South Africa. We all need to continuously analyze the various items in our "knapsacks" that have traveled with us, including our beliefs about gender, feminism, politics, and power (McIntosh). We must spend time making assumptions and privileges visible so that we can process our experiences when studying abroad and engaging in service-learning. Our goal is to interrogate and make unstable conceptualizations of transnational, feminist, solidarity, and praxis for everyone engaged in this ongoing work, including ourselves. The curriculum is designed not only to complement service-learning but also to further the important goal of a critical comparison to help move students from service to solidarity.

Unpack *Here*

We use *unpack here* as a metaphor in that while we are literally unpacking suitcases we are also working with students to unpack privilege. The "here" in the title is about not only their location as students at a university in the US Midwest and in Cape Town but also anywhere they go in the future. The impacts of both the privilege and disadvantage we carry with us differs, and when we are in a different part of the world and in a different context, our relationship to our positionality becomes unsettled, particularly as a new facet of privilege—citizenship and global mobility—becomes visible.

Another important aspect of our feminist pedagogical praxis lies in who we are and the ways we teach together. Our approach centers the ongoing dialogue happening between ourselves and the students. For students, what is visible is how much we make our identities and positionalities a part of the conversation in the room. We offer up our own life experiences in the classroom—friendship, teaching, travel experience, first-generation college experience—making it clear that critical feminist self-evaluation is ongoing. Talking across and through our differences in the classroom is instructive, and it is an intentional pedagogical choice to model this engagement for the students. However, this type of academic collaboration does not come easily in settings that prioritize individualism and competition. Although we traversed our pre-tenure years in a similar time frame, those years were not without the often-fraught senior/junior faculty hierarchies.

Our positionalities are important to note here as they shape the dynamics of how we work together with students and for the ways students view us and our partnership. Danielle is a white, cisgendered, lesbian woman with more pedagogical and study abroad experience. Ayana is a black, cisgendered, heterosexual woman who came to the collaboration with fewer years of experience in these areas. Being in South Africa, race is a particularly salient category to discuss in relation to identity, the history of apartheid in South Africa, and the present-day constructions of race. Students are working through feeling "out of place" or more visible than they do in the United States if they are white. If they are students of color, they are working through feeling for the first time in their lives that they are not easily identifiable as the "other." In our study abroad program, both students of color and white students may experience these kinds of moments as they travel in South Africa, where racial categorizations differ from the United States in both name and relationships of hierarchy and power. As co-instructors, with our own distinct positionalities, we are able to facilitate nuanced discussions of intersectionality and the shifting meanings of their social identities. For Black students from the United States, this hierarchy of lighter- and darker-skinned Black South Africans is both familiar and distinct. This has prompted group discussions in which Ayana has facilitated an examination of colorism and racism as students are experiencing them both in South Africa but also in the United States. For white students, the experience of not being in the majority in terms of race is a new and uncomfortable experience. Danielle processes this experience with the group, and white students develop empathy as their peers explain feeling that same way on a daily basis on campus in the United States.

Unpack in the Classroom

Service-learning, when based in a model of sympathy for a lesser-developed community, serves to reify a dynamic of inequality and, thus, is an obstacle to empathy and solidarity. Empathy is essential to solidarity. Solidarity is essential to social change. As Patricia Hill Collins theorizes:

> Race, class and gender oppression form the structural backdrop against which we frame our relationship—these are the forces that encourage us to substitute voyeurism and academic colonialism for fully human relationships. But while we may not have created this situation, we are each responsible for making individual, personal choices concerning which elements of race, class and gender oppression we will accept and which we will work to change. One essential component of this [individual] accountability involves developing empathy for the experiences of individuals and groups different than ourselves. Empathy begins with taking an interest in the facts of other people['s] lives, both as individuals and as groups. (42)

Empathy is also about seeing others as equal to oneself. More than simply humanizing others and taking an interest in their facts, it involves seeing them as equal. As Collins argues, empathy is a necessary building block in transformative feminist collaborations and praxis.

In our first class session in Cape Town, we begin to unpack students' ideas about Africa by reading excerpts from Larry Krotz's *The Uncertain Business of Doing Good* and discussing the concept of "doing good" that accompanies both missionary work and unexamined, untheorized service-learning. To do this, we address assumptions about Africa that many students have learned through their experiences with popular culture, news media, school curricula, and churches that engage in missionary work, all of these stemming from the idea of the Western savior in relationship to a lesser-developed continent and people. We ask that students actively counter this narrative of Africa. One of the ways we do this is by setting ground rules together, especially in relation to their social media postings; for example, as we move through various spaces in the city, we ask the students to be sure to take pictures *with* people rather than *of* people. Instead of posting random images of unidentified children or strangers, we ask that only pictures where people can be named be posted as this speaks to our goal of building relationships rather than engaging in voyeurism. As we move through the trip, students hold one another accountable when someone in the group is engaging in ways that detract from the goal of intentional relationship building, including posting images to social media or sharing one-sided narratives with friends and family at home.

Though students who have taken classes in women, gender, and sexuality studies; feminist theory; or sociology may be skilled in *naming* their privilege with regard to race, class, and gender, thanks to Peggy McIntosh's foundational essay on privilege, Kimberlé Crenshaw's seminal work on intersectionality, and feminist and critical race theorists who have detailed the institutionalized operations of race over the last four decades, their privilege as US citizens in a global context is less visible to them. Not only have most of them never left the United States, but despite the emphasis on internationalization in education their curricula remain US-centric. Thus, they are less able to articulate *how* their privilege operates in relationship to others as they move through the world. They are less skilled at the kind of individual accountability necessary to build empathy. Therefore, we spend a significant amount of time in our class sessions discussing specific interactions and observations with students, modeling praxis by using personal reflection to analyze past action and inform future engagement. We use essays by Allison Attenello and Joanne Muzak to interrogate service and service-learning, giving attention to how the university frames the value of service-learning, particularly with regard to the benefits for future employment. We unpack the role of service in maintaining structures of inequality when they are not rooted in politics and social change. Tobi Walker's essay on the gendered history of service versus politics and the importance of politics in creating social change helps us to move the discussion to how students have engaged or avoided politics thus far and how they might rethink that in their future work. For example, some of our students see themselves as preparing for a future in social service nonprofit work, others see themselves as preparing for political work, and neither of them sees the connections between those two. We challenge the apparent dichotomy of service work being apolitical and politics as divorced from service.

And, importantly, we address the ways in which their privilege will change as they complete their university degrees and move into what Paul Kivel describes as the "buffer zone." Kivel argues, "This buffer zone comprises all occupations that carry out the agenda of the ruling class without requiring ruling-class presence or visibility. . . . These jobs give them a little more economic security and just enough power to make decisions about other people's lives—those who have even less than they do" (134). We discuss the need to consider how acquiring a four-year university degree will shift their social locations in often subtle but substantial ways. Many may begin their college careers as first-generation college students, for example, but upon completion their social standing has changed, even if initially their economic status has not significantly been altered. Completing their bachelor's degree places them in a privileged category of less than 10% of people globally who will ever attain this status. This can be a difficult transition for students, especially those who identify closely with working-class backgrounds. This connects to our larger discussions of shifting relationships to privilege on the study abroad trip. For many, while paying for this trip may have required economic sacrifice by themselves as well as their families, the fact remains that as citizens of the Global North, they have the ability to travel the world in ways other people do not. Thus, while they may identify as poor or working-class in the United States, that does not translate similarly when situated in global contexts in which their US dollar goes much further and makes them feel wealthy, highlighting the contextual nature of privilege. Finally, if they achieve their intended goals of entering social service nonprofit work or politics, they will be in positions of power where they are responsible for making decisions that will impact entire communities. The shifting landscape of their identities becomes a theme for the courses as we unpack both their globality and their educational and class mobility.

Unpacking/Practicing Partnership and Solidarity

Our goal, eventually, is to see students taking on others' struggles in solidarity. Mohanty argues for a praxis-oriented definition of solidarity in *Feminism without Borders*:

> I define solidarity in terms of mutuality, accountability, and the recognition of common interests as the basis for relationships among diverse communities. Rather than assuming an enforced commonality of oppression, the practice of solidarity foregrounds communities of people who have chosen to work and fight together. Diversity and difference are central values here—to be acknowledged and respected, not erased in the building of alliances. (7)

Solidarity and feminist collaboration are concepts used by theorists and activists to frame not only *how* we do this kind of work but also how we benefit differently from it. Both are central to working in equitable ways that are attentive to operations of power and actively working to alter the legacies of supremacy. As Nagar and her colleagues articulate:

> Deep and sustained collaboration across unequal places can help us appreciate and learn from illegitimized or invalidated knowledges, and it can give us the tools or languages to grapple with our responsibility towards other(ed) worlds, knowledges, and epistemes. The radical potential of a given collaboration stems from this possibility of responsibly and ethically enacting complex, nuanced, and multilingual critical interventions and translations that are impossible to imagine from any single "pure" location. ("Feminisms" 507)

Collaboration requires learning the historical context for the setting in which you will be partnering, which is why we place such importance on the pairings of the readings and site visits in South Africa. Additionally, we extensively discuss the racially polarized history of the country and the similarities to the United States.

South Africa and the United States have parallel histories of anti-Black racism, oppression, and violence. During apartheid South Africa's white minority population enforced segregation, pushing Black and Colored South Africans farther and farther from metropolis centers into rural lands and denying free movement, access to voting, housing, employment, and human rights broadly. This legacy of white supremacy has produced complicated, messy, and artificial structures of race as it has the world over, including in the United States. In South Africa the racial categorizations emerging out of this system of racial apartheid included "Blacks" and "Coloreds"—used to refer to people whose families were brought as slaves from India, Indonesia, or other Indian Ocean islands—and "Whites."

Part of the legacy of apartheid segregation in South Africa is that many of the suburbs, known as townships, are still racially segregated. Manenberg is a Colored township outside of Cape Town contending with the legacies of apartheid as they currently manifest—continued economic exclusion; insufficient housing; precarious access to electricity and water; high rates of gender-based violence, including gang violence; and underfunded schools. Our work in Manenberg, while feminist, on its face does not seem like the usual WGS service-learning project. We counter the expectation that service-learning projects in WGS will explicitly include work that mirrors the subjects of most curricula—gender-based violence, women's health and reproductive justice, women-led businesses or capitalist ventures, and women-based environmental projects, such as access to water. Given expectations of what feminist work looks like, volunteering at the Saartjie Baartman Centre for Women and Children in Manenberg would make sense. However, a site visit to the Saartjie Baartman Centre proved that what the center needs is not *more* study abroad students volunteering. A significant amount of staff time is spent managing volunteers rather than in direct service and programming to their residents. In contrast, because we are in Cape Town when SHAWCO volunteers, who are usually available to tutor students in the SHAWCO Manenberg educational programs, are taking university exams, SHAWCO *does* need more volunteers at this time. Thus, we are able to fill a need for their educational programs.

While tutoring sixth-grade learners may seem like a surprising WGS service-learning project, it is in line with the need to expand what we consider women's activism and Nagar's call for collaboration to resist being formulaic. As the Sangtin Writers affirm, the work of women's activism has to broaden beyond focusing solely on "women's" issues:

> If we are truly interested in bringing about sustainable, long-term socio-political and economic change in the lives of those who have been pushed to the margins, it is essential for all the members of our rural communities—women and men; children, young, and old; *sawarn* and *dalit*; peasants, sweepers, workers, and shopkeepers—to constitute the waves of change. . . . In other words, . . . in order to bring about long-term changes in power relations, Sangtin had to be taken out of the ghetto of "women's problems" and its political struggles had to articulate with wider struggles. (125)

Similarly, our work with sixth-grade learners in Manenberg Primary relates to the wider struggles in the community in important ways. Racial segregation in South Africa is also evident in school structures and funding; Manenberg Primary is a seriously underfunded school in an impoverished Colored township. By the sixth grade, this impacts boys and girls in disparate ways. Girls are more likely to be pulled from the classroom to engage in caretaking for their families; boys are more likely to be pulled from the classroom to engage in income-producing activities. Thus, access to education is a social justice issue affecting everyone in the community in gendered, racialized, and classed ways. By supporting SHAWCO's educational programs at Manenberg Primary, our students are engaged in work geared toward addressing structures of inequality.

We also model feminist collaborations and solidarity in our relationships with staff at SHAWCO Manenberg Primary. We break down the central assumption of the authority and expertise of the professor by modeling the important practice of checking the desire to be in control and being willing to do all the necessary work when working in communities and organizations to which we do not belong. We are present and engaged on site every day with our students. For example, we work with our partners in Manenberg to guide us through interactions with the learners because local staff knows the students' backgrounds, abilities, and needs; moreover, they speak both Afrikaans and English.

In summary, the structure of this service-learning study abroad program is designed to introduce students to the concepts of feminist solidarity and collaboration and to provide a space for them to engage in feminist praxis. During their time working in Manenberg, we model feminist praxis with them as we all use the readings and class sessions to discuss and frame our work with the community. We practice communication and problem solving with our community partners, using feminist theoretical frameworks to guide our work.

Conclusion: What Are We Trying to Repack?

In *Study Abroad in a New Global Century* the authors ask, "Can study abroad be the transformational experience we expect it to be, transforming the American college student into a globally oriented, interculturally competent citizen able to compete in a global economy?" (Twombly et al. 109). We ask ourselves this and similar questions during and after each trip, wondering if we are successful in attaining our goals. In some instances, the answers to these questions do not come for many years after the program and they come in disjointed ways and moments.

The sentiments expressed by students with which we opened this essay include moments when unacknowledged bias and privilege emerge, and they make for unexpected, painful, and awkward interactions. The students come to the program with multiple identities and varying relationships to privilege, and we use intersectional analyses to support them in examining the privilege they carry. However, students' urge to compare the United States and South Africa are to be expected, and unpacking those comparisons offers opportunities for contextualizing how what they are seeing locally reflects larger structures of globalization and the legacies of white supremacy. During these discussions we are able to offer constructive comparisons of the ways that, for example, these structures are shaping access to employment, education, and health care globally in countless ways. Using these productive comparisons we are able to emphasize the need for empathy and solidarity.

We grapple with the complexities of the broad range of emotions and responses students have when studying abroad. Despite the scaffolding of the curriculum, the process of negotiating one's privilege is difficult and follows an unclear path that continues after our return home and well into the future. This proves challenging for everyone, faculty and students alike, and can have unexpected and surprising results. As Kubota writes, "While there is nothing wrong with reaffirming Self, it would defeat the purpose of study abroad's purported benefits if discovering and appreciating the Other did not also occur" (353). Sometimes being in a new context has the unintended consequence of shoring up hegemonic beliefs about US exceptionalism, the supremacy of Western ideals, or racist constructions of the Other.

The students end the trip better able to discuss how their privilege operates; they express humility and the desire to move in solidarity toward social change. Alumni of the program later tell us they travel the world differently, ask different questions both at home and when they travel, and have chosen different career paths as a result of the trip. Our goal is that their future work is framed by the praxis-oriented solidarity and collaboration we have modeled during this service-learning study abroad experience.

As we finalize this essay in 2020, we are writing and reflecting in the midst of the global pandemic, COVID-19. Necessarily, many programs are on hold. This context has highlighted the importance of emphasizing the feminist frameworks and specific strategies for sustaining intentionally collaborative work that can be applied to other service-learning, study abroad, or other community-based programs, including internships.

Feminist curricular programs must challenge the neoliberal agenda of these educational experiences. Students' professionalization and future employment cannot be the only goal; rather, in order to survive and to create the kind of social change that is the result of feminist collaboration, long-term community partnerships based in reciprocity must be developed. At the core of any study abroad, study away, or service-learning program that emphasizes social justice education, transnational feminist praxis, or destabilizing assumptions undergirding service-learning and citizenship must be sustained commitment to building solidarity with local communities.

Finally, the experience cannot stand on its own. It must be accompanied by a careful unpacking of privilege by discussing specific interactions and observations with students and modeling praxis by using personal reflection to analyze past action and inform future engagement based in empathy. Structures of inequality and white supremacy must be examined to contextualize how what students are seeing locally reflects larger structures of globalization and the legacies of white supremacy; this can be accomplished through readings or site visits, for example. Examining local histories and engaging with local activists lays a foundation for building collaborations and moving toward the solidarity that is necessary for survival and social change.

Works Cited

Attenello, Allison. "Navigating Identity Politics in Activism: Leading Outside of One's Community." *Leading the Way: Young Women's Activism for Social Change*, edited by Mary Trigg. Rutgers UP, 2010, pp. 96–106.

Collins, Patricia Hill. "Toward a New Vision: Race, Class, and Gender as Categories of Analysis and Connection." *Race, Sex & Class*, vol. 1, no. 1, 1993, pp. 25–45.

Costa, LeeRay M., and Karen J. Leong, eds. *Women's Studies and Civic Engagement*, special issue of *Feminist Teacher*, vol. 22, no. 3, 2012.

Crenshaw, Kimberlé. "Mapping the Margins: Intersectionality, Identity Politics, and Violence against Women of Color." *Stanford Law Review*, vol. 43, no. 6, 1991, pp. 1241–99.

Kivel, Paul. "Social Service vs. Social Change." *The Revolution Will Not Be Funded: Beyond the Non-Profit Industrial Complex*, edited by INCITE! Women of Color against Violence. South End Press, 2007, pp. 41–52.

Krotz, Larry. *The Uncertain Business of Doing Good: Outsiders in Africa*. Michigan State UP, 2009.

Kubota, Ryuko. "The Social Imaginary of Study Abroad: Complexities and Contradictions." *Language Learning Journal*, vol. 44, no. 3, 2016, pp. 347–57.

McIntosh, Peggy. "White Privilege and Male Privilege: A Personal Account of Coming to See Correspondences through Work in Women's Studies." Working Paper 189. [Wellesley] Center for Research on Women, 1988.

Mohanty, Chandra. *Feminism without Borders: Decolonizing Theory, Practicing Solidarity*. Duke UP, 2003.

Muzak, Joanne. "Women's Studies, Community Service-Learning, and the Dynamics of Privilege." *Atlantis: Critical Studies in Gender, Culture & Social Justice*, vol. 35, no. 2, 2011, pp. 96–106.

Nagar, Richa, and Amanda Lock Swarr. *Critical Transnational Feminist Praxis*. State U of New York P, 2010.

Nagar, Richa, Özlem Aslan, Nadia Z. Hasan, Omme-Salma Rahemtullah, Nishant Upadhyay, and Begüm Uzun. "Feminisms, Collaborations, Friendships: A Conversation." *Feminist Studies*, vol. 42, no. 2, 2016, pp. 502–519.

Sangtin Writers. "Still Playing with Fire: Intersectionality, Activism, and NGOized Feminism." *Women's Activism and Globalization: Linking Local Struggles and Transnational Politics*, edited by Nancy A. Naples and Manisha Desai. Routledge, 2002, pp. 124–43.

Twombly, Susan B., et al. *Study Abroad in a New Global Century: Renewing the Promise, Refining the Purpose*. John Wiley & Sons, 2012.

Walker, Tobi. "A Feminist Challenge to Community Service: A Call to Politicize Service-Learning." *The Practice of Change: Concepts and Models for Service-Learning in Women's Studies*, edited by Barbara J. Balliet and Kerrisa Heffernan. American Association for Higher Education, 2000, pp. 25–45.

10

Transcultural and Transborder Pedagogies in the Feminist Classroom

MONTSERRAT PÉREZ-TORIBIO
and M. GABRIELA TORRES

In *El Mundo Zurdo* I with my own
affinities and my people with theirs can
live together and transform the planet.
—Gloria Anzaldúa, "La Prieta" (1983)

For the past decade, feminist collaborations in the humanities and social sciences at Wheaton College (Massachusetts) have engaged students in site-based and experiential learning opportunities supported by external grant funding. In this essay, two faculty members from the humanities (Hispanic studies) and social science (Anthropology) reflect on their own collaborative practices and show how feminist pedagogies focused on praxis to inform our understanding of teaching and learning. We experimented with experiential feminist pedagogies in two courses: a study away course in urban Miami and a field-based course for decolonial learning in Puerto Rico. The two courses shared common praxis goals—albeit from different starting points—of bringing to the forefront plural understandings of how we learn, how we speak, how we think, and how we engage between ourselves and others. As a whole, both courses strove to enable self-reflexive sites of conversation and negotiation that make possible visions and narratives of agency and resistance.

This chapter juxtaposes two collaborative experiments in feminist pedagogy for teaching students to dialogue with difference. In doing so, it engages the reader in understanding how, in the humanities, feminist learning projects are conceived as acts of learning in praxis. Different approaches arose in part because of disciplinary constraints, the course modality and location, and course learning objectives. In sum:

1. The semester-term program in the city of Miami employed transborder and transcultural feminist pedagogies to link public and humanities with social action. Taking Miami as a dynamic cultural space of postindustrial hybrid art-music-linguistic forms, the students interacted with and learned from local institutional partners to decipher the complex imbrications between the local and the global. Team teaching in Miami focused on transcultural relationships between individuals and communities to interrogate subjectivities forged across differences in the queer, immigrant, and racial nexus. In Miami humanities and social science faculty joined forces to explore how art and humanistic inquiry can shape cultural citizenship and political protest.

2. The short-term field-based course held in Ponce, Puerto Rico, Disaster and Reconstruction: Gender and Post–Hurricane Maria Reconstruction, was co-developed by instructors from Wheaton College and the Pontificia Universidad Católica de Puerto Rico. The course introduced students to research as service practice to support community reconstruction. The field-based experience engaged students in conversations with local community members on gender and post–Hurricane Maria reconstruction. To debrief field experiences, the instructors employed intergroup dialogue to purposefully engage students' own positioning with the study of gender relations. The course was taught in both Spanish and English.

In both courses, we aspired to activate our vision of publicly engaged (Sandlin) feminist pedagogy that crosses or transgresses disciplinary boundaries to link the classroom with the world outside. Our feminist pedagogies foster a "pluralistic mode" of being in the world that embraces contradiction and ambiguity by rejecting easy identity and place categories. Following the challenges set by Teresa de Lauretis's "eccentric subject" and Gloria Anzaldúa's *El Mundo Zurdo* (the left-handed world) to neatly fixed affiliations with a singular feminism, our work in the classroom engaged students in an embrace of multiple queer and BIPOC (Black, Indigenous, and people of color) inclusive feminist ways of being. The "eccentric" political subjects articulated by de Lauretis are in essence transcultural individuals who, though marginalized and displaced, nevertheless transform their subjectivity through struggle, reflection, and (re)interpretation of their spaces of belonging. De Lauretis's conception of the subject's activist resistance to fixity (126) provided a theoretical framework that shaped the practice of classroom-based activism intended to yield multiple and contradictory perspectives. Similarly, Anzaldúa, in her piece "La Prieta," creates a "left-handed world" that goes beyond mere rhetorical expressions of respect for difference, offering a platform to reconstruct a world of collective social justice. Anzaldúa's left-handed world helps us understand the complexity and incompleteness of the human being as a catalyzing force capable of driving social transformation.

We situated our courses in a global/glocal settings (Robertson) where multiple positionings were possible and shaped course experiences to understand how multiple subject positions intersect and shape one another in struggle and in conversation. Our courses also strove to bring this left-handed world into the classroom, creating an activist stance in working in Puerto Rico or Miami or to question the nature of gender-based violence in the United States. In these courses we allowed eccentric and marginalized voices to become crucial elements in addressing the pressing sociopolitical issues of our time. Taken together, the instructors of these courses learned that the transborder, left-handed world that Anzaldúa depicts in her writings prompts a reexamination of the instructor's role and function in the classroom. These collaborative practices united colleagues from different disciplines and backgrounds to reshape student and faculty learning.

We designed courses to allow students and faculty to experience a multiplicity of cultural positions, perspectives, social trajectories, and irreconcilable juxtapositions. This design imperative made possible a pedagogical practice that gave students the ability not only to observe the co-presence of the here and there, self and other, and the center and margin within geographic and discursive spaces but also to understand the multidimensionality of these sites and the tensions and negotiations that arise within them. To conceptualize gender, ethnicity, and culture as unfixed and fluid categories, we experimented with the design of interdisciplinary courses focused on experiential and self-reflexive learning. Focusing on praxis, we examined how bodies, borders, and identities are transformed. We employed a praxis in bell hooks's sense that ruptures traditional pedagogical boundaries of the brick-and-mortar classroom. We taught our students "to transgress" the classroom itself and consider the open world—the stage, the city, or the field site—as their text and learning space. Moving beyond the typical classroom, we asked our students to break away from the normalizing constraints of the teacher as sage, singular explanations for social realities, and the notions that reinforce the fixity of identity.

Engaging our students beyond the classroom, we asked questions about who holds knowledge, how knowledge is transferred, and where and how we learn. Since the inception of these programs, students were exposed to different teaching figures who engaged in dialogue, negotiation, and argumentation in order to enhance their understanding of the topics at hand. The knowledge was not predetermined but rather continuously in flux, transcending boundaries and constructing connections. Collaborative teaching practices allowed knowledge to be in constant motion, crossing borders of thoughts, ideas, and perspectives to create bridges capable of healing and transformation.

Transcultural and Feminist Pedagogy in a Transnational City

Spatial and cultural borders are violently contested today in the United States and globally. Political lines of exclusion and containment are splitting up families, groups, and communities within and across nations, with renewed waves of populist movements and nationalist prejudice. This millennial border politics beckons us scholar-teacher-activists to look deeply into our knowledge dissemination and educational practices to reflect on what it is that we are teaching to our undergraduate students. We must also consider how to respond to and make sense of our violent, fractured, and politically divided world, particularly for those pursuing liberal arts education both inside and outside of collegiate classrooms.

Two of us, Hyun Kim from sociology and Montserrat Pérez-Toribio from Hispanic studies, teamed up to experiment with pedagogies necessary for critical civic engagement and designing the public humanities. For the fall 2019 academic semester, we launched a pilot program titled "Bodies, Borders, and Crossing Cultures: Transnational Activism in/from Miami" for an "Integrated Humanities in Action" Mellon Foundation grant. The cultural landscape of urban Miami is distinctively transnational, one that links geographic areas of "elsewhere" in the Caribbean and Latin America to historically contingent locations of belonging over "here" in this postindustrial, tourism-based, multilingual, multiethnic metropolis. This particular setting served as a primary "textbook" for experimenting with Humanities in Action. In the 2000s, Miami has grown as an intellectual and cultural node with its internationally recognized Miami Art Week, held annually during the first week of December, when this city and Miami Beach become the center of the art world. In this context, we asked our students to apply their in-class reading and learning to their firsthand experiences of living in the city to unravel the dialectical process of culture making through the arts, in which diverse ethnic communities simultaneously influence and change one another.

Guided by the transborder thinking and practice developed by Gloria Anzaldúa in her now–feminist classic *Borderlands/La Frontera: The New Mestiza*, we urged our fourteen students to immerse themselves in a new geographic space that was radically different from the predominantly white liberal arts campus we offer at Wheaton. Of the students who participated in this academic adventure, ten were African American or Latinx, while the others were Anglo-American. All of our students saw the Miami program as an opportunity to live and study in a linguistically and culturally diverse urban environment. The positionality was different for each of them. For instance, Latinx and African American students engaged immediately with Anzaldúa's readings and the complex process of identifying with a dual legacy and with issues of dismemberment, pain, wound, and trauma. On the other hand, Anglo-American and monolingual students, although very mindful and open in their task of decolonizing their minds, found more difficulties when interacting with a predominantly bilingual and diverse population. Nonetheless, all of them reported in their final evaluations how the reading assignments gained meaning when they combined the theory with their volunteer work. This grant gave us educators the opportunity to apply the transborder and queer theory developed by Anzaldúa in her writings to our domestic study away program. Our aim was not only to offer a distinct geographical experience, but also to resignify and transform our students' college educational experience. In order to achieve our goals, it was necessary to undertake a process of decolonization and epistemological transformation of our pedagogy, which involved breaking away from the traditional linear approach to learning and teaching.

To this end, we offered a program with two professors from different disciplines co-teaching classes that were held in a museum where students had the unique opportunity to directly engage with works of art, artists, and curators. In addition to the traditional reading assignments, the syllabus included a carefully curated program of activities that formed part of larger cultural events, which were open to the public and offered by the city of Miami. Finally, we implemented a practical component that allowed students to work and interact with various organizations throughout the city. By taking these steps, we aimed to create a more engaging and immersive learning experience for our students that would expose them to a broader range of perspectives and enable them to develop practical skills and knowledge that could be applied beyond the classroom setting. In this way, our transdisciplinary program, inspired by Anzaldúa's transborder thinking, emerged as a feminist decolonial strategy that questioned the roles of teachers and students in order to create an educational space of resistance and activism. This unexpected site made possible a non-mainstream, non-canonical educational experience: a left-handed, queer, and *prieta* (translated as dark-skinned but denoting the nonwhite) educational program where local knowledge was not viewed in isolation but rather as part of a larger whole. Anzaldúa's work proved to be an invaluable tool for introducing our students to the world of collaborative activism through the humanities and the arts. The initial reading assignment, "La Prieta," served as an excellent example of this value. Anzaldúa's oeuvre expertly blends autobiography, essay, art, poetry, and activism, providing a unique and multifaceted platform for engaging students with the theme of political-national borders and their own personal boundaries. While feminist readings that are excessively theoretical and dense may prove challenging for some students, Anzaldúa's works offer an alternative approach that enables students to explore these topics from a more accessible and direct perspective. Her reading created a need in our students to explore their own experiences and identities within the city of Miami and to consider how they intersect with the social and political landscapes around them.

Our pedagogic goals were woven into four courses: Immigration, Queer Politics and Hispanisms, Interculturality, and a practicum seminar. Some students also took an elective course: a language course (Spanish) or a course on bilingual education. Miami, a pan-Latinx US city with deep cultural and economic ties to Latin America and a pioneer in bilingual/bicultural education programs, offered students the opportunity to fully immerse themselves in Spanish. The inquiry-driven and transdisciplinary nature of the program made all courses intrinsically linked to one another and facilitated an integrative and collaborative teaching/learning experience that generated a dynamic source of project-based knowledge from which students actively explored real-world problems and challenges, acquiring transferable skills.

The field-based practicum course required students to embed themselves and collaborate as volunteers in local communities. For two days per week over ten consecutive weeks, our fourteen students volunteered for and partnered with social and cultural organizations and mentored youths and children from marginalized neighborhoods. All the students found this experiential opportunity to be a refreshing break from classroom-based learning and felt that direct interaction and engagement with community organizations offered personally meaningful and challenging opportunities to negotiate their racial, ethnic, gender, sexual, and linguistic differences.

As volunteers, they became insiders and learned to respect community organizations' missions and values. Over time, they became less timid as outsiders and more comfortable with and curious about cultural differences.

In the current landscape of higher education, there is an increasing demand for undergraduate students to participate in domestic internships and international experiences. However, for the majority of students in our program, the prospect of dedicating a summer to an unpaid internship or studying abroad was unattainable. During their regular semesters at Wheaton, this was practically unfeasible, as students from high-income households with access to personal vehicles were significantly more likely to take advantage of unpaid internships and to benefit from direct networking and experiential opportunities outside the classroom. Our goal was to provide *all* students with the opportunity to connect with nonprofit organizations aligned with their personal interests, such as teaching, mentoring children through music, social work in BIPOC communities, or supporting victims of domestic violence. The topics discussed in the practicum seminar were primarily focused not on exposing students to the professional world but on how these different organizations support the most marginalized and underrepresented communities in the city of Miami. For us, the experiential/practicum component of our program had a clear activist and awareness-raising objective. Our program aimed to bridge theory with practice, academia with activism. We wanted our students to engage in local activism with the potential for transnational impact, working to fight against capitalism in its current phase of neoliberal globalization.

This experiential component of our program was an important aspect of students' growth as learners, inquirers, and activists. Emerging from marginality and displacement, our students experienced class, ethnic, linguistic, and racial divisions separating Miami's communities, to which they were easily able to apply and connect theories and questions debated in class. The direct application of theory to practice not only opened their eyes to understanding how community relationships and development are shaped, but their appreciation of social equity and cultural diversity also increased. Through this practical component, they learned to shift into the transcultural eccentric subject in Miami, à la de Lauretis. Our students became empowered in their postcolonial feminist subject positions as immigrants and transnationals, and their volunteer work enabled them to engage directly with the poor and immigrant children and women who struggle at the edges of "urban ghettos" and "ethnic enclaves" and with queer communities of Miami. The idea of the transcultural eccentric subject thus served as a powerful pedagogical tool to critique cultural hegemony and to break open normative boundaries that exclude, penalize, and oppress "undesirable" postcolonial subjects. Our purposeful play with the concept of the transcultural eccentric subject, which we applied in our teaching/ learning as an epistemological and pedagogical method enabled our students to adopt a critical study of power matrices and cultural flows shaping public and community spaces of Miami. Rejecting voyeurism, tourism, and consumerism, our students were guided to enter into and to occupy different spaces—museums, art exhibits, public gatherings—through participation, conversation, partnership, dialogue, and activism.

For example, as part of their learning, our students participated in important exhibits and community performances such as *Where the Oceans Meet* curated by Hans Ulrich Obrist, which offered our students a direct engagement with the Martinican philosopher Édouard Glissant's ideas about postcolonialism and transculturality. Our students worked through Glissant's relation identity theory where notions of identity are constructed in relation to people, places, and histories, and his transformative concept of tout le monde that offers a vision of the world where cultural diversity flourishes. It is important to mention how our students immediately established direct connections between Anzaldúa's work discussed in class, particularly her left-handed world, and the concepts of archipelago and *opacité* created by Glissant. This was one of the most evident ways for our students to understand the interconnection between feminism and postcolonialism. They saw that it was not simply a matter of multiplicity or painful differences among subjectivities but rather a matter of power interactions, and how postcolonial feminism can help us understand power and its complex layers in multiple subject positions, demonstrating that the member of a minority culture is not always powerless.

Through talks, videos, literary texts, and paintings, students engaged with Glissant's ideas of shifting and porous borders—geographic, national, cultural, social, racial, ethnic, and linguistic—and how crossing borders has shaped our world. Glissant proposes to read the world as an archipelago open to change, where very diverse parts can also be intimately linked to one another to create something new. According to this archipelagic thinking, culture and identity become positive products of a complex and multiple set of histories and circumstances as long as we approach the specificity of communities as closely as possible to avoid "the danger of being bogged down, diluted, or 'arrested' in undifferentiated conglomerations" (142). Glissant's notion of opacité, a fundamental form of resistance to assimilation and cultural appropriation, was also key to the civic engagement component of our program. The students met personally with writer and intellectual Raphael Confiant, who was Glissant's close colleague and friend and who learned firsthand about his literature and revolutionary vision of the Creolité movement. Glissant's and Confiant's ideas about the powerful and contradictory experience of contact among cultures—acquired in the Interculturality course—served as a theoretical framework to explore other inquiry-based activities that explored the historical legacy of trauma caused by migration, slavery, colonialism, capitalism, and the structural and institutionalized forms of oppression created by these processes.

The conversation with Confiant set the tone for our subsequent readings on culture and language as focal sites of colonial repression and resistance. On this occasion, students read Ngũgĩ wa Thiong'o's "Imperialism of Language: English, a Language for the World" and Anzaldúa's "How to Tame a Wild Tongue" to discuss how language is intertwined with a person's identity and how, by keeping our mother/wild/queer tongues, we can resist and challenge linguistic and cultural oppression. These readings inspired deep discussions and reflections on the importance of preserving minority languages and the need for cultural and linguistic resistance in an increasingly globalized world.

During Miami Art Week 2019, our students encountered the critical works of local and international artists, writers, activists, educators, and community leaders and joined in public dialogues about power and political crisis, conflict, and transition. The panel discussion "Stonewall at 50: What Now?" (held at Art Basel); "Black Talk, Back Talk: Capacities of Criticism" and "Black Art in America" (included in the PRIZM Art Fair); Dick Jay's series of artworks titled *Plantation Island*; and Deborah Oropallo and Andy Rappaport's video *FLIGHT (2019)* (where the consequences of mass migration and global displacement were brought to life) offered artistic spaces to stir student's reflections and understanding of themselves as active individuals and changing agents.

It is also significant that we held all our core classes for the semester at The Bass, which is Miami Beach's premier contemporary art museum. The museum was pried open, figuratively and pedagogically, as a democratizing space in order to *query* and *queer* the conventional institutions—such as the gallery, the curated arts space, the university, and the classroom—where learning focuses on methodologies to decipher how knowledge is produced through conversations about various meanings of "art and design." The optional courses (Spanish courses and bilingual education) with small groups of three and four students were held at the Miami Beach Regional Public Library, where students were able to use its library services and its cultural programming. The open space of the public library enabled them to interact with those from underprivileged backgrounds or without computer access at home. Spanish served as the primary language of communication at the library. The majority of young people using the library were Latinx and Latin American immigrants. Therefore, our students were able to interact with other students, many of whom had received bilingual education in Miami, making the library an invaluable setting for learning Spanish through local immersion while simultaneously gaining insight into the history and implementation of the city's bilingual programs.

By taking liberal arts collegiate classes into the public sphere, our overall aim was not merely to deconstruct ideologies and discourses about *difference*. Nor was it to valorize the right for all individuals to be different. Rather, we experimented with our feminist conception of educational activism—drawing on Gloria Anzaldúa's transborder thinking and practice—with the larger goal of valuing and imagining cultural pluralism and mutual understanding that are so urgently needed in a democratic world. If students are to understand that others' agency and cultures are as important as their own, they would also readily see that multiple and different cultures are not separate or extrinsic from their own or from those of others. Moving beyond the "self–other" and the "own–foreign" binary pitfalls, we wanted to create opportunities for our students to experience the value of hybridity (in the semiotic and symbolic mode of interpretation, à la Bakhtin) and transculturality so that intermixing, entangling, sharing, and crossing over and across difference becomes essential for envisioning, living, and shaping a kinder and more just world.

Feminist Pedagogy in
Disaster and Reconstruction

Hurricane Maria was one among multiple crises that have shaped the physical and social landscape of Puerto Rico. When we visited, the country was changing rapidly as out-migration fueled by unemployment and underemployment on the island led to a constricting school system, long delays in basic services (police, health, and government), and the rapid privatization of public services like electricity. Mutual aid associations were also aplenty, resulting from reduced state involvement in local communities and a general sense of economic uncertainty. Nearly two years after the hurricane, it was clear that colonial history was being played out with a lack of government funding that translated into a continuing neglect of services for women subject to gender-based violence. To understand how persons are emplaced into "positions through practices of political and personal dis-placement across boundaries between . . . bodies and discourses" (de Lauretis 145), two Latinx instructors from Wheaton College (M. Gabriela Torres and Raquel Ramos) and a Puerto Rican instructor from the Pontificia Universidad Católica de Puerto Rico (Waleska Sanabria) co-designed this course in 2019. In *Disaster and Reconstruction: Gender and Post-Hurricane Maria Reconstruction* we asked, how do we learn about the gendered impacts of the social changes compelled by the natural and social disarray post-Maria? Teaching about the impacts of disasters required engaging students with the layers of complexity that can be best done *in situ*. Teasing out the political dimension and historical roots of colonial marginalization (e.g., chronic underfunding of services, extractive and exploitive industries) that was expressed as gender inequities post–Hurricane Maria, we experimented with a collaborative method to teach and learn about the expression of the eccentric subject. To do so, we employed the following practices: (1) a commitment to multiple raced and gendered perspectives engaged through intergroup dialogue that took place with students as we drove home at the end of fieldwork (Zúñiga et al. 2007; Freire 1970); (2) explicit use of evidence-based pedagogy from cognitive theory to make visible the dynamics of culture and gender; (3) the collaborative positioning of the instructor as curator-in-process, where students were able to add and take away from the content; and (4) the activist practice of research service.

The composition of the team as bilingual and transcultural was intentional for teaching with a decolonial goal of working with marginalized populations in mind (Castillo). Working with thirteen intercultural students from our residential liberal arts college, and with four field research students from south-central Puerto Rico, we actively engaged as instructors in conversation using the intergroup dialogue pedagogical feature of the course. Together we conceived of fieldwork as participatory, responsive to community needs, and cognizant of power inequalities. To understand the work of social reconstruction and gender-based violence, the instructors engaged artists, activists, community members, policy makers, and researchers into conversations that were observed and filmed by students. The work of the instructors was curatorial, collaborative, and inspired by the concept of a *fugitive anthropology* envisioned by Berry and her colleagues (Berry et al. 2017). The collaborative knowledge creation put our own perspectives into conversation with those who were working to counter colonial forces through local activism.

To make the dynamics of culture and gender visible, the course employed pedagogy that draws from cognitive theory and the practice of intergroup dialogue to outline for students how knowledge acquired in the field is connected to ourselves as particularly positioned and raced bodies. Specifically, the course relied on James Lang's *Small Teaching* toolkit. We engaged students with structured opportunities to practice reflective writing on field experience with immediate instructor feedback (134), and scaffolded experiences for students to offer self-explanations of their learning and define their fieldwork of choice to peers (156). Student reflections on fieldwork were assigned through prompts that were devised from reading their work and were organized to support the development of their chosen mode for their final project. As an example, filmmakers were asked to transition their reflection toward writing the treatment of their future films and defining which field sites enabled them to better present the visual narratives they envisioned in their work.

Curatorial work of the instructors included organizing and defining site visits: visits with local public intellectuals, the Federal Emergency Management Agency (FEMA), police and court officers, artists, and activists; just-in-time offers of social science methods (interviews, surveys, social service inventories, textual analysis); and exposure to varied cultural performances and installations. The structured juxtaposition of experience coupled with structured reflection, mapping, and regular feedback enabled students to construct different narratives of disaster and reconstruction that can be repurposed by Puerto Ricans toward their own aims in community reconstruction. One example is the production of a twenty-two-minute documentary titled *Aguante* (Resistance), which Dominick Torres (no relation to the coauthor) completed during his course of study.

By their own accounts, this work was both exhausting and expansive for students. They were challenged because they were managing cultural, religious, gender, and linguistic differences and because they were forced to consider uncomfortable realities about their own position as US citizens in a colonial context. In the post–Hurricane Maria Puerto Rican climate, where grass roots became the principal solace of local populations, our role as part of a colonial enterprise was ever present. This positionality was different for students with Puerto Rican, Black, and Anglo-American heritage. For instance, those who had Puerto Rican heritage engaged in a complex process of identification with the dual legacy in their diasporic position and the importance of Spanish in Puerto Rico as compared to mainland Puerto Rican communities. In contrast, the experiences of Black students were often uncomfortable because in Puerto Rico they were dually identified as colonial-adjacent and racially likened to Black Puerto Ricans, who are regularly discriminated against.

Using dialogue and decentering the idea of the epistemic primacy of the academic voice, we worked to decolonize our methods, learning, and teaching to embrace the insight from the uncertainty and discomfort we found in our own reactions. In this effort, an acceptance of the unknown in learning experiences was crucial as knowledge production took place in dialogue with the local activists and not prior to it. Enabling students to reflect on their understanding of persons (including themselves) as they are placed into subject positions (in intergroup dialogues and social mapping) puts into practice what de Lauretis expressed in theory: the subject or self is perpetually in process of becoming.

Concluding Thoughts:
Experiments in the Feminist Classroom

Our main goal was to offer our students and colleagues an educational and advocacy platform that embraced fluidity, multiplicity, and instability as a starting point that not only makes transformation possible but also enables political resistance to oppression. For both courses, the plurality possible in co-teaching and collaboration beyond the classroom were key to bringing activist practices into the classroom and providing students with real-world connections to promote self-reflection, dialogue, and classroom-based activist projects. Collaboration between faculty members, staff, and institutional leaders infused multiple and conflicting perspectives into the framing of course development. Our commitment to partnerships and active collaborations affirmed by mutual respect and shared responsibility was central to building community, resistance, and work that could affect positive social change.

Teaching students to "transgress" the taken-for-granted Western-centric categories and discourses of race, gender, sex, class, and ethnicity is one way to enable them not only to critique power and injustice but also to foster self-reflexive activism that works to reshape the self and the society. hooks understands that this kind of reflexive practice bestows learners with the "gift and practice of freedom," which we find aspirational, and our pedagogical aim is to foster students' self-actualization as citizens of the world—active learners who understand and value the role of activism and resistance in shaping our history and promoting community engagement. If we can facilitate their enactment of agency as learners and citizens, we can impart the kind of education that we aspire to teach in our students and for ourselves. Faculty and instructors also need to experiment with pedagogies for "freedom" through transformative pedagogies, which we think can be delineated in eccentric discursive positions that are sites of resistance and agency. In both courses outlined in this chapter, de Lauretis's conception of the subject's activist resistance to fixity shaped the practice of classroom-based activism: In Puerto Rico students negotiated their identity and the public health need to act through research; in Miami students combined activism and academic work to explore their own experiences and identities to consider how they intersect with the social and political landscapes around them; and in playwriting students negotiated complicated narratives of the self to compose a production that aimed to reshape the narrative of sexual violence. In all cases, students managed their own "un-fixity" and the ways their site for action refused clear definition. In all courses students learned that their activist political positionings have unintended impacts that yield multiple and contradictory perspectives. Importantly, they also learned that taking an activist stance allows different and marginal voices to become crucial elements of the new narratives we can construct to address pressing sociopolitical issues of our time head-on.

Works Cited

Anzaldúa, Gloria. "La Prieta." *This Bridge Called My Back: Writings by Radical Women of Color*, edited by Cherríe Moraga and Gloria Anzaldúa. Kitchen Table: Women of Color Press, 1983, pp. 198–209.

Anzaldúa, Gloria. *How to Tame a Wild Tongue. Borderlands La Frontera: The New Mestiza*. Aunt Lute Books, 1987, pp. 53–64.

Berry, Maya J., et al. "Toward a Fugitive Anthropology: Gender, Race, and Violence in the Field." *Cultural Anthropology*, vol. 32, no. 4, 2017, pp. 537–65.

Castillo, R. Aída Hernández. "Against Discursive Colonialism: Intercultural Dialogues as a Path to Decolonizing Feminist Anthropology." *The Pluralist*, vol. 16, no. 1, 2021, pp. 58–74.

De Lauretis, Teresa. "Eccentric Subjects: Feminist Theory and Historical Consciousness." *Feminist Studies*, vol. 16, no. 1, 1990, pp. 115–50.

Freire, Paolo. *Pedagogy of the Oppressed*. Continuum, 1970.

García, Antonina, and Patricia Sternberg. *Sociodrama: Who's in Your Shoes?* Praeger, 2000.

Glissant, Édouard. *Poetics of Relation*. U of Michigan P, 2006.

hooks, bell. *Teaching to Transgress: Education as the Practice of Freedom*. Routledge, 1994.

Lang, James M. *Small Teaching: Everyday Lessons from the Science of Learning*. Jossey-Bass, 2016.

Ngũgĩ wa Thiong'o. *Moving the Centre: The Struggle for Cultural Freedoms*. Heinemann, 1993.

Robertson, Roland. "Glocalization: Time-Space and Homogeneity-Heterogeneity." *Global Modernities*, edited by Mike Featherstone et al. Sage, 1995, pp. 25–44.

Sandlin, Jennifer A., et al. "Mapping the Complexity of Public Pedagogy Scholarship: 1894–2010." *Review of Educational Research*, vol. 81, issue 3, 2011, pp. 338–75.

Torres, Dominick, director. *Aguante*. Vimeo, 2021, https://vimeo.com/455604003.

Zuniga, Ximena, Biren A. Nagda, Mark Chesler, and Adena Cytron-Walker. "Intergroup Dialogue in Higher Education: Meaningful Learning about Social Justice." *ASHE Higher Education Report* 32, no. 4 (2007): 1–128.

PART III

Organic Collaborations, Collective Feminist Transformations

11

Widening the Circle

Collaborative Learning Within, Between, and Beyond Classrooms

CHRISTINE KEATING

A key insight of both feminist and critical pedagogy is that the classroom can be a place of anti-hierarchical possibility, innovation, and transformation, even within the hierarchical institutionalized settings of the university. Drawing on the work of Paulo Freire, María Lugones, and Ann Russo, this essay explores the possibilities and challenges for building praxical collaborations between teachers and students. In particular, I suggest that experiments in classroom design can help enable processes of anti-hierarchical dialogue and decision making, resistant engagement, and community building in ways that highlight the praxical impact and relevance of feminist learning.

Brazilian educator Paulo Freire is one of critical pedagogy's most influential theorist-practitioners. Work inspired by Freire's writing and praxis has been pivotal in many struggles for liberation around the world. His book *Pedagogy of the Oppressed* is a particularly important text in the development of critical pedagogic praxis. In it, Freire argues for the importance of paying close attention to questions of pedagogy in struggles for liberation. For Freire, education—whether in the classroom or in social movement settings—is profoundly political. He distinguishes between two kinds of education: education as the practice of domination and education as the practice of freedom. In his framing, education as the practice of domination indoctrinates people into the world of oppression by "producing particular subjects: those who will be obedient to authority" (76). Underpinning education as domination is an approach to teaching that Friere calls the "banking method," in which teaching "becomes an act of depositing, in which the students are the depositories and the teacher is the depositor" (72). In this pedagogic interaction, students are trained to obey authority and teachers are trained to think of themselves as those who can and should command obedience. What is particularly pernicious in this approach is that such a training in hierarchy is often cast as benevolent and for the good of the student. Freire notes, however, that "one does not liberate people by alienating them. . . . Those truly committed to the cause of liberation can accept neither the mechanistic concept of consciousness as an empty vessel to be filled, nor the use of banking methods of domination (propaganda, slogans—deposits) in the name of liberation" (51).

In contrast to education as the practice of domination, Freire argues for an education geared to liberation. For Freire, the link between theory and practice underpins such liberation, which he defines as praxis: "the action and reflection of men and women upon their world in order to transform it" (51). Key to education as the practice of liberation is what Freire calls the "problem-posing" approach," in which people "abandon the educational goal of deposit-making and replace it with the posing of the problems of human beings in their relations with the world" (79).

In this framework, instead of banking subject matter into the students, the problem-posing teacher presents material to students and asks them to consider it in relationship to their own knowledge and experience and then "reconsiders her earlier considerations as the students express their own" (82). Indeed, while the banking approach is marked by "monologue, slogans, and communiques" from the teacher, the problem-posing approach is marked by dialogue between the students and the teacher. Knowledge is not something "given" from the teacher to the students; instead, it is something they create together. Through such dialogue, the hierarchical and dichotomized relationship between teacher and student has the possibility of being transformed. According to Freire, "The teacher-of-the-students and the students-of-the-teacher cease to exist and a new term emerges: teacher-student with student-teachers. The teacher is no longer merely the-one-who-teaches, but one who is himself taught in dialogue with the students, who in turn while being taught also teach" (80). Instead of a relationship that acculturates and accustoms both teachers and students to hierarchical ways of being and interacting, the teacher-student relationship becomes one that orients both toward anti-hierarchical modes of interaction and toward praxical modes of knowledge production.

In his account, Freire focuses on how teachers can foster liberatory educational exchanges by rejecting top-down, banking modes of instruction and replacing them with a problem-posing approach. Such a shift, in his description, largely hinges on the ability, the commitment, and the actions of a willing instructor who would both initiate and structure the new liberatory dynamic in the classroom. Less clear, however, is the role that a student might play in initiating or fostering such a shift. Who is the student in the liberatory classroom? What are their possibilities for resistant engagement? María Lugones's essay "Feminist Learning in Academic Contexts: A Paradox" helps to unpack those questions. Reflecting upon the US academy, she explains that teachers and students occupy two sets of roles: one that casts the teacher in the role of an authority figure (within the institutionalized confines of the university) and the student as subordinate and another in which the teacher occupies the role of employee and the student of client. In the authoritarian version of the roles, the teacher is understood as an adult, mature thinker with the responsibility to guide the student, who is in turn understood as a child or immature thinker in need of guidance. In the clientistic version of the roles, the teacher is understood as a professional employee of an institution who provides a valuable service to the institution's customers, its students (30–31).

Lugones notes that that the authoritarian and the clientistic conceptions of the teacher-student relationship are in considerable tension with each other and that their tense interplay depends in part on the political and social positioning of the students and the teachers themselves (31). For example, she writes:

> When a teacher is a radical of sorts and the student is someone who is very successful in and unproblematically "of" the status quo (non-political, etc. . . .), it is the clientistic relation that dominates the "lived" side of the relationship. When the position is reversed, the teacher is unproblematically of the status quo and the student is a radical of sorts, it is the authoritarian side of the relation that dominates. (31)

Lugones highlights the student's agentive (if constrained) role in both of these encounters. In the first scenario, the teacher is pressing for a liberatory praxis that can be hindered or constrained by the student's demand for status quo approaches to the material and pedagogic interaction. In the second scenario, when a student presses for a more radical approach to the subject matter or to the teacher-student relationship, the status quo teacher can use their institutionally backed authority to block such a move.

Lugones calls not for a synthesis of the roles but for a rejection of them. She argues that the role-proscribed nature of the teacher-student relationship conditions how we understand who we are and what we are doing together in the classroom in ways that move against the possibility of feminist learning. When conceptualizing ourselves and each other in terms of the roles prescribed by the university, we meet as teachers and as students in the classroom, "not as people with particular histories, positions in the class system, positions in the racial state; [not] as having faced particular acts of victimization, as having enjoyed particular privileges, as having particular interests, as having participated in particular struggles . . . [nor] as particular individuals moved, for example, by their interest to reconstruct the gender system." Instead of meeting as who we are in all our complexity and difference, and in our liberatory commitment to understanding and challenging inequitable relations of power, teachers and students meet as institutionalized role-players in a restricted encounter that constrains both what the teacher and student can learn from their interaction, as well as the effects it can have on their respective liberatory transformations. Lugones explains that in such situations:

> The student, the institutional customer and the institutional subordinate, comes to learn what the institutional employee and the institutional authority already knows. . . . When the knowledge is "passed on," the knower can remain unchanged with respect to her structure of desires, beliefs, character, etc. and the knowing does not have any practical effects either in the personal life of the learner or the practical life of the learner. (31)

Lugones argues that the project of feminist learning—that is, learning that is committed to the praxical task of "revolutionizing the construction of gender" (30)—is possible only if we meet, not as teachers or students as they are defined in the academy but, in her words, "as resistors, imaginative risk-takers, creators of double visions, creative individuals willing to analyze, question and re-create the gender-system" (33).

As resistors, people are motivated to come together by the desire for particular changes "in oneself, in one's relations to others, and in the socio-political and economic structures that shape one's life with others" (32). Toward these goals, Lugones suggests, both teachers and students can work to turn "hopelessness into hope, powerlessness over our situation into power over it, despair and lack of self-respect into pride and a good sense of one's integration, acquiescence into action, mystification and psychological oppression into active, critical, creative understanding" (32). Feminist thinking in the classroom, as Lugones describes it, is deeply and inextricably praxical. It is, in her words "done in the midst of practice" and "informs practice and is informed by it" (29). The close connection between theory and practice puts feminist thinking in tension with the US academy's institutionalized efforts to separate the two. Given this tension, and the institutionalized challenges that it brings, Lugones concludes her essay by asking, "Can we resist the meaning given to our coming together and to ourselves in the coming together? Can we resist the meaning given to our learning?" (33). For Lugones, answering yes to these questions means that we come together, not as teacher and student but as "companions in resistance," searching together for new ways of interacting, new ways of understanding reality and perceiving the world, and new ways of living.

In her book *Feminist Accountability Disrupting Violence and Transforming Power*, Russo draws on her own thirty years of experience in activist organizations and in feminist classrooms in Chicago to explore the possibilities for a feminist politics of solidarity and accountability. She begins by asking, "What does it take to build movement communities to struggle against the injustices we face and to create the social change we envision necessary for the world in which we want to live—a world with love, liberation, and justice at its center?" (1) In exploring this question, Russo writes about shifting from a position of ally—which implies a privileged position outside of the oppression at hand—to a position of "co-struggler," one that roots solidarity in "people's active participation in collective efforts and struggles to transform oppressive systems, working side by side with those most impacted" (27). She explains that "co-strugglers are compelled to action . . . because we have vested interest in challenging and transforming these systemic injustices because of their profound impact on people's identities, relationships, and communities, including our own" (27).

For Russo, the feminist classroom is an important space for collaboration as co-strugglers. She writes that in "[my] work as a teacher, I seek to create learning spaces where participants—teachers and students alike—can see ourselves individually and collectively as deeply embedded in the systems that we also have a stake in changing" (70). Echoing Lugones's emphasis on the importance of self-transformation to such work, Russo suggests that in learning spaces such as the classroom, we "have the opportunity to remap our identities and affinities and, in turn, to expand the possibilities for building mutuality, for living within an ethic of interconnectedness, and most significantly, for taking accountability for our own role in maintaining and reproducing the power lines that create . . . harm and violence" (68). She calls the approach she takes to building such spaces "embodied pedagogy," meaning "a pedagogy that creates spaces for participants to share, to witness, to cultivate empathy and accountability in response to systemic pain and suffering" (70).

A key component of Russo's embodied pedagogy is the work of challenging the systems—including the systems of knowledge production—that teach those with privilege and power (or who are striving for it) to distance ourselves from the suffering of others. Russo writes that these systems "train us to see ourselves as outside of the situation and as distant and separate from the people harmed and from the structural power lines, inequities, and injustices" that cause harm. With the aim of disrupting such distancing in the classroom, Russo writes that she "encourages students (and myself) to be persistent and consistent in asking ourselves always: How am I feeling about what has happened? How am I impacted by this situation? How am I implicated within the specific situation and in the broader one? How can I act from that location and with the knowledge and perspective of those most impacted?" (76). Dialogic questions like these enable the teacher and students to meet as co-strugglers in the classroom, motivated to work together for change because neither are willing or able "to tolerate the injustices that we experience and witness, that create such pain, sadness, and broken-heartedness, and that are caused by . . . systems of domination" (70).

For Freire, Lugones, and Russo, the classroom is a vexed but important site for radical praxis. Challenging the theory–practice divide in the classroom, for these theorists, in part hinges on reworking the institutionally hierarchicalized roles that student and teacher are expected to play toward the possibility of relations grounded in liberatory dialogue (Freire), in resistant relationality (Lugones), and in deeply felt solidarity and accountability (Russo). The classroom, however, is more than just the potential site of reworked relationships; the space itself can help shape and enable such reworkings. In *Design for the Pluriverse: Radical Interdependence, Autonomy, and the Making of Worlds*, Arturo Escobar argues that when we design spaces, we create "structures of possibility" that engender particular relations and ways of being (111). As such, he notes, design has politico-ontological consequences that can be both constraining and enabling (1). Feminists have long been cognizant of the impact of classroom design for the possibilities of collaborative praxis. Indeed, the paradigmatic model of the feminist classroom design is a circle formation in which no one is at the front of the classroom and no one is at the back. In the rest of this essay, I argue that in addition to being co-learners, co-resistors, and co-strugglers, we become co-designers as well, working to widen and deepen our collaborative feminist learning circles in, between, and beyond the classroom. I will share three examples of such co-designing projects and discuss some of the nuts and bolts of our process.

Co-Designing a Disability Justice Classroom

A disability justice framework shifts questions of access from being an individual responsibility to a collective responsibility (Sins Invalid, 2019). Drawing on work of the Sins Invalid Collective and of the Generative Somatics Disability Justice committee (Bundalli et al. 2018), I have collaborated with students to co-design our classrooms in a way that can foster our collective responsibility for each other's flourishing in the classroom. At the heart of this project is the following question: How can we design a space where we can work toward disability justice by collectively learning about and supporting one another's bodily needs and strengths? Here is how we addressed that question during a Race, Gender, and Technology class.

To begin our discussion, I asked each student to write down their access needs along with any potential ways that we could collectively support those needs as a class (Sins Invalid 30). To give them an example, I shared my hearing loss with the class and explained ways they could collectively support me in the classroom by using (and passing to the next speaker) the remote microphone that streams into my hearing aids. For those who did not feel they had any particular access needs at the moment, I asked them to follow the disability justice practice of saying not that they did not have needs, but rather that their needs were being met at the moment. Such language underscores that a person's access needs may change over time and from place to place.

After everyone finished writing, I asked them to share what they had written (with the option to pass if they were uncomfortable sharing with the group). After hearing from each other, we briefly brainstormed together some initial ways we could design our classroom to be one in which we weave together our needs and strengths in ways that are inclusive, accessible, celebratory, and creative. For our next class meeting, I compiled our access needs and ideas cards into a group list and distributed them to everyone in the class. We then discussed the list in its entirety, with several people adding new needs and ideas to the list. Next, we broke up into groups, supplied with poster board papers and markers, to sketch some possible classroom designs. I urged the groups to feel free to be creative and to include ideas that might seem "impossible" as well as those that might be easier to implement together as a group.

Coming back together as a large group, we shared our designs and collectively decided on ideas to try in our classroom redesign. Our classroom itself presented a challenge as the room was organized with stadium-style tables, ascending toward the back, and the tables were fixed (though the chairs were not). The size of our class was also a challenge: There were also almost fifty of us! In the words of Arturo Escobar, "In modern society we design ourselves, although not under conditions of our own choosing" (117). We did not let these adverse conditions stop us, though, and we made several design interventions, including bringing the chairs from the upper half of the classroom down to the front so as to approximate a circle. It was our hope that such a circle, large and imperfect as it might be, would not only support dialogue in the class but also enable those with hearing loss (it turns out there were a few of us) to see each other's faces more easily. We kept a door and a window open to facilitate the flow of air in the room. We asked everyone not to wear scented perfumes or lotions. We decided to work in small groups as much as possible. We also committed to taking stretch breaks to make sure that people who might need to move could do so. For each class, we designated a notetaker so that if people were sick or had to miss a class for some reason, they could be sure to have a sense of what went on in discussions. Throughout the class we reevaluated and assessed these redesigns, incorporating some new practices and modifying those that were difficult to implement. For example, after a while it became difficult to bring and return all the chairs to the front, so we opted for turning our chairs around to see each other in place. We also had periodic check-ins about our evolving access needs.

By working together to design a disability justice classroom, we were not only able to transform the physical space of our classroom—a transformation we recommitted to every time we turned the chairs toward one another, opened the window, or reminded each other that it was stretching time—we were also able to build a disability justice community in which questions of need and access became a collective responsibility and an opportunity for creative praxis.

Expanding the Classroom Circle

Myles Horton, popular educator and founder of the Highlander Folk School in Tennessee, explains that "during movement times, the people involved have the same problems and can go from one community to the next, start a conversation in one place, and finish it in another" (84). To the extent that we are teaching in "movement times," our classrooms can very much be part of these extended conversations. Indeed, digital pedagogic technologies enable us to link classrooms together across distance, expanding the boundaries of the classroom, challenging the theory-practice diving, and breaking down the barriers between movement-based and academy-based dialogues. I have had the good fortune to be a part of two collaborative teaching collectives that have worked to link classrooms to each other and to broader movements. The first is the feminist technology collective Femtechnet, which takes up questions of digital technology from a feminist and antiracist perspective (femtechnet.org). As part of the work of that collective, we initiated and co-designed a linked course called Dialogues in Feminism and Technoculture, which brought together classes at schools such as Ohio State, the University of California, Penn State, Yale, the University of Toronto, and the University of Washington, as well as in people's living rooms. The class garnered much national attention for its innovative, collaborative approach to large-scale online learning. The second, more loosely organized collective, is the LGBTQ+ learning collective, which brings together teachers and students from across the globe who are interested in sharing resources, ideas, and approaches to learning about LGBTQ+ politics. As part of that collective, Zein Murib, Julie Moreau, and I linked our LGBTQ+ politics classes at Fordham University, the University of Toronto, and the University of Washington, with the goals of learning about LGBTQ+ politics in different regions as well as of generating multi-sited, complex, and energizing conversations, that, to draw on Horton, could be started in one classroom and finished in another.

One of the primary ways that we linked the three LGBTQ+ classrooms was through a LGBTQ+ politics map. On the map, we—students and professors alike—marked a place of importance to our lives (e.g., a hometown, a country of origin, a residence hall, etc.) and shared what we know about LGBTQ+ lives and politics in that place. Because we generated the content of the map ourselves, the LGBTQ+ politics map functioned as a collaborative and participatory tool to learn about each other's contexts. Feminist critical pedagogy scholar Judy Rohrer argues for what she calls an "it's in the room" pedagogical framework that takes up "the power of recognizing that whatever the social justice topic is that we are studying (gender oppression, ableism, racism, colonialism, heterosexism, classism, etc.), it is almost always in the room in some form or another" (577). The goal of the map was to recognize—and create dialogic space for—the different places that we bring into a room when we enter it.

Many theorists and activists have critiqued the Eurocentricity of LGBTQ+ organizing and discourse, highlighting the ways that a focus on Global North organizing in the United States, Europe, and other countries of the Global North both eclipse and obscure the important political work of activists in the Global South as well as non-heteronormative ways of living and relating. Further, there is a related critique of what Mary Gray calls the "metrocentricity" of city-centeredness of LGBTQ+ politics, in which rural spaces are assumed to be outside the purview of LGBTQ+ political engagement, except as places to be left (22). Even though the classrooms in the network were themselves located in large cities in the United States and Canada, many of the students in the classrooms were from all over the world, and many were from small towns and rural spaces. With the help of the LGBTQ+ politics map, we worked to challenge and critically expand the restricted geographical imaginary of much LGBTQ+ political discourse.

In order to build the map, we created a Google Form with several categories that when answered would be linked to a specific marker on the map. We emphasized that students could participate anonymously if they would prefer. The following are the categories that we used:

- Name (if you would like to share it)
- Preferred gender pronouns (if you would like to share it)
- College/University (if you would like to share it)
- Place (this place could be a household, a neighborhood, a region, a city, a country, etc.—be specific as possible!)
- Why is this place important to you?
- What is happening here with respect to LGBTQ+ politics (widely understood)?
- Is there anything else you'd like to add (a picture, a recording, etc.)?

Figure 11.1 shows a screenshot of the map.

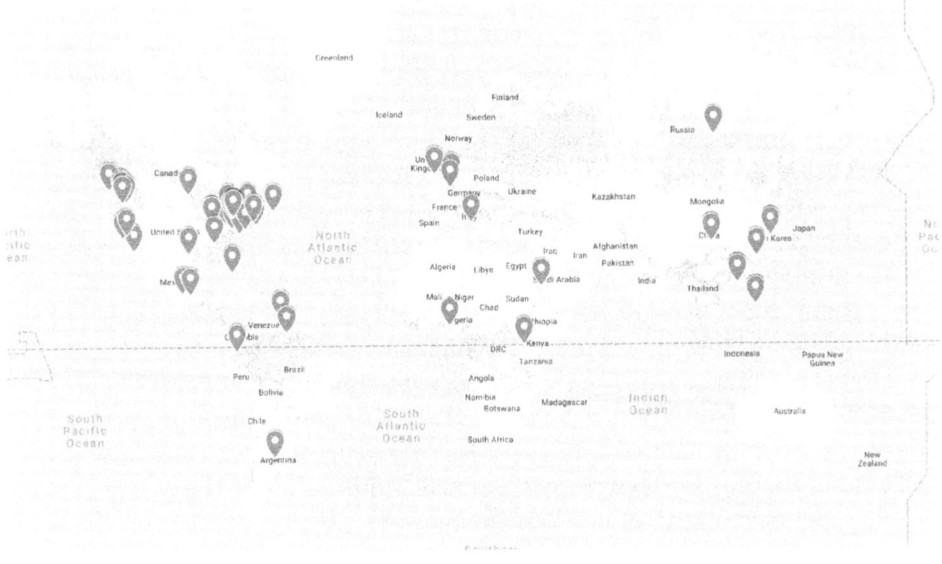

FIGURE 11.1. LGBTQ+ Politics Map. Google Maps (2020), retrieved March 18, 2024, from https://www.google.com/maps/d/u/0/embed?mid=1PLsO_XykkgL d2RKHCtYUjl44JXg&ehbc=2E312F.

Together with our readings, the LGBTQ+ politics map served to ground our class dialogue in the particularities of our contexts. Throughout the course, we would think about the readings in relation to the places we had shared and learned about. The map also served as a basis for one of our assignments: For a response paper, we asked the students to study their classmates' descriptions and write a short paper about what they learned about LGBTQ+ politics from them. We encouraged students to include questions they would like to ask their classmates about their different places. In class we discussed these questions together. In part because of our sharing and learning about each other's responses, not only were we able to have a sense of "movement" discussions that moved across time and space in each other's lives, but also our conversations with one another were grounded in a curiosity about and commitment to each other's places, including places that are all too often assumed to be outside the purview of LGBTQ+ political engagement.

Co-Designing Democracy

A third example of collaborative, praxical engagement comes from a course in which we were exploring approaches to democracy that aim to increase people's direct involvement in decision making about aspects of their own lives. In particular, we were examining Iceland's "crowdsourced" design process in which Icelanders used both face-to-face and social media methods to get broad input from people in order to draft the constitution. Although the Icelandic people approved the new constitution, the final passage of the constitution is stalled in the Icelandic Parliament, blocked in part by political and economic elites whose interests would be challenged by both the content of the new constitution and its participatory, non-elite-led process. There is a vibrant, ongoing movement to keep the constitutional reform process alive, however, with groups such as Stjórnarskrárfélagið (the Icelandic Constitutional Society) and Samtök kvenna um Nýja stjórnarskrá (The Woman's Association for the New Constitution) leading campaigns, protests, and large outreach initiatives to push for its passage. One of the groups working to generate continued momentum for the constitutional reform process is KRIA, which gathers, preserves, and makes digitally accessible materials related to that process in an archive. An exciting aspect of KRIA's work is that it echoes and draws upon an open-ended participatory approach that animated the constitution-writing process. For example, KRIA's organizers host "tagathon" events, where people come together to share, sort, and tag the materials related to the constitutional reform process that they have gathered.

As part of our class's research into this struggle, we had the opportunity to link our classroom to the constitutional reform movement in Iceland by participating in one such event during our class. Such a collaboration gave us the opportunity to experience working side by side on a project that went well beyond the boundaries of our classroom itself. In order to facilitate our collaboration with the archives, KRIA organizers Eileen Jarrett and Ann Lally joined our class to lead us in a tagathon. They brought coffee and doughnuts that the Greater Icelandic Club of Seattle made to celebrate the event. To begin, Jarrett and Lally discussed the importance of the archiving project to both the constitutional reform efforts in Iceland and to struggles for participatory democratic change more broadly. Next, they taught us how to use the crowdsourcing platform Omeka on our computers and cell phones to navigate the collection and tag materials. We then broke up into small groups and Jarrett and Lally distributed lists of videos, newspaper reports, and articles for us to tag. They stressed that our varying experience with and knowledge of the Icelandic constitutional process was not a hindrance to our participation and, indeed, would be helpful in leading others who might be "outside" to the archives. After we were done, the organizers distributed cards on which we wrote messages and asked questions directed to activists in Iceland involved in the constitutional reform movement. These cards were published on KRIA's Facebook page, where Icelandic activists commented on them and responded to questions. The cards themselves will also become part of the archives. Although we ourselves were located in the classroom, our work moved far beyond its boundaries.

Conclusion

The classroom is a constrained but critical site for feminist collaborative praxis. On the one hand, it is all too often a place that habituates us— teacher and students alike—to non-egalitarian modes of learning, being, and relating, a place where hierarchies are both normalized and normativized. On the other hand, the classroom is a place where hierarchies of role and status can be reimagined and reworked. As the works of Friere, Lugones, and Russo underscore, the classroom is a space to practice new ways of relating to one another. Working against the hierarchical grain of those spaces as co-learners, co-resistors, and co-strugglers, we can nurture our skills in egalitarian problem solving and dialogue, learn about each other as companions in resistance, and develop our capacity for mutuality and accountability.

We can also work together to change classroom spaces themselves. As co-designers we can build classrooms that enable our most creative, resistant, and mutually engaged selves. Taking the classroom as a place of relation seriously means that each classroom is different depending on who is present. As such, the practice of collaborative design is crucial—there is no set formula for what a feminist classroom space is; we must talk and think together to figure out what might work best for each other. For example, in describing their approach to what they call "relational organizing," the LGBTQ activist group Southerners on a New Ground (SONG) write, "One of the most common things groups and members say about why SONG is crucial in their lives is the way that SONG can create a space for conversation and community that makes people feel whole, connected, and courageous." They write that working with people to create such spaces is more like alchemy than like chemistry, because "it is different every time" (Page et al.). Indeed, each time we come together in the classroom (either in person or virtually), we have the opportunity to create the space anew, structuring possibilities for collaboration, care, and dialogue among us. Together we can experiment with ideas and practices—trying some on and discarding others—as we try to find the alchemy that best fits who is in the room and what our collective goals might be. In doing so, we can work to build a "room where it happens!"

Works Cited

Bundalli, Fayza, Yashna Padamsee, Danielle Feris, and Wendy Elisheva Somerson. "Bringing a Disability Justice Framework to Generative Somatics Courses." Unpublished document, Generative Somatics, 2018.

Escobar, Arturo. *Design for the Pluriverse: Radical Interdependence, Autonomy, and the Making of Worlds*. Duke UP, 2018.

Femtechnet. http://femtechnet.org. Accessed Jan. 5, 2020.

Freire, Paulo. *Pedagogy of the Oppressed*. Bloomsbury Academic, 2002.

Gray, Mary. *Out in the Country*. New York UP, 2009.

Horton, Myles, with Judith Kohl and Herbert Kohl. *The Long Haul: An Autobiography*. Teachers College Press, 1997.

KRIA: The Icelandic Constitution Archives. http://kriaarchives.com/blog/. Accessed Jan. 5, 2020.

Lugones, María. "Feminist Learning in Academic Contexts: A Paradox." *Breaking Ground*, vol. 13, 1992, pp. 29–33.

Page, Cara, Suzanne Pharr, Paulina Helm-Hernandez, and Caitlin Breedlove. "ALCHEMY: The Elements of Creating Collective Space," Sept. 2019, https://southernersonnewground.org/wp-content/uploads/2019/09/SONG-Alchemy-The-Elements-of-Creating-Collective-Space1.pdf.

Rohrer, Judy. "'It's in the room': Reinvigorating Feminist Pedagogy, Contesting Neoliberalism, and Trumping Post-Truth Populism." *Teaching in Higher Education*, vol. 23, no. 5, 2018, pp. 576–92.

Russo, Ann. *Feminist Accountability: Disrupting Violence and Transforming Power*. New York UP, 2018.

Sins Invalid. *Skin, Tooth, and Bone: The Basis of Movement Is Our People*. 2nd ed. Sins Invalid, 2019.

12

"The Most Real Experience I've Had in a Course"

Disrupting Silences and Cultivating Intimacy

EMILY FAIRCHILD, LEEN ALFATAFTA,
SARA YOUNGBLOOD GREGORY,
and CAROLYN BEER

Students often find their way to feminist classrooms via an awareness of inequity and a desire to better understand and articulate their unease. They are intrigued by courses that promise attention on social forces they have seen affect their lives and those of people around them, though they might not yet know that what they are hungry for is the blend of theory and action that liberatory feminist praxis provides—a learning experience that connects new ways of knowing, personal growth, and action for social change (Freire 79). What follows is a description of one such course, born of frustration, collaboratively facilitated, and with transformational effects. It is the story of how three students and their professor drew back the curtain on the power dynamics that shape the academy and cultivated an intimacy that allowed us to explore uncomfortable realities. It is an example of helping one another find the edges of our understanding and supporting our growth into new ways of knowing (Berger 345–48).

Our institution, a small liberal arts college with individualized plans of study, encourages professors and students to co-create small-group tutorials that are part of faculty's teaching expectations. The four of us collaboratively designed the course Marginalized Identities in Academia in response to disappointment with a campus panel on masculinity in higher education. We attended the discussion with the hope that the conversation would confront the ways the academy is shaped by patriarchal privilege and assumptions.

Instead, the experiences described by the (all cis men) professors on the panel reinforced the connection between masculinity and academia and failed to critique how their proximity to the image of the "ideal professor" served their careers and everyday lives (Hirshfield 205). Not only did we believe the topic demanded additional attention that more accurately emphasized the serious challenges of navigating higher education from different social positions, but we also wanted to develop the course to send a signal to the campus community that an intersectional feminist examination of the question deserved institutional recognition. The students did not have the language to explain these processes at the beginning of the course, but in a matter of just a few months, they developed a rich understanding of the hidden dynamics of knowledge production that inspired them to conduct original empirical research, undertake campus activism, and reflect on the structures that shape undergraduate education through the process of writing this chapter.

Feminist instructors often hope that their courses will be transformative. We want our students to learn more than a defined set of concepts—we want to guide them to develop a critical lens, empower them to apply the material outside of class, and for coursework to encourage active, informed citizenship. Feminist pedagogical literature outlines these goals (Fisher 20; Sandell 181; Shrewsbury 8), gives suggestions for how instructors might achieve them (Bricker-Jenkins and Hooyman 40; Ryan 23; Sandell 182; Winkler 66), and reports on the success or effects of feminist teaching (MacDermid et al. 37; Mahraj 17). We join the conversation by addressing calls for student-professor collaborative learning and extend this work to collaborative writing about learning.

Specifically, we offer *intimacy* as a pedagogical goal that emphasizes emotional connection, trust, and responsibility to others. Intimacy in this sense is an extension of previous attention on emotion in transformative teaching, such as Thompson's teaching with tenderness, "an embodied way of being that allows us to listen deeply to each other, to consider perspectives that we might have thought way outside our own worldviews, to practice a patience and attentiveness that allow people to do their best work, to go beyond the given, the expected, the status quo" (1). This includes both a reunification of the realm of intellect with that of feeling and challenging the binary often imposed in academic spaces that separates emotion from scholarship (Boler 110). We argue that cultivating intimacy enhances learning and beckons intervention in the patriarchal structure of the academy (as well as intervention in whatever inequities are implicated in course material).

Importantly, we did not design the course with the intention of explicitly studying feminist collaboration or pedagogy. Rather, this essay developed organically as we found ourselves sharing reflections on how we were affected. Near the end of the term, we saw the call for papers about transformative feminist collaborations and felt uniquely positioned to contribute a piece that both described and exemplified our collaboration. Our readings on marginalized identities heavily influenced the students to consider their undergraduate status as a dimension that is typically excluded from knowledge production and, therefore, one that should be included in the collection. Our subsequent class meetings included work toward articulating the meaning and outcomes of the connection we shared, ultimately arriving at the concept of intimacy as foundational of our experience. It was a next step, but not a leap, to move from the collaborative work we had done to co-constructing an essay.

In one of our writing sessions, Leen reflected, "This was the most real experience I've had in a course." Her phrasing struck us, and we exchanged examples that fleshed out how we were impacted. It was "real" because it connected to our lives at the college. The students realized that the few faculty members they regularly approached to support campus-wide initiatives or to pressure the administration were untenured faculty from historically marginalized groups. Inadvertently, they were contributing to the uneven distribution of service work and requesting faculty put themselves in precarious positions. We also reflected on authors' narratives around finding appropriate mentorship to overcome racialized barriers (Castro 173–88) and the challenges of service expectations (Pyke 83–95) as related to our future selves. Reading firsthand accounts of scholars' difficult work experiences was eye-opening for the students who were interested in academic careers. "Real" also meant the ability to bring our whole selves to the conversation without intellectual pretense or fear of criticism based on our identities. Throughout, the course brought "realness" in revealing/disrupting the inequities that maintain conventional academic value systems and shifting our understanding of the history of knowledge production. It is our hope that the following pages convey how the collaborative spirit of our meetings—in the context of studying hierarchies in the academy—created an emotional connection that improved our scholarship and transformed our relationships to each other, ourselves, our campus, and our future feminist endeavors.

Our Feminist Classroom

We approached this learning experience committed to engaged pedagogy and the challenge of self-actualization that bell hooks discusses in *Teaching to Transgress* (13–22). We embraced all participants in mind, body, and spirit with the aim of meaningful education that can improve our lives. Each of us came to the course out of concern for how gender, race, and class affect students' and professional scholars' careers in higher education. Moreover, we were all living in this context. We embraced one another's differences and made space for our life histories, thinking through our personal formation as entangled with the social and historical processes ordering the academy. Whereas politics of respectability typically govern academic spaces, in our class we prioritized what bell hooks has called "radical openness." We dwelled in these sites, dissecting conventional expectations and imagining emancipatory alternatives. How might our marginality enable, generate, and sustain these alternatives? What might we learn about inequity in our own community? How might the material inform the students' remaining time in college and future career choices? We took the subject seriously and expected that we would be dealing with difficult material—sexism, racism, ableism, settler-colonialism, classism, and homophobia—that would affect us personally.

We set the stage by being explicit about the critical lens and collaboration the course required: It would give a backstage, or "behind-the-scenes," view of the academy and we would challenge the dominant model of instruction by deemphasizing the professor's role as expert. Moreover, there would be shared responsibility to excite learning rather than an expectation that the professor is responsible for classroom dynamics (hooks, *Teaching* 8). We acknowledged that we brought various racial, gender, sexual, religious, and class positions, as well as different statuses on campus, and committed to respecting those as sources of knowledge while actively working against reproducing the inequities we would study. Establishing these features of the course on the first day grounded us in the shared goal and approach.

We found that speaking of our identities allowed for a rich understanding of the material. Connecting readings to our own lives, we learned about students on campus who were unsupportive of an event about Palestine that Leen had planned and about Emily's experience as the only known lesbian to earn tenure at our college. As one of the first Palestinian students to attend her college, Leen, alongside other Palestinian women from her cohort, regularly mobilized the student body to stand with Palestinians facing settler-colonial dispossession, which often elicited interpersonal and institutional backlash. The ability to share her perspective and be embraced by the group was critical for Leen's definition of our space as feminist. Likewise, it was important that Emily, as the professor, be as willing as the students to disclose details of how her queer identity shaped her career. To ask the students to be vulnerable without the same from the professor risks coercion (hooks, *Teaching* 21) and, in the case of the study of social positions in the academy, missed opportunities for learning.

Practically, we shared the work of constructing the class. In investigating how knowledge production has been policed in ways that keep minority scholars from full participation in the academy, we turned to narratives written by scholars at the margins of the profession—those with minority identities who had been denied opportunities, held to exceptional standards, or not given the support their colleagues received. Emily suggested two core texts: Gutiérrez y Muhs and her coauthors' *Presumed Incompetent: The Intersections of Race and Class for Women in Academia* and De Welde and Stepnick's *Disrupting the Culture of Silence: Women Navigating Hostility and Making Change in Higher Education*. The first presents personal narratives of academic women of color, and the second provides sociological research on patterns of gendered inequality and suggestions for addressing these phenomena on readers' campuses. The students chose which chapters they would read on a weekly basis to build the curriculum according to their interests. For instance, after we discussed a narrative that introduced "other mothering," the group wanted to learn more about students' expectations for personal support from women faculty of color, a racialized and gendered phenomena that frequently increases faculty workload in emotionally drain- ing ways. Their concern for the unrecognized labor that marginalized faculty contribute was also reflected in a desire to learn more about service over- loads—how they are unevenly distributed and recognized among faculty with different identities. While potential directions for future study could be evident during the body of our discussions, we saved time at the end of each session for consideration of connections across readings and decisions about where to go next. The process of planning the subsequent week was a vibrant space for reflection and a tool for synthesizing the material. It also gave the students a sense of empowerment they had not felt in other courses. In addition to the core texts, we all regularly shared articles from *The Chronicle* and InsideHigherEd.com that provided examples of inequity in the professoriate; framing the relevance of articles for our discussions was a way the students enacted their collaborative investigation of the issue. The students also devised their requirements: full participation in discus- sions, reading summaries shared weekly, and an empirical research project that they would present to the campus community. These choices were the result of conversations about the students' shared commitments to student activism—they wanted to use what they learned in the course to engage a material reality on campus in the hopes of contributing meaningfully to their community.

The material we studied enhanced the feminist goals we brought to the course. We thought and talked about how feminist approaches can be used to uncover inequality in classrooms, interactions with colleagues, and institutional procedures. As Nicole Seymour's review of relevant literature on the feminist classroom describes, we worked to flatten hierarchies, validate lived experience, emphasize self-reflection, and empower students to find and use their voices (188). Key to this was centering marginalized voices via the personal narratives in *Presumed Incompetent*. As hooks argues, personal testimony is "fertile ground" for the production of liberatory feminist theory (*Teaching* 70). In this case, women of color telling their stories makes transparent how one might navigate the academic world and can serve as a tool for others (Gutiérrez y Muhs et al. 504). These narratives exposed the structural violence waged against academics from historically marginalized groups and troubled perceptions of academic worlds as egalitarian utopias, isolated from contexts where injustice is more likely to be recognized. In effect, these narratives insist not only that configurations of power permeate academic worlds but also that the two are intimately connected and co-produce one another. The testimonies are both models (and warnings) for other academics navigating similar terrain, and in naming the inequities, their publication is itself an act of resistance. We felt solidarity with the authors of the pieces we read and were inspired to investigate how the phenomena we studied might occur on our campus. Examining patterns of discrimination, implicit biases, and microaggressions strengthened our commitment to creating spaces where all voices were heard and respected. We could not read of these experiences without a keen awareness of how we might reproduce similar phenomena in our classes and advising relationships.

We therefore mobilized to collect systematic data. The empirical research project the four of us designed was a way to make a theory-practice link that was consistent with feminist scholarship. Our discussions of unequal service burdens on women and people of color (Castro 174–75; Harley 21; Pyke 83), the emotional labor expected of these faculty (Baldwin and Griffin 59–60; Bellas 97; Kupenda 22–23), and contrapower harassment (Lampman 241) led the group to become curious about how the formal advising system at our college was constructed and how the labor was distributed among faculty. All professors at our college are also advisors. While there is administrative effort to distribute them evenly, students can choose advisors, and there is great variation in the resulting relationships, ranging from minimal semesterly contact to close mentor-mentee relationships. What their goals are, and how they are accomplished, are developed by the student and faculty member on an individual basis, meaning all advising relationships are unique. The students became interested in how this work might be unevenly experienced. Specifically, advising likely takes an emotional toll on those faculty who are especially invested in their students' well-being, academic participation, and career path and those who have greater numbers of advisees. Moreover, these are professors who are likely to occupy marginalized social positions vis-à-vis gender, race, and sexuality. We designed a study to examine faculty advising behaviors and emotional investment in their advising relationships via a campus-wide survey sent to all faculty. Sara and Leen presented the findings, including analysis by race and gender, in an open campus forum. It is notable that we could not complete data collection and analysis during our semester. However, the team continued to work on this project for an additional year, and to facilitate community discussions, without course credit. We view our efforts as a political exercise informed by a feminist ethic of care and inspired by the scholars' narratives we studied.

Thus far we have presented a brief overview of how our roles in the course, the material we studied, and the theory-practice link were a manifestation of feminist pedagogy. In what follows, we describe the intimacy we cultivated and the transformations we experienced in order to demonstrate the power of student-professor collaborations that disrupt cultures of silence around power inequities in academe.

Intimacy: Embracing Rich Interpersonal Connections

A deeper level of sharing and a willingness to reveal aspects of ourselves made it possible to get to know each other in ways not typically available in the classroom. Each meeting began with informal conversation about our school and personal lives. We supported one another's pursuits by offering resources we thought would be helpful for other coursework and attending campus events that we each sponsored. These efforts, including time spent together outside the classroom, built trust that made us able to deal with difficult material in an honest way. In knowing one another well, we could better help incorporate new understandings into our conceptions of ourselves and ideas about what we wanted from our experiences in college. Moreover, our substantive focus required that we critically examine our own context. Our readings and discussions alerted us to patterns we had taken for granted. Untenured faculty, despite having a more demanding workload, were primarily the ones performing service work. Similarly, at a time when campuses across the United States were undergoing a reckoning with histories of anti-Blackness and Indigenous genocide brought about by the Black Lives Matter movement and the Dakota Access Pipeline protests, the handful of faculty of color on our predominantly white campus were assumed to lead the work of repair. In this way, we believe our personal connections supplied a footing for self-actualization (hooks, *Teaching* 15–21). We would not let each other get away with avoiding challenging opportunities for growth.

Our approach to one another was consistent with hooks's description of a love ethic that utilizes "care, commitment, trust, responsibility, respect, and knowledge" (*All About Love* 94). Further, we identified comradeship and confidentiality as key aspects of what it meant to apply a love ethic to the classroom, ultimately conceiving of what we shared as *intimacy*. There is a particular kind of closeness that develops when studying topics that directly engage shared oppression. Our class material consistently reminded us of the pressures working against those identities we carry, and we shared examples of how they affected us personally. We could be vulnerable due to our trust in the group and understanding that, though our positions were diverse, they were linked in their marginalization from the dominant model of the academy. Thus, we were jointly fighting oppressive forces as we strategized how to have successful academic careers as women and sexual, racial, and religious minorities.

Our intimacy was a foundation for our learning. Usually, when we share our experiences regarding our encounters with systems of oppression, we are met with pushback from those whose privilege is made apparent. This frequently turns the classroom into a battlefield, where our words are met with aggression, or a graveyard, where we are silenced. Comradeship, confidentiality, and trust made our course unique because it de-weaponized the conversations. In classrooms we had previously experienced, we entered conversations critically disengaged because we found reification of structural hierarchies. Here, we no longer had to worry about justifying our lived experiences, qualifying our marginalization with explanations or proof, or fighting for validation. We found solidarity and mutuality that redressed the troubles we encountered in our other learning spaces. The purpose was no longer defensive or combative; it was inquisitive and collaborative. We recognized that our discussions brought us closer to the "edge of knowing" (Berger 338). The edge is a space for growth, not rebuttal; it is a space to unpack the limits of our knowledge and push the boundaries. When we did that, we also followed Berger's advice of being "good company at the edge" (347). This meant acknowledging the difficulty of arriving at this new unknown territory, offering support in the form of affirmation and thought-provoking questions, collective reflection, and laying bare the complexities to build new possibilities together.

Identifying and speaking of our relationships were part of our collaboration. We regularly acknowledged that we were fighting oppressions from varied angles with varied amounts of power and that what we shared to this end was confidential. This allowed the professor and students to be vulnerable with the recognition that their experiences are situated differently in the institution. One is not closer to the truth, but together they provide multiple perspectives that lead to a richer understanding, moving us all closer to hooks's goal of self-actualization and connecting "the will to know with the will to become" (*Teaching* 19). The classroom model that relies on hierarchy and transmission of knowledge produced by others disavows such emphasis on emotional connection and shared pursuits. We therefore see claiming the concept of intimacy in relation to learning as a feminist act that acknowledges—and embraces—the personal connections among students and professors that lead to collaborative learning.

Transformations: Learning, Becoming, and Connecting

We believe the intimacy of the class, through its emphasis on mutual vulnerability and collective well-being, resulted in a transformative experience and led to radical interconnections within our group and regarding our faculty-student relationships broadly. Normative, hetero-patriarchal frames shape most classrooms. Interconnections among and between professors and students are expected and often encouraged, as long as they uphold the hierarchies—raced, gendered, tenured, or otherwise—according to which academia was designed. Our radical interconnections, however, intentionally disrupted hierarchy as we centered marginalized voices, crossed and questioned the boundaries of professional status, critiqued disciplinary tactics guised as "collegial" comportment, and allowed expertise to be told firsthand by the authors we read and by each other. We extended these connections beyond our small group: sharing our awareness of campus power dynamics and acting as agents of change within our institutions by launching a faculty-wide survey on the formal advising system and sharing our results with administrators, faculty members, and students. We also left as transformed learners, excited to cultivate and model connections across social positions in our future pursuits.

Before giving examples of these, however, we want to note that becoming coauthors on this project was in itself a recasting of traditional power roles in academic scholarship. As a group, we put ourselves in equal roles of responsibility, scholarship, and authority when writing this essay, which we also view as an example of a radical interconnection that resulted from our class. None of us intended to embark on a writing project about pedagogy. Rather, this essay is an unplanned result of feminist pedagogy. That is, Leen, Carolyn, and Sara were motivated to share what they learned. We acquired "knowledge we aren't supposed to have" about the realities of marginalized scholars, yet it was knowledge that improved our studies and lives and informed our career choices. We wondered, Why haven't undergraduates been more involved in these kinds of conversations?

Though feminist teaching empowers students in the classroom, most published work on feminist pedagogy lacks student voices (Seymour 190). Instructors write about the possibilities of feminism for improving education (see Salazar 136; Sandell 185), or their own transformative experiences (Colwill and Boyd 226–27; M. Wallace 184), or they offer directions for employing feminist principles (Carter; Crabtree and Sap 135; Magnet 10; Scanlon 9), but we rarely hear from students outside of their campus spaces. Where student voices are included as authors (rather than being reported by instructor-authors), they are current or former graduate students (Chow et al. 260; Grauerholz and Copenhaver 319). These pieces often reflect on experiences planned by the professor (Chow et al. 260) or are collaboratively designed in order to write about the process of collaboration (Pileggi et al. 34). It is significant that the effects reported here were identified and described by undergraduate student authors to communicate to others how our practice of cultivating intimate learning transformed us. As students, we resist the idea that there is an appropriate age or educational level to begin practicing radical pedagogy. We invite instructors not only to consider what knowledge might remain inaccessible to undergraduates but also to seek opportunities to build intimacy that would allow exploration of guarded topics.

Awareness of Identity-Based Power Dynamics

The first way we note that we were transformed by the class is most directly linked to the class material: we developed an awareness of how identities shape power dynamics at play in campus interactions. We began to appreciate nuance within the category of "professor" and to better understand the ways in which inequality can manifest. For example, Leen, whose campus job required her to attend all-campus faculty meetings, began noticing how issues of seniority, tenure status, gender, and parental status affected who attended, who spoke, and the content of their comments. As she witnessed motions made and votes taken, she directly observed how the most powerful faculty can build campus policy that serves their circumstances.

We also learned about professorial appointments, responsibilities, and institutional power. It was quickly evident that the tenure process had been a mystery to the students, including teaching/research/service expectations. In fact, Leen, Carolyn, and Sara reported confusion about the meaning of tenure and academic ranks altogether. The insight we gained helped us appreciate the pressures on our professors and understand that they do not always have the job security we might assume. Carolyn, a Spanish major, realized she had significantly benefited from the work of adjunct faculty. She previously had not understood this status or the way it differed from other faculty. Recognizing that the status of professor is not homogeneous not only helps students gauge professors' responsibilities and level of institutional influence; it also exposes their precarious status as university workers.

We believe that our connections to our professors were enhanced by gaining this awareness. Learning that the role of the professor involves more than teaching helps students understand the time constraints professors are working under, which in turn helps them develop more realistic expectations of their professors when it comes to grading speed, requests for letters of recommendation, and after-hours correspondence. We developed increased compassion for how life circumstances, relationships with colleagues and students, and the structure of the college affects professors' ability to do their job. For instance, Sara became aware that she previously held expectations of her advisor that focused on the work she expected the advisor to do for her without proper consideration of the advisor's time and other commitments the advisor may have had as a professor and parent. This stemmed from seeing her advisor as a mother figure while also not accounting for the fact that she *was* a mother. With a better understanding of her advisor's workload, and how being seen as a mother figure likely increases that load, Sara adjusted her expectations and behavior. Learning about this as students who experience marginalization made us feel closer to minoritized faculty. While they navigate different bureaucracies, the potential for alienation and feeling overwhelmed are similar. Our "backstage" knowledge gave us common ground for connecting as more than students and professors but as individuals resisting a system hostile to divergence from the white male professorial ideal.

Shifting Identities

Our newfound awareness catalyzed a shift in our identities from learners to activists and allies for marginalized professors, students, and staff on campus. As we studied examples of minority faculty being presumed incompetent (Douglas 57–58; Kupenda 22; Lugo-Lugo 43–44; Wallace et al. 428–36), we were moved to actively intervene when witnessing behavior or talk that we know contributes to images of incompetence. This was a conscious transformation in which we began to think of ourselves as "co-conspirators" in a movement to combat silence around issues of identity and power on our campus.

The students found themselves doing consciousness-raising, both on and off campus. When students complained about faculty not participating in evening club events, they reminded their peers that faculty have a range of professional and personal commitments that might keep them from attending, despite supporting their causes. Upon hearing advisors referred to as "my second mom" and "everybody's mom," Leen explained the concept of "other-mothering," the gendered and racialized nature of this behavior, and how it keeps some faculty from professional advancement. Realizing that students play a role in the tenure process via course evaluations and review letters inspired a sense of responsibility to take action by informing our peers about the gravity of our feedback. We were moved to stand in front of our classes at the end of the term and encourage our peers to write thoughtful comments that would be helpful for evaluation committees. We formed connections with other students as we taught them about how our lives as students are situated in an institution designed for white, male, able-bodied workers who are not required to devote significant amounts of time to caregiving—or to proving they are competent experts in their field. We encouraged other students to increase their awareness of power inequities on a daily basis and make visible the ways our institution may disadvantage or devalue the labor of professors with marginalized identities.

We also saw allyship in our newly recognized responsibility to participate in hiring and review processes. Our college was undergoing significant growth, and we had more than fifty job candidates on campus the year following our course. We went to job talks and asked questions of the candidates. We saw participation in faculty searches as a civic responsibility and encouraged others to attend talks, meet with candidates, and give the hiring committees feedback, particularly involving how candidates could contribute to a more diverse campus community. Further, we wrote letters for tenure files, something we had not considered doing in the past.

Taken together, as co-conspirators we strengthened our connections with faculty, helped other students consider how they relate to faculty, and became better connected to the college as an institution. We felt accomplished as agents of positive change affecting the systems of inequality we had been studying.

Knowledge We Are Not Supposed to Have

In all, we have come to see our enhanced awareness of campus inequities as a type of knowledge we are not supposed to have—a knowledge that provides an opportunity for political change. Through our course we were able to interrogate the configurations of power underpinning the formal advising system at our university. The uneven distribution of labor reflected the gendered and racialized sensibilities often invoked in our course readings. The insights we gained mobilized us. We were empowered to disrupt the culture of silence that ignores the way the academy is a gendered and racialized organization in favor of purporting to be a meritocracy (De Welde and Stepnick 11–14; Harris and Gonzalez 1–2).

Our writing this essay is one form of this political action; it is an opportunity for students to be part of an inclusive scholarly team and contribute to the academic conversation. We see this essay serving as a bridge connecting the graduate students and faculty already writing about these issues with folks at earlier career stages who could benefit from considering the power dynamics of the profession. It is our hope that our story will encourage others to offer graduate and undergraduate courses that directly address inequities in higher education. To Freire, critically examining one's contextual reality is essential for education to truly become a practice of freedom (140). We all deserve to understand the power dynamics shaping our lived experience so that we can help each other survive and thrive in academia.

A second type of knowledge we gained is about the type of learning that challenges student-professor hierarchies around knowledge creation. Though we entered with "feminist" identities, we now identify as "feminist learners" who are capable of working *with* faculty in the pursuit of transforming the material conditions of higher education. We typically do not have opportunities to get to know professors beyond their formal role as authority figures (when we do, it is often because they have invested uncompensated labor in supporting our co-curricular activities). We practiced a feminist ethic of care by jointly investing in and laboring toward each other's well-being, which allowed for critical growth not found in other courses, even at our very progressive liberal arts college. Our narrative is a testimony to how student-faculty collaborations go beyond learning and teaching but are also sites "for creating the personal relationships, networks, knowledge base, and skills required to build solidarity and enact change in the U.S. higher education system" (Steffen 24).

Conclusion

Our experience taught us that we can all be members of a community committed to collaborative search for truth and to acting in solidarity with marginalized groups—within and beyond the academy. Prior to the course, we did not have the same feeling of agency, responsibility, or activism in our education. This class felt meaningful to us as learners because we were able to direct our course of study and see the impact of our education. The course has had a particularly long-lasting impact, and we continue to work together to apply both our knowledge and our feminist-learner approach in professional settings. We believe our experience confirms the effects of feminist pedagogy that many writers expect, and we offer this essay as a personal narrative informing the project of liberatory feminism, one that adds intimacy as a critical component of pedagogy.

The interconnections resulting from this experience have a broad range and wide reach. We obviously developed connections with one another; we were co-creators of our learning process and of the resulting activism. We also created a forum for community building and discussion around advising. The presentation of our research was well-attended and involved discussion among students, faculty, and administrators about how gender and race can affect advising relationships. This is an example of the connection we made with our institution as well. As we learned about the structure of higher education, we employed our feminist perspective to become active participants in college-wide initiatives. Finally, but not of least importance, this course resulted in connecting us with other feminist scholars. We felt as if a curtain had been lifted on how universities function and what it is like to be a professor. As members of this community, why hadn't anyone shared this information with us before? We see tremendous power in exposing undergraduates to personal narratives and scholarship on inequalities in higher education, as well as in allowing us to be part of this conversation.

It is this filling in of silences that led us to discover the transformative power of intimacy in education. We encountered traces of these silences when we attended the masculinity panel. The traces became the substance of our line of inquiry, which prioritized counter-narratives emanating from the margins of the academy. Centering personal experiences gave us insight into the hierarchies that shape our lives as students and professors and created a context for a particularly deep connection. In disrupting the culture of silence in higher education, we discovered the power of extending vulnerability to intimacy. Intimacy involves a sense of togetherness that is not captured by vulnerability's confessional mode. Intimacy nurtures mutual stakes, mobilizing a desire to address harm and an impulse for repair.

We would like to conclude with two notes about how the topic and size of our course relate to its applicability. While we focused specifically on the social position of women of color and higher education, the course topic does not have to be so obviously connected to students and professors for the relationships in the group to benefit from a shared sense of learning about what they "aren't supposed to know." We hope that instructors will not only consider how the structure of the academy obscures inequalities that affect students' learning experiences in the ways we have noted but also that they will examine the myriad cultures of silence specific to their fields and campuses. As instructors invite collaboration and connection across status, they challenge the power dynamics dominant in the academy. In this way, the intimacy we propose is a method of approaching one's role as professor and relating to students that can be applied in larger classes as well. Continued exchange about these practices and outcomes will further develop intimacy as a collaborative achievement that stretches current ideological limitations on how academia should function.

Works Cited

Baldwin, Candice, and Monica Griffin. "Challenges of Race and Gender for Black Women in the Academy." De Welde and Stepnick, pp. 55–66.

Bellas, Marcia. "Emotional Labor in Academia: The Case of Professors." *Annals of the American Academy of Political and Social Science*, vol. 561, 1999, pp. 96–110.

Berger, Jennifer Garvey. "Dancing on the Threshold of Meaning: Recognizing and Understanding the Growing Edge." *Journal of Transformative Education*, vol. 2, no. 4, Oct. 2004, pp. 336–51.

Boler, Megan. *Feeling Power: Emotions and Education*. Routledge, 2004.

Bricker-Jenkins, Mary, and Nancy Hooyman. "Feminist Pedagogy in Education for Social Change." *Feminist Teacher*, vol. 2, no. 2, 1986, pp. 36–42.

Carter, Angela. "Teaching with Trauma: Disability Pedagogy, Feminism, and the Trigger Warnings Debate." *Disability Studies Quarterly*, vol. 35, no. 2, 2015, https://doi.org/10.18061/dsq.v35i2.4652.

Castro, Corrine. "Characteristics and Perceptions of Women of Color Faculty Nationally." De Welde and Stepnick, pp. 173–88.

Chow, Esther Ngan-Ling, et al. "Exploring Critical Feminist Pedagogy: Infusing Dialogue, Participation, and Experience in Teaching and Learning." *Teaching Sociology*, vol. 31, no. 3, 2003, pp. 259–75.

Colwill, Elizabeth, and Richard Boyd. "Teaching without a Mask? Collaborative Teaching as Feminist Practice." *NWSA Journal*, vol. 20, no. 2, 2008, pp. 216–46.

Crabtree, Robbin, and David Sapp. "Theoretical, Political, and Pedagogical Challenges in the Feminist Classroom: Our Struggles to Walk the Walk." *College Teaching*, vol. 51, no. 4, 2003, pp. 131–40.

De Welde, Kristine, and Andi Stepnick, eds. *Disrupting the Culture of Silence: Confronting Gender Inequality and Making Change in Higher Education*. Stylus Publishing, 2015.

Douglas, Delia. "Black/Out: The White Face of Multiculturalism and the Violence of the Canadian Academic Imperial Project." Gutiérrez y Muhs et al., pp. 50–64.

Fisher, Berenice. "What Is Feminist Pedagogy?" *Radical Teacher*, no. 18, 1981, pp. 20–24.

Freire, Paulo. *Pedagogy of the Oppressed*. Continuum, 2007.

Grauerholz, Elizabeth, and Stacey Copenhaver. "When the Personal Becomes Problematic: The Ethics of Using Experiential Teaching Methods." *Teaching Sociology*, vol. 22, no. 4, 1994, pp. 319–27.

Gutiérrez y Muhs, Gabriella. Afterword. Gutiérrez y Muhs et al., pp. 501–4.

Gutiérrez y Muhs, Gabriella, et al., editors. *Presumed Incompetent: The Intersections of Race and Class for Women in Academia*. Utah State UP, 2012.

Harley, Debra. "Maids of Academe: African American Women Faculty at Predominately White Institutions." *Journal of African American Studies*, vol. 12, no. 1, 2008, pp. 19–36.

Harris, Angela, and Carmen Gonzalez. Introduction. Gutiérrez y Muhs et al., pp. 1–16.

hooks, bell. *All about Love: New Visions*. William Morrow, 2000.

hooks, bell. *Teaching to Transgress: Education as the Practice of Freedom*. Routledge, 1994.

Hirshfield, Laura. "Not the Ideal Professor: Gender in the Academy." De Welde and Stepnick, pp. 205–14.

Kupenda, Angela Mae. "Facing Down the Spooks." Gutiérrez y Muhs et al., pp. 20–28.

Lampman, Claudia. "Gender Differences in Faculty Responses to Contrapower Harassment." De Welde and Stepnick, pp. 241–52.

Lugo-Lugo, Carmen. "A Prostitute, a Servant, and a Customer-Service Representative: A Latina in Academia." Gutiérrez y Muhs et al., pp. 40–49.

MacDermid, Shelley, et al. "Feminist Teaching: Effective Education." *Family Relations*, vol. 41, no. 1, 1992, pp. 31–38.

Magnet, Shoshana, et al. "Feminism, Pedagogy, and the Politics of Kindness." *Feminist Teacher*, vol. 25, no. 1, 2014, pp. 1–22.

Mahraj, Katy. "Dis/Locating the Margins: Gloria Anzaldua and Dynamic Feminist Learning." *Feminist Teacher*, vol. 21, no. 1, 2010, pp. 1–20.

Pileggi, Victoria, et al. "Becoming Scholars in an Interdisciplinary, Feminist Learning Context." *Feminist Teacher*, vol. 26, no. 1, 2015, pp. 29–52.

Pyke, Karen. "Faculty Gender Inequity and the 'Just Say No to Service' Fairy Tale." De Welde and Stepnick, pp. 83–95.

Ryan, Jennifer. "Writing the World: The Role of Advocacy in Implementing a Feminist Pedagogy." *Feminist Teacher*, vol. 17, no. 1, 2006, pp. 15–35.

Salazar, María del Carmen. "A Humanizing Pedagogy: Reinventing the Principles and Practice of Education as a Journey toward Liberation." *Review of Research in Education*, vol. 37, 2013, pp. 121–48.

Sandell, Renee. "The Liberating Relevance of Feminist Pedagogy." *Studies in Art Education*, vol. 32, no. 3, 1991, pp. 178–87.

Seymour, Nicole. "The Interests of Full Disclosure: Agenda-Setting and the Practical Initiation of the Feminist Classroom." *Feminist Teacher*, vol. 17, no. 3, 2007, pp. 187–203.

Shrewsbury, Carolyn. "What Is Feminist Pedagogy?" *Women's Studies Quarterly*, vol. 21, nos. 3/4, 1993, pp. 8–16.

Steffen, Heather. "Inventing Our University: Student-Faculty Collaboration in Critical University Studies." *Radical Teacher*, vol. 108, no. 1, May 2017, pp. 19–27.

Thompson, Becky. *Teaching with Tenderness: Toward an Embodied Practice.* U of Illinois P, 2017.

Wallace, Miriam. "Beyond Love and Battle: Practicing Feminist Pedagogy." *Feminist Teacher*, vol. 12, no. 3, 1999, pp. 184–97.

Wallace, Sherri, Sharon Moore, Linda Wilson, and Brenda Hart. "African American Women in the Academy: Quelling the Myth of Presumed Incompetence." Gutiérrez y Muhs et al., pp. 421–38.

Winkler, Barbara Scott. "Raising C-R: Another Look at Consciousness-Raising in the Women's Studies Classroom." *Transformations: The Journal of Inclusive Scholarship and Pedagogy*, vol. 8, no. 2, 1997, pp. 66–85.

13

Facilitating Feminist Collaborations in Undergraduate Education

Models for Research and Internships in Gender and Women's Studies

LETIZIA GUGLIELMO, JORDYN ALDERMAN, JEREMY HALL, BRAYDEN MILAM, and ANDREA PUTALA

In her 1987 article "What Is Feminist Pedagogy?" Carolyn M. Shrewsbury identifies feminist pedagogy as "a crucial component of a feminist revolution" (13), with classroom practices grounded in engagement, reflection, and activism (6). Teacher-scholars have continued to engage in, expand, and apply to a growing number of contexts the liberatory, decentered, and activist potential of feminist pedagogical strategies and theories, demonstrating how students take more active roles in and responsibility for their own and their peers' learning and identifying opportunities for applying that learning outside of classroom settings. Within these teaching and learning environments, feminist pedagogy is quite often supported by collaborative classroom practices that may find their foundations in consciousness-raising groups associated with feminist activism and by feminist rhetorical strategies like intervention and interruption that highlight and amplify marginalized voices and perspectives (Crabtree, Sapp, and Licona; Byrne; Chick and Hassel; Ewell; Guglielmo; Hassel, Reddinger, and van Slooten; Reynolds; Rinehart; Ryan).

Developing as a separate pedagogical thread within higher education and connected to Ernest L. Boyer's call for more engaged undergraduate education in the early 1990s, high-impact learning practices (HIPs) have grown across colleges and universities, facilitating experiential learning experiences that move student learning outside of the traditional classroom. According to the Association of American Colleges and Universities (AACU), HIPs may include first-year experiences, learning communities, writing-intensive courses, collaborative assignments and projects, undergraduate research, service learning, community-based learning, internships, and capstone courses and projects, with the goals of "increas[ing] rates of student retention and student engagement." Notably, various studies also identify increased "student-reported learning gains" in key areas among those who participate in undergraduate research opportunities, especially for first-generation college students and students from minoritized or underrepresented groups (Berkes; Lopatto; Sell, Naginey, and Stanton; DeCosmo). Research further indicates that combining two or more HIPs, including collaborative approaches or work in teams, positively impacts students' integrative learning, "enabling college students to gain understanding across the disciplines so that they may address the challenges and complexities facing an increasingly complex and globalizing world" (Mumford, Hill, and Kieffer 28).

In truth, as Karen Bojar and Nancy A. Naples write in the introduction to their collection, *Teaching Feminist Activism*, gender and women's studies and experiential education have long been connected, supporting academic programs in the discipline with "activist-oriented pedagogical strategies" (2). Michele Tracy Berger and Cheryl Radeloff explore the challenges that gender and women's studies students often face in articulating how and why this work is relevant and meaningful outside the classroom. Fully capturing this theory-activist link, the authors argue, "Students pursuing questions in women's and gender studies are part of an emerging vanguard of knowledge producers in the US and globally . . . trained to consider how their efforts in the classroom can be translated to affect the status of women and men (and anyone outside the gender binary) beyond the borders of their college or university" (5). As teacher-scholars in the discipline are aware, graduates who enter professional fields with gender studies coursework are better positioned to foster diversity, equity, and inclusivity in the workplace and in their communities (Colatrella). In addition to the language and strategies Berger and Radeloff provide on how to apply learning outside of classroom contexts, they invite students to identify as "change agents," defined as "an undergraduate who has strong experiential learning capabilities and a commitment to public engagement beyond the borders of the academic classroom" (25).

Responding to Naples and Bojar's call "to take up the challenge of teaching feminist activism experientially," in the pages that follow we share and reflect on three models for undergraduate research and internships and argue that when these HIPs are created with collaborative inquiry as a primary objective and guided by a decentered feminist pedagogy in which students are coequal teachers and knowledge creators, such projects have the potential to foster increased activism and engagement among undergraduate students and to support the "change agency" Berger and Radeloff describe. In the sections that follow, we, as former undergraduate students and as the instructor, reflect on our experiences engaging in HIPs and the ways they facilitated feminist collaborations that shaped both our learning and future work.

Undergraduate Research and High-Impact Practices

Letizia: As a teacher-scholar of writing and rhetoric and gender and women's studies, I have blended HIPs into my pedagogy across disciplines for many years, including through collaborative learning, reflective writing, writing-intensive courses, and, later, through undergraduate research projects funded and supported by my university. In 2016 I was invited to serve as editor-author for a two-volume reference set exploring misogyny in American culture to include both long-form essays and short case studies on the topic. Having previously worked with students on smaller undergraduate research projects, I envisioned an undergraduate research component of the book project from the beginning as a way to support students in deliberately applying feminist theory outside the classroom. I approached the early stages of planning for the book project with an interest in and a rough idea of what undergraduate research might look like. Because I was regularly teaching in our Gender and Women's Studies (GWST) program, specifically a course on gender in popular culture, I also knew I could invite a collaborative team of undergraduate researchers to contribute to this work.

A growing body of research identifies undergraduate research projects as HIPs that can significantly shape student learning and engagement. Undergraduate research typically includes "student participation with faculty in research and creative projects that are not associated with any lecture course" (Berkes 2) and can bridge the gap between classroom learning and real-world application. According to Richards and colleagues, "When students are effectively mentored in undergraduate research and creative activity they report ownership of the work, a deep sense of satisfaction, and high levels of self-efficacy" (5). One significant facet of projects like these, according to the AACU, is their ability to "involve students with actively contested questions." Grounded in gender and women's studies scholarship, one of this project's primary goals included expanding and complicating definitions of misogyny, a timely and contested topic given the political and cultural climate and use of the term *misogyny* by various media outlets during and after the 2016 presidential election. Within this context, participation in the project allowed undergraduate researchers to contribute to and inform public conversations on misogyny and would move the work of their GWST courses outside of the classroom, as we illustrate in later sections of this chapter.

The first team of researchers explored misogyny within radio and journalism by focusing their essay on the history, current trends, impacts, and responses to misogyny in US American culture. This team, including Andrea, had enrolled in my Gender in Popular Culture course, and they were completing our program's GWST minor in their third or fourth year of undergraduate coursework. Because this two-volume set included reference essays intended to offer a comprehensive introduction to misogyny for upper high school and beginning undergraduate readers new to the topic, the project was ideal for GWST minors who were near-peers to the target audience and who had previous coursework in gender and women's studies, media studies, and critical and rhetorical theory, as well as experience in advanced writing and research.

Following completion of Gender in Popular Culture in spring 2017, I reached out to members of the team individually to invite them to be part of the project based on their achievements in and contributions to the course. My institution's Office of Undergraduate Research provides a variety of funding for undergraduate research projects, and this project was supported by a Creative Activities and Research Experiences for Teams (CARET) grant, which funds books and other research materials, students' travel and expenses for conferences, and a course release for the faculty mentor. Beginning that summer, we engaged in a scaffolded and collaborative research and writing process, which included a reading, discussion, and writing schedule through the summer and fall semesters. Throughout the process, team members identified and shared additional readings and resources as they collaboratively drafted and made decisions about content for the chapter. Given the amount of work this team was doing on the chapter, and later in preparing for two professional conference presentations and an on-campus undergraduate research symposium, I also created a directed study course so that the students could earn academic credit for this work as part of the GWST minor. Because the research grant supported a course release for that semester, the directed study did not significantly shift my teaching load.

Guided by a collaborative and decentered feminist pedagogy in which students are coequal teachers and contributors to knowledge creation (Chick and Hassel; Turpin), the course syllabus included a collaboratively developed reading list and schedule drawn from texts the four of us had identified during our research and preliminary drafting of the chapter. Assignments included drafts of the chapter that the group was working on along with drafts of content for our collaborative conference presentations. Our biweekly meetings provided opportunities for discussion and for reflecting on content in preparation for those presentations. Although some of the work for the chapter started during the summer, the directed study for the fall made sense for a few reasons—namely, because not all team members had enrolled in summer courses. It also prepared students for the conference presentations that would take place during the spring semester after the bulk of the chapter had been written, allowing students to draw on content from the chapter and begin to reflect on the research and writing process.

In the second phase of the project, once the twenty-four essays and case studies for the two volumes were drafted and revised, I invited a second team of undergraduates to the project. Brayden and Jeremy, who were enrolled in our general education course in GWST, Love and Sex, had interest in undergraduate research opportunities and graduate study, and came to the project recommended by colleagues. Brayden and Jeremy worked collaboratively on a comprehensive chronology of key events connected to the chapters and case studies and a list of organizations focused on addressing and working against misogyny, gender bias and discrimination, and violence against women. They supplemented content with additional research as needed; however, the project's chapters served as the primary source of content. This work was ideal for first- or second-year students who did not yet have extensive content-knowledge in GWST but whose participation in the project could contribute to early and increased engagement and change agency. Like their peers, Brayden and Jeremy also engaged in a scaffolded reading, writing, and revision process, which involved splitting up the book's chapters and case studies to allow each of them to specialize in topics (about twelve or so) as they identified content for the chronology and list of organizations. Over the course of about nine weeks during the fall semester, they each contributed to a shared document, and, collectively, the three of us offered feedback in the document and via email. Another planned outcome for this undergraduate research project included presenting their work as a poster session at our university's undergraduate research symposium and at the National Conference on Undergraduate Research (NCUR). These presentations—both the planning and preparation as well

as the experience of sharing the work in multiple public scholarly venues—
extended the context for their discussions and analysis and their engagement
with GWST content outside of the classroom.

Created with a commitment to decentered, collaborative work, these
projects facilitated research and writing processes that allowed team members to engage with scholarly sources, negotiate revisions, and contribute
to collective inquiry and knowledge creation. Furthermore, because the
book project was already under contract with a publisher, all team members were guaranteed publication of their work to wider audiences when
the two-volume set was published in 2018. Most significantly, however,
in preparing content for the book project and working collaboratively on
how to adapt that content for new audiences, the group anticipated and
prepared for audience questions and blended reflection on the process with
their analysis of theory and practice. These projects provided additional
opportunities to apply feminist and intersectional theory and classroom
content with one another and with a broader public.

Internships in Gender and Women's Studies

Internship opportunities also constitute HIPs and remain a growing component of undergraduate education across disciplines. They also have been
a consistent feature of programs in gender and women's studies, facilitating
students' work as activist-scholars and change agents, often in collaboration
with established organizations in movements for social change (Naples and
Bojar, "Teaching"; Naples and Bojar, "Feminist"; Taylor and de Laat). While
serving as the coordinator of our GWST program, I invited students to
apply for and co-create a pair of undergraduate internships in spring 2019
that allowed them to work directly with our program rather than with
an external organization. These "atypical" internship opportunities served
a dual need in our program. They did the institutional work of campus
and community outreach, marketing, and recruitment, and they offered
students an opportunity to apply classroom theory and learning outside
of the classroom, as well as mentored leadership roles and collaborative
problem-solving work (Taylor and de Laat 105–6).

As part of our GWST minor, students have the option to complete a
three-credit-hour internship course taught by the program coordinator, who
mentors interns in connecting theory and practice while guiding reflective inquiry. The final project for the course invites interns to combine
research, reading and analysis of texts connected to the topic of the internship (e.g., the history of feminist bookstores), and reflection about on-site
experiences. In applying the theoretical knowledge they have gleaned from

course readings, research, and reflection on the internship experience, the final essay demonstrates engagement with and analysis of the intersection of theory and practice. Typically, the site director or internship contact is responsible for supervising and evaluating specific internship tasks. However, because the interns were working directly with me as the program director, another program faculty member taught the internship course during that semester to ensure that the interns had multiple mentors and advocates during the experience.

Jordyn and Brayden each brought experience to these roles. Jordyn was completing our certificate in Gender and the Workplace and already worked at our campus women's resource center. A team member on the misogyny research project, Brayden was completing minors in both GWST and computer science. Although the interns had a great deal of leeway in negotiating the content and design of specific deliverables created as part of the internships, including in their collaboration at the intersection of their work, I titled the internships and their primary areas of focus with the goal of connecting internship work with marketable and transferable skills they could include on a resumé and point to in future professional contexts. Brayden was our social media, marketing, and archives intern, and Jordyn, our community outreach and engagement intern.

In addition to an ambitious list of internship tasks and deliverables, Jordyn and Brayden were also responsible for creating an internship site plan designed to prepare future interns for engaging in and extending this work. Similar to the undergraduate research teams, here too, Brayden and Jordyn collaborated to apply their classroom experiences to publicize the work of the GWST program, to articulate the value and purpose of coursework in GWST, and to recruit peers to share these experiences. Working directly within the program and with the program coordinator and faculty, however, allowed them to move outward as change agents while still engaging the support of faculty and classroom networks.

A Dialogue: Centering Reflections and Lived Experiences

Returning to foundations of feminist pedagogy, including a collaborative and decentered ethos through which students are coequal teachers and contributors to knowledge creation (Chick and Hassel; Turpin), we turn toward the works of Lopatto and Berkes that investigate students' self-reported gains related to HIPs through shared authority and amplifying individual lived experience. Guided by bell hooks, we strongly believe that "all efforts at self-transformation challenge us to engage in ongoing, critical self-examination and reflection about feminist practice, and about how we live in the world. This individual commitment, when coupled with engagement in collective discussion, provides a space for critical feedback which strengthens our efforts to change and make ourselves anew" (24–25). We also draw on the work of Mendoza and Louis, who note the importance of asking students "to reflect on the meaning and purpose of their learning" (20), especially as it relates to the kinds of HIPs we describe in this chapter. As an essential part of the writing and learning process, we engaged deliberately in extended reflection at various points throughout our feminist collaborations, fostered by conversations with each other, preparation for conference presentations and program events within the GWST program, and as part of the writing process for this chapter. Because the process for writing and publishing can often be lengthy, we have had the benefit of many years of reflection and professional experience since the start of the project to extend the feminist collaborations we began in 2017 and the collective meaning-making that has grown out of that work. We have chosen to share content in this next section as a dialogue in order to represent our individual lived experiences and to deliberately illustrate how these feminist collaborations continue to shape our thinking and meaning-making.

Letizia: In our initial reflection for this chapter, I shared a set of questions with each of you guided by Berger and Radeloff's overview of internal strengths and external skills developed through women's and gender studies coursework (147–75) as a foundation for reflecting on these experiences. When you think about your undergraduate research or internship experiences, what was valuable about the experience, and in what ways does that experience remain significant for you?

Brayden: My introduction to the GWST program was a pivotal point for me as a person and scholar, and I am lucky it occurred so early—sophomore year—in my college career. I was raised as a white, cis woman in a middle-class household in the "nineteenth most conservative county in the United States," as my father liked to proudly boast. I discovered during my junior year of high school that I was not as straight as I originally thought and, during my sophomore year of college, that I was not into the gender binary as I originally thought. I enrolled in a history course with another GWST instructor, and she encouraged me to pursue a PhD. I realized I needed to publish and engage in research and enrolled in the Love and Sex course with her. For a girl growing up and finding herself in the heart of the Bible Belt, it was radical to hear people comfortably speak about decentering and intersectionality. Participating in the misogyny research project and internship were formative and impactful experiences that completely shifted the course of my undergraduate career. GWST courses and the publication project provided collaborative, nurturing spaces to reflect on my own identity and build my scholarly foundation on the works of theorists and activists like Judith Butler, Kimberlé Crenshaw, Patricia Hill Collins, Angela Davis, Gloria Steinem, and bell hooks. These experiences helped me find my voice and actively disrupt the conversations happening in my other programs, most of which were firmly rooted in patriarchal and heteronormative standards.

Letizia: Berger and Radeloff specifically point to the kind of change agency Brayden is describing: extending the work of GWST courses outside of the classroom and shaping disciplines in the process. They define "change agents" as "an undergraduate who has strong experiential learning capabilities and a commitment to public engagement beyond the borders of the academic classroom" (Berger and Radeloff 25). How did your participation in these HIPs as undergraduates foster your change agency?

Jeremy: At twenty-three or twenty-four as an undergraduate, I was older than most of the people in the class. I had a background in biology and was not focused on anything related to gender and women's studies at that point in my college career. Participating in the research project was difficult and challenging, but it also gave me insights about our country and the world in general and made me ask, "What can I do better? What is my contribution?" Working on the book project made that effort more conscious, intentional, and purposeful. I had conversations with my family and other people about the project, and my involvement gave them an opening to engage in this conversation. Through the research experience and presenting at the undergraduate research symposium and NCUR, I gained insights on how to connect on these sensitive topics. The experience has also been helpful in my professional work as a victim advocate and had a profound effect on the trajectory of my life.

Letizia: A number of researchers who explore "student-perceived learning gains" from participation in undergraduate research identify many of the skills you describe as outcomes of participation in undergraduate research, including, among others, research, analysis, and critical thinking as well as writing, public speaking, and presentation skills (Berkes 2). They also point to the kind of "self-awareness and understanding" that Jeremy is describing (11). Given the grounding of these projects in feminist theory and practice, however, the ways that you each are pointing to change agency moves this work into the space of activism.

Andrea: The undergraduate research experience prepared me for similar conversations and helped me realize that decentering myself was necessary when tackling texts and ideas that were crucial to activism and research within marginalized communities. The research experience and my GWST coursework shaped how I asked questions, the authors I sought out, and my positionality within the various intersections of what I was writing. I have such bad impostor syndrome, and being around peers who were in a similar space academically helped me move out of that mind-set. Like Jeremy, I was older than many of my classmates and in a different place in my life. Going into the project, I asked, "Why me? What do I bring to this? What can I contribute?" The project gave me a space to really think about what I contribute and that what I say matters.

Letizia: Mendoza and Louis specifically point to the significance of undergraduate research experiences and the development of students' scholarly voices, especially for underrepresented students and those from minoritized backgrounds (18–19). They describe "scholarly voice" as "an individual's identity and positionality within the discipline. It evolves and develops through the recursive process of academic apprenticeship" (19). Notably, they argue that in addition to developing a scholarly voice, what is critical for students is having their voice and their experience validated (19).

Andrea: Yes, that voice in your head that says, "This is not your space." As an undergraduate, having a space to contribute to was huge. I cannot fully articulate how proud I was of myself and how proud others were of me for jumping into the academic research process and pushing myself past what felt comfortable, which included presenting our work on a panel at the Southeastern Women's Studies Association Conference. Preparing for the presentation and being able to answer questions from the audience gave me the confidence to say, "This is what I have to contribute." Owning this experience changed the trajectory of my life and gave me the courage to apply for a master's program in American studies and complete the degree.

Letizia: What was the impact of an internal internship and our feminist collaboration? To what extent did our campus become a site for activist work and change agency?

Jordyn: I had a very different introduction to our institution and even to the GWST program because many of my family members went to HBCUs [historically Black colleges/universities], and I am one of the only cousins that went to a PWI [predominantly white institution]. Coming into this space, I wanted to make it my own. I wanted to develop my voice in a space that may not have been meant for me. The internship invited a lot of creativity. It allowed me to think outside the box and have an impact on the GWST program. This was enriching because as a student, you do not always feel you could impact the university or the community. Brayden and I realized through our collaboration that there were no existing campus groups to facilitate communication and community for GWST students, and we created those spaces by starting a women's studies honor society and a student organization. We wanted our peers to feel connected with like-minded individuals pursuing similar goals. The internship allowed me to ask, "What do I want the next brown girl to come into this position to feel and to experience? How do I want her to evolve with this work just like I did?" That opportunity was important not only for my undergraduate work but in other professional spaces.

Letizia: Each of you points to multiple gains or outcomes from these feminist collaborations regarding the language you gained from the content of the project and course material in gender and women's studies and how they shaped the conversations you had. Another outcome relates to your ability to create and facilitate feminist rhetorical spaces, spaces you were not only stepping into but also creating and holding as spaces for other people's contributions. These included rhetorical and physical spaces for marginalized voices and for developing your own voices as activist-scholars. Bradley and colleagues explore the impact of undergraduate research on participants and, specifically, the significance of these experiences when students are supported by multi-mentoring networks. Their findings reveal that peer mentoring was less common in undergraduate research experiences outside of the sciences (40). However, here we demonstrate the significance of collaborative teams grounded in feminist theory and pedagogy in expanding those mentoring networks and the peer support that students receive in projects like these. Furthermore, your reflections reinforce the intellectual inquiry and change agency that can be fostered within those peer mentoring networks, especially when the feminist pedagogical foundation of this work creates opportunities for students to co-create and shape these experiences and contribute to the projects in meaningful ways, as Jordyn described.

Shanahan and coauthors identify ten practices important to undergraduate research, including "for UR [undergraduate research] mentors to build community among members of the research team. In addition to fostering appropriate social-emotional ties with their undergraduate researchers, mentors who work with more than one student at a time often help build trusting interpersonal relationships among the team members" (366). They continue: "In guiding each other, peers and near-peers learn the content and skills more deeply and may even develop their own pedagogy" (366). One of the other insights I have also heard in our ongoing conversations is how working in teams allowed you to recognize various strengths you each brought to the projects, strengths you recognized in your peers but perhaps had not recognized in yourself, whether these were research and writing skills, technical skills, organization and grounding, creativity, idea generation, and the ways you were motivated by conversation.

Jeremy: We all seemed to have a similar outcome, one that we may not have seen happening but that changed our lives in ways that we could not or did not expect, including in education, career paths, or how we navigate the world. We described being more confident in what we say and how we say it given how our work on the projects shaped content knowledge on these topics. As Andrea said, the projects provided a space to experiment with finding your voice, and for me that was the push that sparked confidence.

Andrea: Projects like these create a safe space but still push you. They draw ideas out of you that you might not have thought of on your own.

Letizia: Reflecting on this work over three years later through the writing process for this chapter has allowed us not only to describe or provide examples of our feminist collaborations but also to theorize them in practice. As we describe the feminist collaboration made possible through these projects and experiences, we also continue to actively engage in and foster it among ourselves as coauthors. With these reflections and experiences in mind, we ask, "What are feminist collaborations? What is feminist about these collaborations?"

Jordyn: One word that keeps coming to mind is "community." We built a community of like-minded individuals who genuinely care for each other and for future scholars committed to intersectional feminism.

Jeremy: The word that comes to mind is "equity." We put in significant work and were supportive of each other no matter the circumstances. That is what the feminist movement is about. We aspired for equitable situations and embodied that with these projects from the beginning. We identify across the gender spectrum, are here to support each other, work together, and make adjustments when needed. The intersectional approach to the project allowed us to focus on gender but also made sure to account for intersections of multiple facets of identity, including race and economic status. This project has always been fair and collaborative and a safe space to express yourself and any problems you had.

Brayden: Feminist collaborations are about creating equitable communities. We came into these projects wanting things to be fair, wanting our voices to be heard, and recognizing that we have a stake in this work. We also wanted a collaborative space to build long-term connections.

Andrea: So much continues to come out of these conversations. Maybe I could not articulate it myself, but there was always someone who could, and then we bounce ideas off each other. These feminist collaborations allowed me to be seen and validated and know that our voices matter.

Letizia: As I listened to what each of you has shared in these conversations, I realized that the feminist collaborations I envisioned for the projects grounded in feminist pedagogy took shape in ways I had not imagined. My aim was for a feminist, decentered approach to engaging in this work where everyone could find their voice, work together, and engage in collaborative meaning-making. I did not fully envision how these feminist collaborations would extend for all of you beyond the projects you worked on and how they reinforced this community. Another outcome of working in feminist collaborations like these as undergraduates through HIPs is the equitable community and rhetorical spaces you will create going forward. Being part of feminist collaborations like these not only fosters change agency, but it also creates the possibility for extending the impact of those feminist collaborations in new spaces with new commitments as you each have illustrated.

Conclusion

As our reflections make clear, feminist collaborations like these have the potential to increase student engagement, self-efficacy, self-confidence, and activism in ways that realize the potential of HIPs and experiential learning, "provid[ing] a space and structure for students to articulate their own activist and theoretical positions by thinking critically about their experiences" (Tice 124; see Richards et al.). These reflections illustrate how HIPs grounded in feminist theory and pedagogical practice and guided by intersectional feminism create opportunities for change agency and for asking, as Jeremy does, "How can I make this better? What is my contribution?" Furthermore, these comments speak to the importance of peer relationships and peer mentoring in HIPs and the value of decentered collaborative partnerships that foster integrative learning across disciplines and creative responses to complex problems (Palmer et al.; Mumford, Hill, and Kieffer 28). Essential to these collaborative partnerships is conversation. As we have discovered in the writing of this chapter, and as Andrea reminds us, we are not alone in our research and writing but are in continuous conversation with each other and the theorists and activists whose work we engage with. We recognize the potential impact for projects like these to provide, as Brayden explains, space to reflect on identity and to build scholarly foundations that allow students to shape work in other disciplines and professional spaces. Finally, and most significantly, as Jordyn illustrates, we cannot yet imagine the impact of inviting undergraduates to shape spaces and conversations where they may not see themselves reflected. In continuing to foster change agency in a complex world, we must, as teacher-scholars, explore creative opportunities for access, equity, and inclusion in experiential experiences like these.

Works Cited

Association of American Colleges & Universities. "High-Impact Practices." Association of American Colleges & Universities 2018. https://www.aacu .org/resources/high-impact-practices.

Berger Michele, Tracy, and Cheryl Radeloff. *Transforming Scholarship: Why Women's and Gender Studies Students Are Changing Themselves and the World.* Routledge, 2011.

Berkes, Elizabeth. "Undergraduate Research Participation and Learning at the University of California, Berkeley." Center for Studies in Higher Education Research and Occasional Papers Series. Spring 2009. https://www.researchgate.net/profile/ Gregg-Thomson/publication/237506421_A_Student_Experience_in_the_ Research_University_SERU_Project_Research_Paper/links/00463525d89 6044106000000/A-Student-Experience-in-the-Research-University-SERU -Project-Research-Paper.

Bojar, Karen, and Nancy A. Naples. "Introduction: Teaching Feminist Activism Experientially." Naples and Bojar, pp. 1–6.

Boyer, Ernest L. *Scholarship Reconsidered: Priorities of the Professoriate.* Carnegie Foundation for the Advancement of Teaching, 1990.

Bradley, Evan D., et al. "The Structure of Mentoring in Undergraduate Research: Multi-Mentor Models. *Scholarship and Practice of Undergraduate Research*, vol. 1, no. 2., 2017, pp. 35–42.

Byrne, Kelli Zaytoun. "The Roles of Campus-Based Women's Centers." *Feminist Teacher*, vol. 13, no. 1, 2000, pp. 48–60.

Chick, Nancy, and Holly Hassel. "Don't Hate Me Because I'm Virtual": Feminist Pedagogy in the Online Classroom." *Feminist Teacher*, vol. 19, no. 3, 2009, pp. 195–215.

Colatrella, Carol. "Why STEM Students Need Gender Studies: Gender Studies Scholarship and Practice Contribute to Student Development and to Faculty Networking." *Academe*, vol. 100, no. 3, 2014, pp. 26–30.

Crabtree, Robbin D., David Alan Sapp, and Adela C. Licona. *Feminist Pedagogy: Looking Back to Move Forward.* Johns Hopkins UP, 2009.

DeCosmo, Janice. "Leveraging Undergraduate Research to Foster Diversity and Achieve Equity." *Scholarship and Practice of Undergraduate Research*, vol. 1, no. 4, 2018, pp. 3–4.

Ewell, Barbara C. "Feminist Pedagogy in Cyberspace: Learning to Teach (a Little) Differently." *Works and Days*, vol. 16, nos. 1/2, 1998, pp. 99–114.

Guglielmo, Letizia. "Classroom Interventions: Feminist Pedagogy and Interruption." *Who Speaks for Writing: Stewardship in Writing Studies in the 21st Century.* Peter Lang, 2012, pp. 102–111.

Hassel, Holly, Amy Reddinger, and Jessica van Slooten. "Surfacing the Structures of Patriarchy: Teaching and Learning Threshold Concepts in Women's Studies." *International Journal for the Scholarship of Teaching and Learning*, vol. 5, no. 2, 2011, pp. 1–19.

hooks, bell. *Talking Back: Thinking Feminist, Thinking Black*. Sheba, 1989.

Lopatto, David. "Undergraduate Research as a High-Impact Student Experience." *Peer Review*, vol. 12, no. 2, 2011, pp. 27–30.

Mendoza, Susan G., and David Louis. "Unspoken Criticality: Developing Scholarly Voices for Minoritized Students through UREs." *Scholarship and Practice of Undergraduate Research*, vol. 1, no. 4, 2018, pp. 18–24.

Mumford, Karen, Stephen Hill, and Laurel Kieffer. "Utilizing Undergraduate Research to Enhance Integrative Learning." *Council on Undergraduate Research Quarterly*, vol. 37, no. 4, Summer 2017, pp. 28–32.

Naples, Nancy A., and Karen Bojar. "Feminist Pedagogy and Teaching Activism: An Introduction to a Special Section of This Issue of *Feminist Teacher*." *Feminist Teacher*, vol. 14, no. 2, 2002, pp. 101–105.

Naples, Nancy A., and Karen Bojar, eds. *Teaching Feminist Activism: Strategies from the Field*. Routledge, 2002.

Palmer, Ruth J., et al. "The Influence of Mentored Undergraduate Research on Students' Identity Development." *Scholarship and Practice of Undergraduate Research*, vol. 2, no. 2, 2018, pp. 4–14.

Reynolds, Nedra. "Interrupting Our Way to Agency: Feminist Cultural Studies and Composition." *Feminism and Composition Studies: In Other Words*, edited by Susan C. Jarratt and Lynn Worsham. Modern Language Association, 1998, pp. 58–73.

Richards, Rosalie, et al. *Handbook of Mentoring Undergraduate Research*. Georgia College and State University. 2014. https://www.researchgate.net/publication/ 271908543_Handbook_of_Mentoring_Undergraduate_Research.

Rinehart, Jane A. "Collaborative Learning, Subversive Teaching, and Activism." Naples and Bojar, pp. 22–35.

Ryan, Jennifer D. "Writing the World: The Role of Advocacy in Implementing a Feminist Pedagogy." *Feminist Teacher*, vol. 17, no. 1, 2006, pp. 15–35.

Sell, Andrea J., Angela Naginey, and Cathy Alexander Stanton. "The Impact of Undergraduate Research on Academic Success." *Scholarship and Practice of Undergraduate Research*, vol. 1, no. 3, 2018, pp. 19–29.

Shanahan, Jenny Olin, et al. "Ten Salient Practices of Undergraduate Research Mentors: A Review of the Literature." *Mentoring & Tutoring: Partnership in Learning*, vol. 23, no. 5, 2015, pp. 359–76.

Shrewsbury, Carolyn M. "What Is Feminist Pedagogy?" *Women's Studies Quarterly*, vol. 15, no. 3–4, 1987, pp. 6–14.

Taylor, Judith, and Kim de Laat. "Feminist Internships and the Depression of Political Imagination: Implications for Women's Studies." *Feminist Formations*, vol. 25, no. 1, 2013, pp. 84–110.

Tice, Karen. "Feminist Theory/Practice Pedagogies in a Shifting Political Climate." *Feminist Teacher*, vol. 14, no. 2, 2002, pp. 123–33.

Turpin, Cherie A. "Feminist Praxis, Online Teaching, and the Urban Campus." *Feminist Teacher*, vol. 18, no. 1, 2007, pp. 9–26.

14

Weaving the Maps

Tales of Survival and Resistance

ISIS NUSAIR

This essay is part of a feminist collaboration that Laila Farah and I started in 2018 to write and direct, a one-woman performance titled *Weaving the Maps: Tales of Survival and Resistance*. Laila performed the piece that is based on our work and research for over two decades with Iraqi, Palestinian, and Syrian refugee women. Laila worked with Palestinian women in refugee camps in Lebanon and created several ethnographic projects, including *Living in the Hyphen-Nation*. My doctoral research focused on the gendered politics of location of three generations of Palestinian women in Israel, some of whom were internally displaced (see Nusair, "Gendered Politics of Location"). Following the 2004 release of the pictures of torture by US troops in Iraq, I wrote an article on the gendered, racialized, and sexualized torture at Abu-Ghraib (see Nusair, "Gendered, Racialized, and Sexualized Torture") and have been conducting research since 2007 with Iraqi women refugees in Jordan and the United States (Nusair, "Negotiating Identity"). Haunted by images of the mass exodus of Palestinians from the Yarmouk refugee camp in 2012, and of tens of thousands of refugees from Syria crowded into inflatable dinghies trying to cross the Aegean Sea from Turkey to Greece, I started the research with refugees from Syria in Germany in 2015. As these refugees continued to challenge with their feet the border regime that refused to allow them to seek asylum in Europe (see De Genova), they lay bare questions about collective accountability and what it means to stand in solidarity.

Weaving the Maps is a collaborative project about survival, resilience, and resistance. Research and performance in this context span the continuum of archiving, recording, telling, sharing, and trusting. It is as much about sharing our research as it is about our own survival in continuing to do this work in privileged academic settings in the United States. This performance is in part about the "stories of our own lives and trajectories; the languages, yearnings, and hauntings that we come from and that breathe inside us;" and how they "mold in critical ways the 'projects' that we come to and how we shape those projects" (Nagar, "Editor's Interview" 73). Navigating these terrains requires new modes of envisioning and collaboration that cross disciplinary boundaries of social science, humanities, and the arts. Laila's previous research and her experience as a scholar-performer contributed to developing the performance. I was trying to reach a wider audience beyond the academy to share my research and was looking for new tools and vocabulary to speak about it. Our friendship, political commitments, and years of activism made the emergence of this project all the more necessary and possible.

Weaving the Maps is a multimedia performance with four movements. The first focuses on symbolic and actual processes of veiling and unveiling within the context of historic Orientalist and neoliberal power structures currently at play in the Middle East and North Africa. It addresses myths/assumptions/colonial fantasies of the audience and what needs to be de/reconstructed as we tell these tales. The emphasis is on making connections between the "here" and "there" and on simultaneous linking and breaking of binary spaces. The second movement examines gendered bodies as sites of violence. We write/tattoo the narratives on the body and make links between violence and military aid and budgets. We trace how violence and the consequences of war are linked to the enactment of geopolitical power structures on the body. The third movement addresses narratives of crossing, displacement, and forced migration. It traces the constant moving, multiple displacements, and links between boots, boats, borders, and bans. The last movement looks at the present and future and the challenges of remaking life, stitching survival from the fabric of women's experiences and memories. It weaves the maps of resilience and resistance and traces the sites and routes for creating systems of accountability, movement building, coalitions, and solidarity.

First Movement: The Act of Unveiling

The first movement focused on the unveiling of colonial fantasies and breaking binaries between East/West, us/them, here/there (see Abdulhadi, Alsultany, and Naber). Our weaving entailed threads of poetry, music, song, visual art, maps, testimony, tattooing, and inscription on the body. It moved away from Orientalist representations of the region and challenged preconceived ideas about Arab and Muslim women (see L. Ahmed, *Women and*

Gender in Islam; Abu-Lughod). By linking the "here" and "there" through drawing on the narratives of the women themselves to make these connections, this feminist collaboration expanded to include all of us in this conversation/narration.

Blumer and coauthors argue that reflexivity, being aware of one's positionality, and growth are crucial to collaboration. They identified themes consistent with feminist theory and practice, including acknowledgment of power, nonhierarchical relationships, self-reflexivity, intertwining the personal and political, empowerment, inclusion, sharing vulnerabilities, camaraderie, and support. In "Collaboration across Borders," Nagar warns against reflexivity mainly focusing on examining the identities of the individual researcher rather than on the ways those identities intersect with institutional, geopolitical, and material aspects of their positionality. She argues that this kind of identity-based reflexivity fails to address how our ability to align our theoretical priorities with the concerns of communities whose struggles we want to advance is connected to the opportunities, constraints, and values embedded in our academic institutions. Collaboration, for Benson and Nagar, is about forging alliances and redefining methodologies that seek to reconstitute the norms, structures, and content of feminist knowledge and political agendas in anti-hierarchical ways. They urge us to create new spaces for collaboration to reimagine and coauthor new forms of academic knowledge production and where collaboration could play a critical role in generating new conversations and knowledge across different borders (see Alexander and Mohanty).

Our collaboration is about practice, resistance, and transformation where there is no privileging of positionalities. Keeping in mind Benson and Nagar's emphasis on accountability to the people with and for whom the performance is imagined, we were aware from the beginning of the ways personal narratives are influenced by the sociopolitical contexts in which they emerge and the power differentials between us and the women we conduct research with. According to Laila Farah ("Living in the Hyphen-Nation"), the writing of *testimonio* and the performance of personal narrative is never a straightforward process: "The work of inserting and interweaving ourselves and our people, our pasts and presents, our intimacies and complicities into what we narrate teaches us how to be more honest and attentive knowledge makers, and it also makes us grapple more deeply with the ever-present possibility of epistemic violence in our narration" (Nagar, "Editor's Interview" 75).

Since I conducted the interviews that shaped the performance's narratives in Arabic (we are both native Arabic speakers), questions remain about the possibilities and limitations of translation. Nagar discusses the question of languages that "lend themselves more readily to ethical thought," and the possibilities of co-producing intellectual work in several languages and sites, in ways that could consistently wrestle with questions of ethics and responsibility in relation to interpretive communities that are multiply situated (75). One thing that audience members commented on after each performance related to the eloquence of these narratives, as if the narratives of these refugee women should be anything but "eloquent" considering their experiences and what they had to go through to arrive at these vastly different locations. *Weaving the Maps* is a communal project that involves working with our audience to understand, act, mend fences, and heal. The layers of tracing these narratives not only intensify these encounters but also simultaneously rupture and connect our different yet overlapping positionalities (Laila's mixed heritage of having a Lebanese father and an American mother and I as a Palestinian living in the United States since 1993).

The different experiences of these Iraqi, Palestinian, and Syrian women; the way they depict different forms of violence enacted on their bodies; and the personal and political connections they make between narrating and resisting, telling, and acting brought theory and activism into praxis. Collective action is about moving out of our comfort zones and packaged modes of "consuming refugee crisis." Representations of refugees in the media are intended usually to shock. "Visual images of 'third-world' suffering in Western media—of the dead, wounded, starving—constitute generic decontextualized horrors that elicit pity and sympathy, not discernment and assessment" (Espiritu and Duong 587). These firsthand narratives are not spectacles to be consumed and narratives to be recycled. They urge us to act and stand in solidarity. The four movements enact different locations for mapping, tracing, and ethically listening and acting. When asking Naya, a Palestinian woman from the Yarmouk refugee camp in Syria, about why she wanted to share her painful yet resilient story, she responded by saying, "I hope. . . ." What does she hope for? What is she charging us with? How could that hope be actualized in part through this collaborative project?

Our collaboration brings about a transnational feminist praxis that crosses boundaries in the ethical re/telling of these stories. Espiritu and Duong trace the lines of countertopography that focuses on alliance building and the transnational feminist potential in collaborative work. The performance marks the intersectional sites of gendered power and resistance to racism, imperialism, and colonialism through examining how they are produced and contested on the local, regional, and transnational levels. This is an "unveiling of colonizing frameworks . . . of different ways of being and of representing that being. . . . This constant switching of papers, codes, and languages creates whole new forms of epistemic knowledges and how to body forth these knowledges" (Farah, "Dancing on the Hyphen" 324).

Our collaboration emerged in part as an act of political resistance while former president Donald Trump was in power and as the "refugee crisis" discourse was intensifying. In January 2017 the Trump administration issued an executive order that banned foreign nationals from seven predominantly Muslim countries from visiting the United States for 90 days, suspended entry to the country of all Syrian refugees indefinitely, and prohibited any other refugees from coming into the country for 120 days (ACLU). European Union countries enforced entry restrictions on refugees, including those coming from Syria in 2016 and 2017. Germany and Sweden took the majority of refugees from Syria, with Germany taking about one million and Sweden 250,000 (see Ostrand). This performance also emerged in response to the lack of public accountability regarding the US-led invasion of Afghanistan in 2001 and Iraq in 2003 and continued US political and military support to Israel.

Laila and I collaborated on writing and producing the performance across our different training and modes of communication. We created space for each other, built on our strengths, and were ready to listen, experiment, and move out of our comfort zones. This was Laila's first collaborative performance, and I ventured into a new territory of script writing, directing, and stage management. Our commitment to the project, the people we conduct research with, and to each other kept us going. The work always had a different intensity when we met to revise and practice before each performance. Crossing over distance and finding ways to connect and bridge gaps was a challenge we had to deal with since we did not have the luxury of being in the same place except for a few weeks every year. The intensity of meeting to write and perform was doubled by the intensity of the narratives themselves and the questions at the core of our collaboration with regard to who speaks for whom and how to body forth our knowledges to enact our vision for justice and change.

Weaving the Maps was performed four times in 2019. We had three performances at college campuses in the United States and one at the Interdisciplinary Studies Conference in the Netherlands. The performance is yet to be translated back to Arabic and performed with refugee communities. The work on the translation and the ability to continue to perform were halted because of COVID-19.

These performances, at times raw and challenging, connected us with the audience in ways that are hard to replicate online. Our ability to directly engage with the audience made it possible to hear their reactions at different stages of the performance and to trace the connections they made between what was happening in Iraq, Palestine, Syria, Haiti, and at the US-Mexico border. The audience became part of this collaboration as they were actively engaged in the talk-back sessions in asking questions and challenging the normalized and dominant representations of migrants and refugees as "predators," victims, or helpless "others." Most importantly, they were able to relate these narratives back to their lived experiences.

The Second Movement: Gendering the Body

The second movement focused on bodies as sites of resistance and the context in which our work emerged. It exposed the challenges of remaking/reconstructing our lives and the possibilities for crossing/bridging and building community (see Alexander; Mohanty). The collaboration is in part a product of the insistence of the women interviewed to make their stories heard. They bore the brunt of war and forced displacement on their bodies (see Dubravka). Some were raped, and some witnessed or experienced unspeakable forms of violence. The expectation is that they should remain strong and keep their families together, or as put by Salma, "Iraqi women are like iron and their burden is heavy." Espiritu defines "critical juxtaposing" as an epistemological and methodological enjoining of "seemingly different and disconnected events, communities, histories and spaces in order to illuminate what would otherwise not be visible about the contours, contents and afterlives of war and empire" (21). Shalhoub-Kevorkian adds that "one hears one's own life in the stories of others; there seems an infinite continuum of memories and experiences. Sometimes you lose track of which memory is your own and which belongs to someone else" (195). This is an example of grafting history and stitching together continuum of memories and experiences communally and in public (Espiritu and Duong). The whisper, listening to the silences, thinking about how we talk about refuge, surviving war, and whether we actually survived becomes part of the intimacy of these spaces that is crucial for collaboration.

"The narratives are words written on the body, cartographies etched on the skin, under the skin" (*Weaving the Maps*). They create interwoven connections with the audience about the challenges that the refugee women face with regard to continuums of violence and multiple forced displacements (see Cockburn; Kelly), the transient nature of being a refugee, and the challenges associated with the asylum-seeking process. Emphasizing the violence enacted on the body, Rahma,[1] a Palestinian woman who was born in 1925, wondered where the line between a refugee and non-refugee starts and ends. This line also extends to include us and the audience regarding where the line between victim and survivor, spectator and performer starts and ends. Rahma said:

> We tried to leave Nazareth [in 1948]. We tried to leave. Do you remember Deir Yassin? There were attacks on women and one woman's belly was cut open. I was pregnant with my first child. I told my husband, "What do you want? Do you want them to come and open my belly?" I was quite pregnant at the time. So many people died as they tried to flee. Our relatives could not come back. . . . This affected me a lot, . . . yet despite being the only one who stayed, I feel displaced and like a refugee.

Collaboration is about redefining the terms of crossing boundaries between us, the women we conduct research with, and the audience. Ours is a performance about refuge (literally and metaphorically) that stands in juxtaposition to the destruction, disruption, displacement, and dispersal of war. The women described how they held on to life, or as Jamila expressed it, "I cry bitterly for myself, the homeland and what happened to us. . . . I used to walk on the edge of the sword to survive." Salma stopped wearing colors; now she wears only black. She described the forms of violence she had to live through following the US-led invasion of Iraq in 2003. Salma shared how her young son would look out from the balcony and ask her about the dismembered body parts scattered in the street, thinking they were broken dolls that needed to be put back together. She wondered about what it means to talk with me about rape for the first time. How could one find the vocabulary to talk about such horrors? How do you "live" with what happened? Salma shared how when she was first told that she was coming to the United States, she said, "No, . . . America destroyed us; why would I come here to seek safety? I am very isolated in this country. I thought I would be free."

Collaboration is rooted in ethical commitments and responsibility, especially that some of these women, or others like them, might be living in our own communities. They are not an "other" in a distant land. The performance allowed for the narratives of the six women from these different locations to intersect. They posed questions about what it means to lose a home and search for another. Suha's astute analysis of militarization and war in Iraq; the challenges she faced as a divorced single mother throughout these transitions of seeking refuge, first in Jordan and later in the United States; and her coping mechanisms and endurance brought these questions back to the audience. She said, "We grew up with war and bombing and something died inside. We lived from one war to another; we were barely living."

The integration of the narratives and the constant movement on the stage between these different locations, each depicting part of their experiences, challenge the audience's preconceived notions about Arab and Muslim women. We worked on making these narratives come to life on the stage while maintaining the temporal, transient, yet permanent nature of these lived experiences. We moved away from static and rigid representations of the refugee experience and focused on the movement between these different sites and multiple displacements to show the dynamism and connection between them, us, and the audience.

Dealing with our own traumas of growing up in war zones and of doing research with refugees, our collaboration was as much about survival as it was about healing. Dreiffus-Kattan analyzes the role of creativity in healing grief, trauma, and loss. The three rings of collaboration (Isis and Laila; us and the women refugees we conduct research with; us, the refugee women, and the audience) intersected as we were all impacted, albeit differently, by what is shared through these narratives. Collaboration in this context requires being in motion and crossing the boundaries between our different locations. It simultaneously creates multiple displacements, ruptures, and the ability to bring us together to enact collaborative modes of being and doing (S. Ahmed). As we draw and connect between them, we wonder, "What are homelands, brick or mortar? Who draws these borders and how are we to cross them? Who is counted, legitimized, or excluded from them?" (*Weaving the Maps*).

Choosing from hundreds of interviews I conducted with Iraqi, Palestinian, and Syrian women over the last two decades, Laila and I created a flow of selected narratives. We wrote and edited together. With minimalist stage props and different lighting effects handled by me, Laila changed her dress, posture, and accent when representing each of the six women. She wore different scarves and robes, drawing on Jananne Al-Ani's work disrupting the "normal cliche of the veil being something that's either oppressive or subjugates women" (Al-Ani, "Without Boundary: Seventeen Ways of Looking").

We leave an open suitcase on the stage. It is nearly empty except for a scarf, a pair of boots, slippers, and many questions that Laila shares with the audience about the baggage we/they carry and what we carry or leave behind. Our aim is to move away from objectification and a passive-looking practice into a more inclusive and engaging one. We present different levels of simultaneous engagement on screen and on stage, including imagery, commentary, and discussion questions that connect the six narratives. They weave the theories that foreground the analytic frame between the pieces (Farah, "Dancing on the Hyphen"). These are discursive, politicized performative spaces where the poem, song, image, and map come together to tell these stories.

The performance aims to invoke a certain relation with the audience about what is shared and acknowledged. The symbolism of the suitcase, scarf, boots and constant movement on the stage connects the private with the public, the intimate with the mundane. We focus on body politics—stitching, carving, itching, and the marks they leave behind. We connect the doing with the moving, and the telling with survival. These dynamic narratives move back and forth in time and between spaces. They resist erasure and call for accountability as a set of frameworks and practices for community- and movement-building against oppression and violence (Russo). Laila asks and we ask, How can we challenge and transform these systems of oppression and violence?

Gendered forced displacement does not operate in a vacuum. It is a product of social and geopolitical power structures that shape people's lives. The women in these six narratives bring these stories to the stage and talk back to the audience. Espiritu and Duong emphasize the importance of feminist collaborations in the formation of ideas and arguments that advance a reflexive reading of power and privilege. The performance as well as the talk-back sessions opened the space to think about the power structures embedded in these collaborations and whose voice we hear in the end. We work with the audience in thinking about how to produce collective knowledge that is critical and engaging, political and creative. Some faculty collaborated with us before the performance and shared discussion questions with their students about the links between the course material and the performance.

As the performer, Laila, becomes one of many collaborators in engaging with the audience, she adds a fourth layer of performative reflexivity of poetics to the three categories of reflexivity described by Lash—cognitive, aesthetic, and hermeneutic (Farah, "Dancing on the Hyphen"). The audience performs by being present and willing to engage the material. "It is precisely for this reason that the 'bridge-builders' Hu-DeHart refers to are the ideal performatively reflexive community, with shared, or minimally parallel, experiences for engaging in this important dialogic activism" (341). Laila Farah adds that the different levels of collaboration and talking back taking place on stage in addition to the one we hold with the audience at the end of the performance expand on these topics and shared pedagogical instances to establish shared experiences not just identifications. We use "back/forth, both/and from script to analysis, performance to post-show discourse, experience to action" to enact "resistance, and a transformative poetics of political dissent." Representation "translates into the realities of political, sentimental, and moral gestures and agendas for action" (342).

Laila Farah conceptualizes performance, both as a pedagogical tool and as a call to action in a coalition-building move where the "deliberate decision to incorporate these intersectionalities becomes an overtly political tool as well as a teachable one" (319). These intersections are between us, the women we conduct research with, and the audience. Audiences with little or no exposure to these stories are suddenly offered an intimate view of life on the ground, "made 'real' in the flesh" (319). In this collaborative performative reflexivity, "the global is connected to the local that is part of a transborder poetics whose aim it is to transform, disrupt, and reconnect" (320). The performance also offers an opening for the audience to engage with these "multilayered narratives, come to their own analysis and action, and formulate a new kind of reflexivity for themselves" (330). Collaborative actions and political mobilization could be the final "axis of analysis." In this way, the audience becomes willingly and wittingly "reflexive, desirous of movement within their own subjectivity as local and global citizens for social change" (341).

The Third Movement: Narratives of Crossing

In this collaborative intimate space for meditation and thinking about possibilities for transformation and change, we draw on Anzaldúa's work on mestiza status and how it could enable us to recognize the power that resides on a border. In what she calls *nepantlera subjectivity*, Anzaldúa wonders about how we can deconstruct hegemonic systems and connect to people's political struggles and then cross over and negotiate through these limitations. As the narrative of border crossing continues to unfold, "the process of the telling itself is infused into each incarnation—this script merely being one of them" (Farah, "Living in the Hyphen-Nation" 179). In describing her crossing, Naya said:

> It takes a long time to decide to leave. We weren't sure what was about to happen next. Fear was the only reason for leaving. I refused the idea at the beginning. I did not have the heart for it. . . . This was my first trip. I do not know the sea. I only know al-Sham (Damascus). When you leave all this behind, you refuse to go back. There is no more pain, no more fear, yet the knot in the stomach is always there. You eat while thinking of those you left behind.

Naya attempted in 2015 to cross the Aegean Sea from Turkey to Greece with her son, who was a toddler at the time. They nearly drowned twice. She recounted how she met a group of people on the trip and how the men did not want her to come with them because her son was sick and she might slow them down. She described the scene before the third sea crossing, when some passengers recited, "Surat Yasin and others were cursing God."

We wonder about how military aid, budgets, and profits are enacted on these bodies and why they are criminalized and prevented from crossing these borders in more legal, safe, and humane ways: "The Muslim ban, the travel ban, ICE deportations, family separations and illegal incarcerations, DACA and ending immigration to the US. How movement building is manifested? How are coalitions built across borders? How is accountability enforced? Over here is over there. Where do we go with our resistance now?" (*Weaving the Maps*). These questions and others like them shaped the performance and connected the different narratives together. They were our window to connecting with the audience and thinking collectively about transformation and change. We worked "within, between and behind these affected spaces" to think about "homemaking, healing and survival strategies" (Espiritu and Duong 588).

These narratives transform the "transience enforced by their continuous evictions into the permanence of home, not as a static identity-place-nation, but as a site of dynamic affective, social relations and connections" (Salih 742). Salih investigates the potential of the ordinary as a horizon for a radical political imagination. Her emphasis is on narratives that displace nationalist affects by opening other types of affects nested in the concreteness of ordinary relations, attachments, and responsibilities. These processes, adds Salih, extend through the private and the public, the individual and the collective connecting the ordinary and the eventful in a life continuum. Naya's image of water coming up to her neck while holding her toddler high so that he would not drown is intensified when she describes how when they were shot at by the coast guard, he was separated from her. Not knowing whether he was dead or alive, it took her three days to find him. These haunting images remain with the audience and are juxtaposed later in the narrative when Naya jokes about how the first thing her uncle said after she arrived at his place at the end of her long journey from Syria to Europe was that she "stinks" and how happy she felt to finally be able to shower and cook a hot meal.

Feminist pedagogy, with its focus on "embodiment, at the level of both the individual and the social, often draws explicitly on the emotions and feelings as resources, both for understanding and as sources of strength in creating new models for pedagogy itself and in envisioning alternative futures" (Woodward 72). The emphasis here is on feminist pedagogy and offering different models for the production of knowledge that are collaborative, with "collaboration fundamentally underwritten not by hardware or software but rather animated by an ethos, by ideas and ideals that guide the work, and by relationships that are in great part affective" (72). Collaboration has epistemological and ethical dimensions where affect and impact on the audience are achieved through accumulation and where the co-creation of these intellectual, pedagogical, and performative spaces give more life to the temporary connection between audience and community (Woodward). This "public intimacy is both built through *convivencia* and creates *convivencia*, which carries with it the affective overtones of trust and vitality" (79). Our performance has the potential to create intellectual intimacy, collaborative discussions, reflection, and action. It attempts to build relations and creates emotional bonds to generate solidarity in response to lack of engagement and accountability "through feeling as well as thought and analysis" (85).

This collaborative performance provides hope and intimate spaces to 'learn from below' and co-determine the specific ways in which we can be "accountable to people's own struggles for representation and self-determination" (Visweswaran qtd. in Nagar, "Collaboration across Borders" 357). The question remains on how to conceptualize the different sites of border crossings that challenge othering and objectification and emphasize the "sustained building and nurturing process" of feminist solidarity (Prasad and Zulfiqar 728).

The Fourth Movement: Remaking Life/Stitching Survival

Laila Farah ("Stitching Survival") wonders about how to achieve an embodiment that continues to resist erasure. How can we resist erasure through creativity and collaboration? And how are we to relate to the praxis of challenging power hierarchies and "accepting vulnerability as a radical stance through enacting an ethical and more mutually hospitable way of being in the world" (Nagar, "Editor's Interview" 80)? We needed that collectivity to bring our work together, to heal and survive. Our aim is to continue to collaborate in order to expand the space for these conversations and push at these borders.

The fourth movement in the performance focuses on collaboration and resistance through making art and stitching survival on the stage and in our lives. The last narrative, and the only one not based on an interview conducted by me, weaves the six narratives together. It focuses on Azza Abo Rebieh, who was detained in Syria post-2011 because of her art-making and activism. Since the start of Syria's uprising, her artwork "held up a mirror to a society in turmoil." She risked arrest by painting graffiti murals about the protest movement. While in prison for her activities, her art became a "mirror for fellow prisoners who had none" (Sinjab and Barnard). "I drew them so they could see themselves. I drew them all in shaded black and white"

(*Weaving the Maps*). Azza spent seventy days cramped into a small, filthy cell with fifteen other women. They went on a hunger strike, "demanding only that their families be told their whereabouts. Some refused medicines, risking death from heart conditions and epilepsy. She describes how at first, she felt blocked and depressed, but then the work began to flood out" (Sinjab and Barnard). Azza created a series of more developed etchings of her prison experience and continued to make art about the women she met in detention. Her prison art hangs on the wall of her living room in Beirut, Lebanon, along with olive pits and yarn from the prison-worn blankets.

Azza continues to produce her art, and we continue to weave the maps and tell the tales of survival and resistance. Her art mirrored her resistance and survival together with the fifteen other women she was imprisoned with. It also became a mirror to us and the audience as we continue to stitch, mend, repair in an attempt to survive. We end the performance and this essay with a poem by Lisa Suheir Majaj about the art of repairing with gold:

Kintsukuroi
> *The art of repairing with gold*

What beauty
> in breaking—
spirit's vessel
> shattered
> > fragility confirmed?

fracture lines
> map tectonics
of damage
a jigsaw of breaking
> laid bare

yet rivulets
> gleam
through shards
a geography
> of mending

> as breath
that uneven melody
haunted by broken notes
> rises, splintered, striving
> > toward song

Note

1. Pseudonyms are used throughout for all five interviewees.

Works Cited

Abdulhadi, Rabab, Evelyn Alsultany, and Nadine Naber. *Arab and Arab American Feminisms: Gender, Violence and Belonging.* Syracuse UP, 2011.

Abu-Lughod, Lila. *Do Muslim Women Need Saving?* Harvard UP, 2013.

ACLU. "Timeline of the Muslim Ban." https://www.aclu-wa.org/pages/timeline -muslim-ban. Accessed Jan. 6, 2019.

Ahmed, Leila. *Women and Gender in Islam.* Yale UP, 1992.

Ahmed, Sara. *Living a Feminist Life.* Duke UP, 2017.

Al-Ani, Janaane. "Without Boundary: Seventeen Ways of Looking." https://www .moma.org/audio/playlist/196/2621. Accessed March 26, 2024.

Alexander, Jacqui. *Pedagogies of Crossing: Meditations on Feminism, Sexual Politics, Memory, and the Sacred.* Duke UP, 2005.

Alexander, Jacqui M., and Chandra Talpade Mohanty. "Cartographies of Knowledge and Power: Transnational Feminism as Radical Praxis." *Critical Transnational Feminist Praxis,* edited by Richa Nagar and Amanda Lock Swarr. State U of New York P, 2010, pp. 23–45.

Anzaldúa, Gloria. *Borderlands/La Frontera: The New Mestiza.* Aunt Lute Books, 1987.

Benson, Koni, and Richa Nagar. "Collaboration as Resistance? Reconsidering the Processes, Products, and Possibilities of Feminist Oral History and Ethnography." *Gender, Place, and Culture: A Journal of Feminist Geography,* vol. 13, no. 5, 2006, pp. 581–92.

Blumer, Markie L. C., et al. "Creating a Collaborative Research Team: Feminist Reflections." *Journal of Feminist Family Therapy,* vol. 19, no. 1, 2007, pp. 41–55.

Cockburn, Cynthia. "The Continuum of Violence: A Gender Perspective on War and Peace." *Sites of Violence: Gender and Conflict Zones,* edited by Winona Giles and Jennifer Hyndman. U of California P, 2004, pp. 24–44.

De Genova, Nicholas. "The 'Migrant Crisis' as Racial Crisis: Do Black Lives Matter in Europe?" *Ethnic and Racial Studies,* vol. 41, no. 44, 2017, pp. 1–18.

Dreiffus-Kattan, Esther. *Art and Mourning: The Role of Creativity in Healing Trauma and Loss.* Routledge, 2016.

Dubravka, Zarkov. *The Body of War.* Duke UP, 2007.

Espiritu, Len Ye. *Body Counts: The Vietnam War and Militarized Refugees.* U of California P, 2014.

Espiritu, Yến Lê, and Lan Duong. "Feminist Refugee Epistemology: Reading Displacement in Vietnamese and Syrian Refugee Art." *Signs,* vol. 43, no. 3, 2018, pp. 587–615.

Farah, Laila. "Dancing on the Hyphen: Performing Diasporic Subjectivity." *Modern Drama*, vol. 48, no. 2, 2005, pp. 316–45.

Farah, Laila. "Living in the Hyphen-Nation." *Counterpoints*, vol. 169, 2002, pp. 179–95.

Farah, Laila. "Stitching Survival: Revisioning Silence and Expression." *Silence, Feminism, Power*, edited by Sheena Malhorta and Aimee Carrillo Rowe. Palgrave Macmillan, 2013, pp. 239–51.

Kelly, Liz. "Wars against Women: Sexual Violence, Sexual Politics, and the Militarized States." *States of Conflict: Gender, Violence and Resistance*, edited by Susie Jacobs et al. Bloomsbury Academic, 2000, pp. 45–65.

Majaj, Lisa Suhair. "Kintsukuroi." https://baladimagazine.com/kintsukuroi/. Accessed Oct. 14, 2024.

Mohanty, Chandra Talpade. *Feminism without Borders: Decolonizing Theory, Practicing Solidarity*. Duke UP, 2003.

Nagar, Richa, in consultation with Farah Ali. "Collaboration across Borders: Moving beyond Positionality." *Singapore Journal of Tropical Geography*, vol. 24, no. 3, 2003, pp. 356–72.

Nagar, Richa. "Editor's Interview with Richa Nagar." *Journal of Narrative Politics*, vol. 2, no. 2, 2016, pp. 73–80.

Nusair, Isis. "Gendered, Racialized, and Sexualized Torture at Abu-Ghraib." *Feminism and War: Confronting U.S. Imperialism*, edited by Robin Riley, Chandra Talpade Mohanty, and Minnie Bruce Pratt. Zed Books, 2008, pp. 179–93.

Nusair, Isis. "Negotiating Identity, Space, and Place among Iraqi Women Refugees in Jordan." *Doing Research in Conflict Zones: Experiences from the Field*, edited by Dyan Mazurana, Karen Jacobsen, and Lacey A. Gale. Cambridge UP, 2013, pp. 56–77.

Ostrand, Nicole. "The Syrian Refugee Crisis: A Comparison of Responses by Germany, Sweden, the United Kingdom, and the United States." *Journal on Migration and Human Security*, vol. 2, 2018, pp. 255–79.

Prasad, Ajnesh, and Ghazal Zulfiqar. "Resistance and Praxis in the Making of Feminist Solidarity: A Conversation with Cynthia Enloe." *Gender, Work and Organization*, vol. 28, 2021, pp. 722–34.

Russo, Ann. *Feminist Accountability: Disrupting Violence, Transforming Power*. New York UP, 2018.

Salih, Ruba. "Bodies That Walk, Bodies That Talk, Bodies That Love: Palestinian Women Refugees, Affectivity, and the Politics of the Ordinary." *A Radical Journal of Geography*, vol. 49, no. 3, 2017, pp. 742–60.

Shalhoub-Kevorkian, Nadera. *Militarization and Violence against Women in Conflict Zones in the Middle East: A Palestinian Case Study*. Cambridge UP, 2009.

Sinjab, Lina, and Anne Barrnard. "Syria's Women Prisoners, Drawn by an Artist Who Was One." *New York Times*, Aug. 7, 2018, https://www.nytimes.com/2018/08/07/arts/design/syria-prison-artist.html. Accessed March 7, 2019.

Weaving the Maps: Tales of Survival and Resistance. Directed by Laila Farah and
Isis Nusair, performance by Laila Farah, 2019, Denison University, Merrimack
College, and DePaul University in the United States, and the Interdisciplinary
Conference in the Netherlands.

Woodward, Kathleen. "On Feminist Collaboration, Digital Media, and Affect."
Feminist Interventions in Participatory Media: Pedagogy, Publics, Practice, edited
by Lauren S. Berliner and Ron Krabill. Routledge, 2018, pp. 70–90.

Contributors

JORDYN ALDERMAN is a student support coordinator at Georgia State University and is completing a master's degree in clinical mental health counseling from Mercer University. Her research focuses on mental health concerns within the LGBTQIA+ community, multicultural counselor education, reproductive rights, and the social and disability justice aspects of counseling.

LEEN ALFATAFTA is a PhD student in cultural and visual anthropology at George Washington University. Her research pursues themes of affect and relationality among South Asian migrant communities in the Al-Zarqa governorate in Jordan through conventional and experimental ethnographic methods. Leen holds an MA in Arab studies from Georgetown University and a BA in sociology and gender studies from New College of Florida.

MERYL ALTMAN is professor emerita of English and women's studies at DePauw University in Indiana, where she served for many years as director of women's studies. She came to Greencastle in 1990 after teaching at William and Mary and studying at Swarthmore and Columbia, where she earned her PhD in English literature with a dissertation on modernist American poetry. She has written regularly for the *Women's Review of Books* and has published articles about Djuna Barnes, H. D., Faulkner, Sappho, metaphor, and the history of sexuality, and on Simone de Beauvoir, the topic of her book *Beauvoir in Time* (Brill, 2020). Other interests include feminist and queer theory, women's migrant domestic labor, women in China, and gender and sexuality in ancient Greece.

MARÍA CLAUDIA ANDRÉ retired from Hope College in 2020 after teaching there for twenty-five years. She taught Spanish, Portuguese, translation and interpretation, and a variety of topics in Latin American culture and literature. Her research focused on Hispanic American literature and Latin American studies, with a particular emphasis on Latin American women writers. She conducted collaborative research with students in Mexico and the United States, and edited and coedited numerous books focusing on Latin American women writers and women in Latin American and Spanish literature. She received several grants and awards in recognition of her work and her innovative use of technology in both teaching and research, including developing a historical archive featuring women surrealist artists.

ANDREA N. BALDWIN is an associate professor in the divisions of gender studies and ethnic studies and the associate dean for research in the School for Cultural and Social Transformation at the University of Utah. She is an attorney-at-law who also holds a master's degree in international trade policy and a PhD in gender and development studies. She is the founder of the Black Feminist Eco Lab at the University of Utah. Dr. Baldwin was born and raised on the small Caribbean island state of Barbados and considers herself an all-around Caribbean woman and loves everything coconut and *soca*.

CAROLYN BEER is a graduate of New College of Florida, with degrees in gender studies and Spanish. Raised in a Quaker Intentional Community in upstate New York, her interests combine public health and food justice. She has previously worked with community organizations on strengthening local food pathways and community resilience in Florida and increasing the rights and visibility of domestic workers in Lima, Perú. She is currently earning a master's in social impact data science at Vrije Universiteit Amsterdam.

LUISA BIERI is an associate professor of cooperative education, community arts, and performance at Antioch College in Yellow Springs, Ohio, and also serves as dean of cooperative, international, and community-based learning. She holds an MA in comparative women's studies from Utrecht University in the Netherlands and a BA in theater and Latin American literature from Smith College. Luisa developed an award-winning community arts program as an Open Society Institute Baltimore Community Fellow with Creative Alliance. Her training in Theatre of the Oppressed methods with Augosto and Julian Boal has informed her work as a founding member of the Sol Rising healing arts troupe, Theater Action Group, and a recent multiyear collaboration with the Argentine feminist performance troupe Mujeres de Artes Tomar. Luisa's work as a writer and performer has been featured nationally and internationally.

REBECCA DAWSON is an epidemiologist and associate professor in the biology department and global health studies program at Allegheny College. She blogs regularly (beckydawson.substack.com), serves as the research director at the Meadville Medical Center, and is an exclusive contributor at Erie News Now. Rebecca completed a Master of Public Health (MPH) degree at Emory University in environmental health and a PhD in epidemiology at the University of Maryland, Baltimore. She is a coauthor of *Understanding Epidemiology*, the first epidemiology textbook designed specifically for undergraduate students (3rd ed., 2021). Her work has been published in the *American Journal of Public Health*, *Archives of Environmental & Occupational Health*, and *Scholarship & Practice of Undergraduate Research*.

MISTY DEBERRY is an assistant professor in the Department of Performance Studies at New York University after holding a senior lecturer position in the women's, gender, and sexuality studies program at Dartmouth College. She earned a PhD in performance studies from Northwestern University and completed a postdoctoral fellowship in the Department of Literature and the women's and gender studies program at the Massachusetts Institute of Technology. Misty works across the fields of performance studies, Black feminist thought, queer of color critique, and aesthetic practice. Her scholarly and artistic work considers the relationship between blackness, somatics, and psychic violence. Her work has been published in the *Journal for Lesbian Studies*, *The Hemispheric Institute's e-mispherica*, and in the genre-defining performance anthology *solo/black/woman: scripts, interviews, essays* (2014).

DANIELLE M. DEMUTH is an associate professor of women, gender, and sexuality studies at Grand Valley State University in Michigan. She has led study abroad programs in women's and gender studies to Egypt and to South Africa. Her research and teaching come together in curriculum development, curriculum mapping, and assessment of feminist teaching and learning. Her long-term research is centered on examining narratives of lesbian literary history and twentieth-century lesbian novels as case studies in literary history.

EMILY FAIRCHILD is associate director of undergraduate studies and lecturer in the sociology department at Harvard University. She was formerly associate professor of sociology and gender studies at New College of Florida, where she previously served as director of the gender studies program. She is a teacher-scholar who pursues intertwined projects of knowledge generation, inclusive pedagogy, and institutional application. She has most recently written about the unusually accepting student culture around gender at New College, arguing that despite the challenges queer faculty face, this site provides an alternative conception of gender and a model for interactional inclusivity. Her work on gender, culture, and meaning making can be found in *Journal of Contemporary Ethnography* and *Gender & Society* as well as edited volumes on trans studies, higher education, and women athletes.

SARA YOUNGBLOOD GREGORY is a lesbian journalist, author, and graduate of New College of Florida. A former staff writer for POPSUGAR, Sara's work on queerness, culture, and wellness has been published or is forthcoming in *Vice, Cosmopolitan, HuffPost, The New York Times*, and many other media. Sara is the current News and Narrative 2023 Spring Fellow for TransLash Media. Her book, *The Polyamory Workbook,* came out in 2022.

LETIZIA GUGLIELMO is professor of English and interdisciplinary studies at Kennesaw State University. Her writing and research explore feminist rhetorics and pedagogy, gender and pop culture, and student and faculty professional development. Her work has appeared in a variety of journals and edited collections. Book projects include *Immigrant Scholars in Rhetoric, Composition, and Communication: Memoirs of a First Generation*; *Misogyny in American Culture: Causes, Trends, Solutions*; *Scholarly Publication in a Changing Academic Landscape: Models for Success; Contingent Faculty Publishing in Community: Case Studies for Successful Collaborations*; and *MTV and Teen Pregnancy: Critical Essays on* 16 and Pregnant *and* Teen Mom.

JEREMY HALL is a graduate of Kennesaw State University with a BS in psychology and a minor in gender and women's studies. He is currently a victim advocate in Georgia.

K. MELCHOR QUICK HALL is a popular educator, writer, and researcher currently working as a 2023–2025 postdoctoral fellow with Wellesley College's Anti-Carceral Co+Laboratory. She is the founder of Solidarity Arts & Education Decolonial initiatives (SAEDi) Collective, an organization working at the intersection of Black reparations, food sovereignty, and prison abolition movements. Hall is the author of *Naming a Transnational Black Feminist Framework: Writing in Darkness* and coeditor (with Gwyn Kirk) of *Mapping Gendered Ecologies: Engaging with and beyond Ecowomanism and Ecofeminism*, and the co-editor (with Takiyah Harper-Shipman) of the *International Studies Review* 2021 special forum (volume 23, number 4) on "Stripping Away the Body: Prospects for Reimagining Race in IR." Her co-edited volume (with Annie Fukushima), *Decolonial Feminist Genealogies & Futures,* is in production with the University of Illinois Press.

LINH U. HUA is senior instructor of rhetorical arts in the Department of English at Loyola Marymount University (LMU), where she served as a 2022 Faculty Fellow for the Center for Teaching Excellence and the Office of Diversity, Equity, and Inclusion. She earned her doctorate at the University of California, Irvine, in English, specializing in African American and Asian American literary and cultural history, feminist studies, and critical theory under the directorship of the late Dr. Lindon Barrett. Her writing can be found in *African American Review*, *The Feminist Wire*, *Teaching and Emotion* (Jossey-Bass Wiley), *Conditions of the Present* (Duke UP), and *Mapping Gendered Ecologies: Engaging with and beyond Ecowomanism and Ecofeminism* (Lexington Books). She heads the Citation Initiative at LMU (https://www.thecitationinitiative.com/) and is currently working on a manuscript on citation pedagogy and social justice.

CHRISTINE KEATING is a member of the popular education collective La Escuela Popular Norteña and an associate professor in gender, women's, and sexuality studies at the University of Washington, Seattle. Her research is in the areas of feminist political theory, decolonial politics, popular education, and transnational feminist theory. She is the author of *Decolonizing Democracy: Transforming the Social Contract in India* (Penn State UP, 2011). Her coauthored book with María Lugones, *Educating for Coalition: Popular Education and Political Praxis*, is forthcoming with SUNY Press. Her articles have been published in *Signs*, *Political Theory*, *International Journal of Feminist Politics*, *Hypatia*, *Women's Studies Quarterly*, and *New Political Science* as well as in several edited volumes.

BRAYDEN MILAM is a program coordinator at Kennesaw State University. Her research and writing focuses on student success, online and hybrid education, and project management in the humanities and social sciences. She regularly presents her work nationally and internationally, and she has published in a variety of journals and edited collections.

ISIS NUSAIR is professor of women's and gender studies and international studies at Denison University. She is the coeditor with Rhoda Kanaaneh of *Displaced at Home: Ethnicity and Gender among Palestinians in Israel* and translator of *Ever Since I Did Not Die* by Ramy Al-Asheq. She is completing two book manuscripts on Iraqi women refugees in Jordan and the USA, and on refugees from Syria in Germany. Isis is the co-writer/director with Laila Farah of the one-woman performance *Weaving the Maps: Tales of Survival and Resistance*. She is currently researching the body of war in Syrian TV series post-2011. She serves on the editorial committee of the *International Feminist Journal of Politics*. She previously served on the editorial committee of *MERIP* and as a researcher on women's human rights in the Middle East and North Africa at Human Rights Watch and the Euro-Mediterranean Human Rights Network.

MONTSERRAT PÉREZ-TORIBIO is associate professor of Hispanic studies and women's and gender studies at Wheaton College, Massachusetts. Her research is devoted to early modern women's experiences and writings, with publications on women's literacy and the representation of women's economic life in Spanish early modern literature. She is subject editor for Spain and Portugal of the *Routledge Resources Online—The Renaissance World*. She is currently working on an annotated edition and English translation of Alberto Enriquez's rare book published in Brussels in 1627: *Resolución Varonil O viaje que hizo Doña María Estuarda Condesa de Tirconel en traje de varón* (Manly resolution or voyage undertaken by Mary Stuart, countess of Tyrconnell in men's attire).

ANDREA PUTALA currently teaches courses in gender and women's studies at Kennesaw State University (KSU) and completed a BA in English, undergraduate minors in film and gender and women's studies, and an MA in American studies from KSU.

ARIELLA ROTRAMEL is the department chair and Vandana Shiva Associate Professor of Gender, Sexuality, and Intersectionality Studies. They are an interdisciplinary scholar committed to bridging theoretical and practical engagements of identity and social justice issues. Rotramel holds a bachelor of arts degree for an independent program of study (Intersections of Racial, Sexual, and Gender Identities) from the University of Illinois at Chicago, and a doctorate in women's and gender studies from Rutgers University.

ANN RUSSO is director of the Women's Center and a professor in the Department of Women's and Gender Studies at DePaul University. Her scholarship, teaching, and organizing focus on queer, antiracist, and feminist movement approaches to building alliances and coalitions for social change. Her most recent book, *Feminist Accountability: Disrupting Violence and Transforming Power* (2018), explores transformative justice, prison abolition, and community accountability as practices that cultivate communal healing, intervention, accountability and transformation in response to systemic intimate, interpersonal, and state violence. She is also the author of *Communities Engaged in Resisting Violence* (2007) and *Taking Back Our Lives: A Call to Action in the Feminist Movement* (2001), and coeditor of *Talking Back and Acting Out* (2002) and *Third World Women and Feminist Perspectives* (1990). She is also published in a number of books, journals, and feminist periodicals.

KIMBERLY SANCHEZ (she, her, ella) is an intercultural Salvadoran American working in philanthropy. Kimberly's educational background is in political science and public administration. Two years of Public Allies experience fostered a commitment to centering community-identified priorities and working toward mutual partnership. While working as a community engagement professional in higher education, Kimberly was able to learn with students, staff, and faculty. These learnings continue to inform Kimberly's practice.

BARBARA L. SHAW is associate professor and department chair of women's, gender, and sexuality studies at Allegheny College and affiliated with Black studies, global health studies, and public humanities. She coedited *Introduction to Women's, Gender & Sexuality: Interdisciplinary & Intersectional Approaches* (2025; 2020; 2018) and *Feminist & Queer Theory: An Intersectional and Transnational Reader* (2020). She has published on the institutionalization of the field in *Women's Studies Quarterly*. Her research areas are gendered violence and feminist-queer approaches to health/care and sexuality. She recently served as the director of interdisciplinary studies and has co-directed four curriculum transformation projects.

M. GABRIELA TORRES is a transformative leader committed to fostering a more diverse and socially just academy. She is vice provost at Rhode Island College. Dr. Torres's dedication to innovation in transforming access to learning in higher education grew directly from her award-winning teaching and educational development background. As a scholar, she has published over 30 peer-reviewed articles, research reports, and book chapters, in addition to the volumes *Marital Rape: Consent, Marriage, and Social Change in Global Context* and *Sexual Violence in Intimacy: Implications for Research and Policy in Global Health*. Most recently, Dr. Torres has published regularly on antiracist and intercultural teaching and learning, BIPOC mentoring in higher education, and on equity policies. She is currently coeditor in chief of *Feminist Anthropology*.

AYANA K. WEEKLEY is an associate professor in women's, gender, and sexuality studies at Grand Valley State University. She earned her PhD in feminist studies from the Department of Gender, Women, and Sexuality at the University of Minnesota. Her research and teaching interests include feminist periodical studies and Black feminist studies. Dr. Weekley was a fellow in the "Hurston on the Horizon: Past, Present, and Future" NEH Summer Institute. Dr. Weekley's recent scholarly contributions include coeditor of "Revisiting Zora Neale Hurston," a special issue of the *Journal of American Culture*, 2022; contributor to Musial et al., "Black Feminist Thought and the Gender, Women's, and Feminist PhD: A Roundtable Discussion," *Feminist Formations*, 2020; and coeditor of *Women's Magazines in Print and New Media* (Routledge, 2016).

SHARON R. WESOKY earned her PhD in government at Cornell University and is a professor of political science at Allegheny College. Her scholarly work has centered on feminism and gender in contemporary China, examining urban and rural women's organizations as well as Chinese feminist theory. Along with numerous book chapters, she has published articles in *Signs*, *International Feminist Journal of Politics*, and *Asian Studies Review*. Her most recent project was serving as editor and chief translator of a collection of Chinese feminist theorist Song Shaopeng's work *Chinese Modernity and Socialist Feminist Theory* (Routledge, 2023). She is also interested in comparative political theory, especially questions of Buddhist thought and political subjectivity.

Index

The University of Illinois Press
is a founding member of the
Association of University Presses.

———————————————————————

Composed in 11.5/13 Adobe Garamond Pro
with Gotham display
by Jim Proefrock
at the University of Illinois Press

University of Illinois Press
1325 South Oak Street
Champaign, IL 61820-6903
www.press.uillinois.edu